GOVERNMENT–INDUSTRY RELATIONS 3

CAPITALISM, CULTURE, AND ECONOMIC REGULATION

GOVERNMENT–INDUSTRY RELATIONS

Editors: Maurice Wright and Stephen Wilks

Volumes within this series incorporate original research into contemporary policy issues and policy-making processes in the UK, Western Europe, the United States, and South-East Asia.

ALREADY PUBLISHED

Comparative Government–Industry Relations: Western Europe, the United States, and Japan,
edited by Stephen Wilks and Maurice Wright

Government and the Chemical Industry: A Comparative Study of Britain and West Germany
Wyn Grant, William Paterson, and Colin Whitston

CAPITALISM, CULTURE, AND ECONOMIC REGULATION

EDITED BY
Leigh Hancher and Michael Moran

CLARENDON PRESS · OXFORD
1989

Oxford University Press, Walton Street, Oxford OX2 6DP
Oxford New York Toronto
Delhi Bombay Calcutta Madras Karachi
Petaling Jaya Singapore Hong Kong Tokyo
Nairobi Dar es Salaam Cape Town
Melbourne Auckland
and associated companies in
Berlin Ibadan

Oxford is a trade mark of Oxford University Press

Published in the United States
by Oxford University Press, New York

British Library Cataloguing in Publication Data
Capitalism, culture and economic regulation.
1. Capitalist countries. Economic activity. regulation
I. Hancher, Leigh II. Moran, Michael, 1946– III. Series
330.9
ISBN 0–19–827550–1

Library of Congress Cataloging in Publication Data
Capitalism, culture, and economic regulation/edited by Leigh Hancher and Michael Moran.
p. cm.—(Government–industry relations)
Includes index.
1. Trade regulation—Europe. 2. Capitalism—Europe. I. Hancher, Leigh. 1956– . II. Moran, Michael. III. Series.
HD3616.E8C36 1989 338.94—dc19 88–25872
ISBN 0–19–827550–1

Typeset by Cambrian Typesetters, Frimley, Surrey
Printed in Great Britain
at the University Printing House, Oxford
by David Stanford
Printer to the University

Acknowledgements

We are grateful to the series editors for advice and encouragement; to the contributors for their patience and their readiness to accommodate our requests for revising; to Karen Hall and Helen Beresford for their secretarial help; and to Peter Mair, the go-between.

L. H.
M. M.
University of Warwick/University of Manchester

Contents

Notes on Contributors

ALAN CAWSON is Reader in Politics in the School of Social Sciences at the University of Sussex. He is the author of *Corporatism and Welfare* (1982), *Corporatism and Political Theory* (1986), and of a number of articles on state theory, democratic theory, and industrial policy.

COSMO GRAHAM lectures at the Centre for Criminological and Socio-Legal Studies at the University of Sheffield. He has written widely on aspects of public law, notably on the implications of privatization.

LEIGH HANCHER lectures at the University of Warwick. She was Research Fellow at the European University Institute, Florence, from 1979 to 1981 and will be taking up a post as Assistant Director of the International Institute for Energy Law at the University of Leiden in 1988. Her publications include, with T. Daintith, *Energy Strategy in Europe: The Legal Framework* (1986).

MICHAEL MORAN is Senior Lecturer in the Department of Government at the Victoria University of Manchester. His publications include *The Union of Post Office Workers: A study in political sociology* (1974), *The Politics of Industrial Relations* (1977), *The Politics of Banking* (1984), *Politics and Society in Britain* (1985). He is presently completing a cross-national study of the politics of the securities industry.

SOL PICCIOTTO is Senior Lecturer in Law at the University of Warwick. He has written widely on the subject of international law and the international state system.

TONY PROSSER is Lecturer in Public Law at the Centre for Criminological and Socio-Legal Studies at the University of Sheffield. He is author of *Test Cases for the Poor* (1983) and *Nationalised Industries and Public Control* (1986), together with a number of academic articles in the areas of public law, welfare law, and privatization, and is presently a Jean Monnet Fellow at the European University Institute, Florence.

MARTIN RHODES is Lecturer in Politics at the University of Salford. He has written extensively on government–industry relations in Britain and France.

GEOFFREY SHEPHERD was formerly a Senior Fellow at the Science Policy Research Unit at the University of Sussex. He is co-editor of *Europe's Industries* (1983), and author of several articles on industrial policy and industrial adjustment in Europe. He now works for the World Bank.

DOUGLAS WEBBER is currently at the Max Planck Institute for Social Research in Cologne, and from 1985 to 1987 was a Research Fellow in the School of Social Sciences at the University of Sussex. He has published widely on social democracy, employment, and technology policy in the Federal Republic of Germany.

STEPHEN WILKS is Senior Lecturer in the Liverpool University Institute of Public Administration and Management. He is the author of *Industrial Policy and the Motor Industry* (1984) and his recent publications include *Comparative Government–Industry Relations: Europe, the United States, and Japan* (1987) edited with Maurice Wright.

1

Introduction

Leigh Hancher and Michael Moran

Market economies exist in a state of perpetual tension between the freedoms conferred by the private ownership of productive property and the need to impose communal limits on the exercise of these freedoms. The study of economic regulation is largely concerned with exploring and understanding that tension and that study in turn has produced a huge literature. Yet this large literature is marked by a number of distinctive and, from our perspective, limiting features.

First, it is overwhelmingly American—in the sense that it is the product of American scholarship and in the sense that it is concerned with American regulatory processes. This is in part a source of strength, because the United States possesses both the most powerful of capitalist economies and the best examples of regulation conducted as a self-conscious activity. Yet the limitations are also obvious: the questions asked, and the answers given, are disproportionately influenced by distinctively American concerns. A major consequence of this approach is that American analysis has been dominated by the debate about how far regulators are 'captives' of the regulated. As we argue in our concluding chapter this very language of 'capture' is largely the product of peculiarly American constitutional imagery.

A second limiting characteristic of the literature also reflects this American domination: most cross-national comparative work treats the American experience as a model, or at the least as a point of departure. Yet a moment's reflection shows that building a general theoretical account of regulation depends precisely on exploring the significance of such cross-national variations. A third source of weakness is perhaps a product of this neglect of comparative work: theories remain largely underdeveloped. There exists, on the one hand, a vast literature of case-studies on different American regulatory programmes. At the other end of the theoretical spectrum there is an intense search for the 'essential' nature of regulation—involving, for instance, the issue of how far it is shaped by the 'public interest' or by baser motives. Much of this theoretical debate is prescriptive in character. Between the two extremes of detailed case-studies and general theory there still exists substantial scope for the elaboration and testing of generalizations which, while limited in their range, nevertheless go beyond particular historical instances.

This collection of essays was conceived with such limitations in the existing literature on regulation in mind. The strengths and weaknesses of edited collections are well known: no collection can approach the coherence possible in a study conducted by one hand; but a co-operative effort can encompass expertise and knowledge well beyond the capacities of a single individual, and can harness the skills of scholars from different disciplines. We decided to assemble a collection because it seemed that, given the strengths and weaknesses of the existing literature on regulation, the most pressing need was to widen the geographical and substantive range of study. The most important purposes of this collection are therefore to present studies of regulatory processes which make sense in a comparative setting—and, notably in our concluding chapter, to go beyond the detail of case-studies in the search for some middle-range theoretical understanding.

The choice of studies was dictated by the three key concepts expressed in the title—capitalism, regulation, culture. Regulation is a feature of all economies, but as the American case graphically illustrates it is peculiarly important in economic systems marked by the predominance of private ownership and the allocation of resources through markets. It also became clear early in our work that there are distinctive features of regulation in the economies of the most advanced capitalist nations—a distinctiveness which we attempt to clarify in our concluding chapter. In commissioning contributions, therefore, we were guided by a number of criteria. Some were pragmatic. An immediate priority was to generate contributions which could be set alongside existing American material. The 'European' bias of the collection is therefore deliberate. A second criterion was supplied by the decision to focus on regulation in advanced capitalism. The most distinctive institutional feature of advanced capitalism is obvious: it is the organization of capital into a particular legal form, the corporation operating on a giant scale across national boundaries. Our contributors therefore are linked by a common concern with the regulatory implications of the large corporation—whether those implications concern labour markets, as in Rhodes's case; the formulation and implementation of tax regulation, as examined by Picciotto; or the problem of price regulation in a pharmaceutical industry dominated by a single concern, as examined by Hancher. What is more, all the sectors examined are undergoing rapid change—and change is a notorious source of regulatory dilemmas and problems.

Our primary concern was with the regulatory character of market economies dominated by giant corporations—but this of course begs the question how 'regulation' is itself conceived. 'Regulation' is a contested concept. Some would restrict its scope narrowly, identifying as regulation only that process of making and enforcing legal rules. A somewhat more expansive account identifies it with the activity of rule-making generally. We began indeed with the broader 'rule based' approach, but were soon driven to a yet more eclectic position. The reasons for this are elaborated in our conclusion, but they can be briefly summarized. In essence, 'regulation as rule-making', while undoubtedly significant, is inexplicable outside the context of the wider processes of intervention and control in the economies of advanced capitalist nations. The point is made in its most emphatic form by the contributions of Wilks, and by Cawson and his colleagues: in these case-studies it is plain that what is at issue is not just the specification of a set of rules but the character of control over the course of industrial adjustment in economies marked by fierce competition between large firms.

Problems of regulation are, to put it simply, dominated by questions about the control of, or control by, big corporations. But these questions, though they recur, do not present themselves in the same way in all settings. It is the recognition of this variation in setting which lies at the root of our third key concept, culture. The notion of culture as a variable in social explanation is commonly dismissed as a mere residue of what cannot be accounted for by more precise means. 'Culture' is indeed a form of shorthand for a variety of influences, and like any shorthand symbol it sacrifices subtlety in the interests of compression. In essence, when we refer to culture we refer to the rules of the regulatory game. Expectations about the purpose of regulation, about who are the legitimate participants, and about their relations with each other, are subject to great variations—across historical time, across nations, and between different economic sectors and industries. 'Culture' in our title signals an interest in the recurrent tension between the common structural forces shaping regulation in the economies of developed market nations, and the idiosyncracies introduced by unique historical, national, and industrial settings. The vagueness of 'culture' as a concept perhaps explains its relative neglect. Yet it must be addressed in any comparative study as a way of appreciating the varying forces encapsulated in different national, institutional, and industrial settings.

Regulation is indisputably a political process, and it thus exhibits one of the defining features of any such process—it involves the contest for power. As such, its study lies at the heart of the interests of political scientists. But regulation in the economies of advanced capitalist nations has an additional distinctive feature. These nations have, or at least claim to have, political systems in which constitutionalism and the rule of law are paramount features. In other words, even when regulation is not narrowly concerned with rules it is shaped by the legal structures of public power. In short, it is as eminently the domain of the lawyer as of the political scientist. In the study of regulation, therefore, lies an important opportunity for a reconciliation between the long divorced disciplines of law and political science. Consequently, the contributions to this volume are by both political scientists and by public lawyers. In some degree the contents of the individual chapters reflect some obvious differences between the two disciplines. Those writing in the tradition of political science—Rhodes's chapter is perhaps the clearest instance—tend to analyse regulation in terms of its forms, stressing modes of interest articulation and policy implementation. On the other hand those writing in the discipline of public law stress the substantive as well as procedural aspects of regulation, including the *content* of rules and the criteria governing their application. In part these differences in themselves reflect contrasting intellectual traditions. The Americanization of British political science in the 1960s submerged an older European tradition which was more broadly concerned with an institutional analysis of public power—with its embodiment in legal codes and institutions and with its discretionary exercise. This tradition survived in public law, and can be seen notably in the contributions by Picciotto and by Prosser.

The significance of this division between the disciplines of law and politics should, nevertheless, not be overstressed. Moran's essay on investor protection, for instance, is substantially concerned with the elaboration and implementation of legal rules, while Hancher's chapter on pharmaceuticals, though focused on the courts, is partly concerned with the sort of bargaining between powerful actors which would be of central interest to any political scientist. Indeed the most enduring feature of the collection is not so much diversity as the recurrence of a limited number of key themes. We examine these in detail in our conclusion, and here do no more than offer a brief anticipation. Four themes emerge as of special importance.

1. Economic regulation is an activity increasingly dominated by large organizations. Private citizens only matter in so far as they enter regulatory arenas in specific organizational roles.

2. Conventional divisions between public and private spheres of power lose most meaning in regulatory arenas. 'Public' bodies like departments of state routinely represent 'private' interests in the debates surrounding regulation. Formally, private bodies, like trade associations, routinely carry out nominally public roles, such as the implementation of particular regulations.

3. Of all the big organizations involved in regulation, large firms have a peculiar importance. Corporate strategies shape both the working and execution of regulatory policy. Big firms are public institutions, though the degree to which this is recognized varies internationally.

4. Big organizations profoundly influence economic regulation, but they do not everywhere dominate it in the same way. Understanding regulation means understanding how the cultures and structures of critical organizations are shaped—and this demands attention to national setting, historical timing, and the nature of regulatory issues and arenas. The impact of cultural influences on the *organizational* character of regulation is perhaps the most distinctive feature to emerge from the substantive chapters—and, appropriately, it forms a major theme of our synthesis in the conclusion.

The selection and ordering of the individual chapters themselves is governed by the mixture of analytical considerations sketched in the preceding pages. Granted our initial focus on the regulation of economic activity in the most advanced market economies, and a desire to expand the scope of empirical work beyond a focus solely on the United States, our first priority was to present evidence about the character of regulation in the financial sector. This is not only because it is a highly topical area, but also because it is here that many of the structural features of advanced capitalism—fierce competition, large-scale organization, rapid innovation—are most highly developed. As such the sector presents regulators, who must continually assess, reassess, and reformulate governing rules, with a task of enormous complexity. The consequences of their actions reverberate throughout the economy and across national boundaries.

This theme is notably developed in Picciotto's chapter—itself an important exercise in excavation. As its starting-point he takes one of the single greatest structural changes of modern times—the rise of the multinational corporation. His analysis shows how esoteric and neglected debates about taxation regulation actually raise issues central to the power and capacity of nation-states. Moran's contribution has a narrower starting-point—the issue of investor protection—but it uses the issue to explore the impact of structural change on regulatory norms in financial markets.

The studies in Part 2 are chosen and arranged with two particular considerations in mind: they are intended to explore the development of institutionalized interdependence between large organizations in advanced capitalism, and are intended to show the variety of examinations offered by the different disciplinary traditions of political science and law. This explains the choice of two 'mature' technologically advanced industries—automobiles and pharmaceuticals—and one, consumer electronics, which is at the frontier of both technical innovation and international competition. Graham's chapter looks in detail at the legal status of the company, the central institution in the whole collection. Prosser's study is included because, in examining the regulatory implications of privatization, it looks at the consequences of perhaps the single most important development in the structure of developed market economies in the 1980s.

Hancher's, Prosser's, and Graham's contributions all share a distinctively legal perspective: a concern with the impact of different legal traditions, and an emphasis on the importance of institutional arrangements and regulatory procedures. By contrast, both Wilks, and Cawson, Shepherd, and Webber, begin with the phenomenon of structural change in their industries, and chart the way change imposes constraints on actors in both state institutions and in markets. Rhodes's chapter likewise reflects a concern with the impact of structural change, but because it shifts both the area and level of analysis has been segregated into a separate section. His comparative examination of regulation and de-regulation of labour markets is distinguished by its emphasis on the significance of controls within individual firms, and even individual plants. It is also marked by an appreciation of the different national institutional and legal frameworks within which the regulation of labour markets occurs, and by the extent to which these national differences have been partially overriden in the 1980s by common experiences of recession and international competition. Rhodes's examination of the tension between national peculiarity and cross-national convergence is indeed emblematic, for the tensions between the national and the international, the unique and the common, are recurrent features of all the contributions.

Our concluding chapter has a variety of purposes. It is not a summary of the preceding contributions, but it draws on them in order to offer a framework for making sense of existing findings, and as a way of providing an agenda for further research.

PART 1

Financial Regulation

2

Slicing a Shadow: Business Taxation in an International Framework

Sol Picciotto

Introduction

Most studies of economic regulation are confined to a national framework, or perhaps go outside the boundaries of the nation-state for foreign comparisons. Alternatively, specialists in international relations or law deal with the inter-governmental aspects of regulation. In recent years, however, there has been a greater awareness of the interaction of national systems of regulation, especially as applied to international business. Initially this was due to increasing public awareness and discussion of Transnational Corporations (TNCs). More recently, the de-regulation of markets has paradoxically led to a greater awareness of the regulatory frameworks within which market transactions take place, and an increasing interest in the international co-ordination of this regulation.

Both the growth of TNCs and international de- (or re-)regulation are frequently thought to express increasing national interdependence, which has led to some reconsideration of both legal and political processes in terms of transnationalism. In political science, this has meant taking into account the emergence of new transnational actors: the world stage now contains not only governments, but also corporations, pressure groups, and non-governmental organizations. Transnational law identifies an increasingly close interaction between public and private international law, resulting from the involvement of the state and public policy in international private law transactions. In both cases the notion of transnationalism is frequently linked to the view that there has been a weakening of the nation-state resulting from the pressures of increasing national economic interdependence.[1] On closer examination, a number of objections can be made to this view. First, in reality there seems no sign of the national state being weakened: the ideological force of nationalism has certainly continued to grow and with it the legitimizing function and the welfare activities of the state: and these are hard to separate from the more general economic–regulatory role of the state. More seriously, close consideration shows that internationalization is as much a political as an economic process. For example, in the formation of the European Community, probably the most significant catalyst of internationalization in this half-century, the impetus was more political than economic.

Above all, it seems mistaken to assume that developments such as the emergence of TNCs entail a strengthening of international economic ties and a weakening of national political structures. Indeed, both neo-classical and neo-Marxist theories emphasize that the growth of TNCs or multinational enterprise results from the power to take advantage of *differences* in markets, most importantly differences created by state controls and protectionism. In the neo-classical perspective, it is market imperfections (such as technological monopoly, or state intervention) which create the firm-specific advantages which alone can explain the efficiency of the internalization of activities within the transnational firm in place of their performance via world markets.[2] For the neo-Marxist, international uneven development is both created by, and facilitates the domination of, giant finance-capitalist firms.[3] Hence, transnationally organized capital, as represented by TNCs, circumvents and takes advantage of differences in national regulation; while it may desire their co-ordination, it by no means requires their elimination.

What is needed, therefore, is an analysis of changing forms of state regulation within an international context. This analysis should move away from the state-centred perspective which assumes that national regulation and international interdependence are opposed, to emphasize the interaction of national and international regulation. This perspective should enable us to analyse regulatory forms not in terms of the extent to which political structures are adequate to or functional for economic relations, but in terms of the interplay of political and economic factors, as well as allowing a consideration of the contradictions and limits of the regulatory forms themselves.

Conflict and Co-ordination of Regulatory Jurisdiction

An increasingly prominent feature in recent years has been the problem of overlap and conflict of business regulation by national authorities. This is frequently referred to as the problem of extraterritoriality, and is seen as resulting from an aggressive assertion of jurisdiction by regulatory authorities, often American, although US writers point out that business regulation by other authorities, notably the EEC, also has an extraterritorial scope.[4]

The internationalization and liberalization of markets has led to pressures, once again mainly from the US regulatory authorities, for increased international regulatory co-operation. The problem of conflicts of regulatory jurisdiction has a longer history than is sometimes supposed. For example, the revival of US antitrust, in the second phase of the Roosevelt Administration after 1938,[5] involved an attack on many of the cartels that had dominated global industries since the turn of the century, and which had been encouraged or even fostered by European states as a means of largely private industrial 'planning'. The US antitrust attack led some European companies to seek support from their home governments and use their laws where possible in a defensive way. British government intervention obtained the suspension of some US antitrust actions during the Second World War and impeded others during the immediate post-war period.[6] However, since the application of competition laws to regulate industrial structure can be a highly nationalistic and interventionist matter, the internationalization of antitrust has over a long period been marked by relatively little inter-governmental co-ordination and notable conflicts such as over shipping, airlines (the Laker affair and Bermuda II), raw materials cartels (uranium and the Westinghouse affair), and others. More recent efforts at international regulatory co-ordination have focused on financial markets, and have been aimed at activities defined as fraudulent (insider trading, money laundering), and at improving supervision in banking. The US authorities have been especially concerned to try to control the use of financial havens for tax evasion, laundering of the proceeds of crime, and market manipulation. US government pressures on the Swiss authorities produced not only the treaty for mutual assistance in criminal matters, brought into force in 1977, but more significantly the private agreement among Swiss bankers of 1982 which gave the Securities and Exchange Commission (SEC) unprecedented access to Swiss bank account information. Continued conflicts, such as over the Marc Rich case, have required continuing attempts to improve co-operation. Nevertheless, this model has been used to develop administrative co-operation based on information exchange with other states. British government agencies have been won over to this approach, partly as a means of avoiding extraterritoriality conflicts, and have helped the US to obtain mutual assistance agreements with Caribbean island states. Further, in September 1986 a Memorandum of Understanding was signed by the SEC and the Commodity Futures Trading Commission (CFTC) with the UK's Department of Trade, for the confidential exchange of information relating to malpractice in financial markets. Although drafted in legal language, it purported to be a purely practical arrangement between the administrative authorities; but the memorandum is stated to be the prelude to a full-scale treaty.[7] At the same time, a multilateral arrangement for information exchange in relation to insider dealing is under discussion in the Council of Europe, with the participation of the US and other non-European states. In the field of supervision, there have been continued efforts to strengthen the Basle Concordat of bank supervisors, as well as a tentative US–UK agreement on common minimum capital standards for banks, resulting in some concern at the European Commission, which had long wished to develop European standards in this area.

As other chapters in this work illustrate, business regulation in an era dominated by the giant corporation has taken a characteristic bureaucratic–corporatist form. This is also true for the international dimension of regulation. Indeed, in some respects, this characteristic has been imported from the international to the national arena. Many areas of business regulation, though established and operated by national state authorities, have from the beginning had an international dimension, whether through imitation or importation of regulatory models, the application of national requirements to businesses operating abroad, or their modification to avoid restrictions on foreign expansion. In some areas the pressures to develop regulatory practices acceptable or appropriate to the corporate economy came from the global rather than the purely national arena: this was so, for example, in the nineteenth century in relation to the regulation of technical innovation in a framework of protection of intellectual property, and in the twentieth century for the attempt to control bribery and corrupt practices.

The development of international business regulation has not taken place within an orderly framework of international organization providing an international political basis for the rational co-ordination of national state regulation. Rather, there has been a jumble of arrangements, formal and informal, inter-governmental, as well as non- or even quasi-governmental.[8] An important aspect has been the growth of an international bureaucratic–administrative culture, which has both influenced changes in national regulation and developed various forms of international co-ordination. However, due to its narrow political base, international co-ordination has remained a technical and specialist matter. The continued growth of big business has gone hand in hand with its internationalization, and its effective regulation has laid ever greater stress on the bureaucratic–corporatist administrative processes, as well as creating an increasing necessity for internationalization. Equally, the problems of effectiveness and legitimacy of regulation have an international dimension, and their solutions must be sought in an international framework.

This chapter seeks to explore some of these issues in greater detail by an examination of the historical development of the regulatory framework for international business taxation. From its inception, the direct taxation of business profits by national revenue authorities has had to take account of the various forms of involvement of nationally based business with global trading and investment. The patterns of internationalization of business were significantly influenced by the provisions for taxation of business profits or investment earnings made abroad, and by the attempts of national tax authorities to resolve the problem of allocation among the relevant tax jurisdictions of the earnings of international businesses. An important feature was the network of treaties for the avoidance of double taxation, whose principles emerged from the work of an international group of fiscal specialists between the wars, and which were actively implemented by the capital-exporting countries after 1945. This system effectively limited taxation of business profits at source by the capital-importing country and gave priority to the capital-exporting country in the taxation of investment earnings (dividends, interest, and royalties) upon repatriation. However, this allowed internationally organized businesses to channel such returns via third country tax havens, thus providing virtual tax exemption for retained earnings. This apparently privileged position was subject to increasing pressures as debates about fiscal equity and effectiveness grew, and led to more active administrative measures to ensure a 'fair' national tax take from international business. As with other areas of business regulation, a problem of extraterritoriality arose: in this case by the assertion of some state tax authorities in the United States of the right to tax a calculated proportion of the world-wide profits of a multinational company group, under the system of World-wide Unitary Taxation (WUT). On closer examination, the current debate over WUT can be seen to go back to the origins of the discussions over international business taxation, and to reopen some of the broader political and economic issues which had been obscured by a variety of administrative and technical arrangements.

In what follows I will first give a sketch of the recent controversy over WUT, before discussing the historical growth of international business taxation.

The Dispute over World-wide Unitary Taxation

During the 1970s an increasingly publicized dispute developed over the use by a number of state jurisdictions in the United States of the system of World-wide Unitary Taxation, or the apportionment on the basis of a formula of the world-wide taxable income of a unitary business of a TNC. Formula apportionment had originated as a means of taxation of cross-jurisdictional business *within* the United States. As early as the 1870s, the application of state property taxes to railroads began to be done on the basis of the proportion of length of track within each jurisdiction.[9] With the introduction in many states during the 1920s of business taxes based on income, some state tax codes provided for the source of income of a multistate unitary business to be allocated on the basis of the proportion of activities within the state, calculated on the basis of a variety of factors, such as property, sales, purchases, and payroll. In the 1930s, the principles of combined reporting and formula apportionment also began to be applied to affiliated companies under common ownership or control. Notably, this was introduced by California's Franchise Tax Board (FTB), to deal with the practice in the motion picture industry of using affiliate companies incorporated in low-tax Nevada to distribute films made in California, ensuring that the profits accrued to the distribution rather than the production company. Harmonization among the states was largely achieved by the adoption of UDITPA (the Uniform Division of Income for Tax Purposes Act) in the 1960s, under threat of Federal legislation, and of regulations and practices formulated by the Multistate Tax Commission.

The controversy that emerged in the 1970s centred on the application, by California and a dozen other states, of this formula apportionment method to the combined world-wide activities of TNCs engaged in a unitary business. This method cut across the separate accounting method based on 'arm's length' pricing, which had emerged in international treaty practice as the primary basis for the allocation between jurisdictions of the taxable capacity of international businesses.

State World-wide Unitary Taxation does not seem to have resulted from any deliberate or unified policy, but rather from the momentum of the legal and administrative principles, developed within a Federal context, being applied to an increasingly internationalized business environment. In California, the turning-point was the decision of its Supreme Court in 1963 that formula apportionment should be used not merely as an option where separate accounting did not produce an adequate allocation (which had been the FTB's practice), but as a uniform principle for any unitary business.[10] The case concerned oil drilled in California and sold at the well-head to independent third parties; the taxpayers, not the FTB, wished the oil-drilling activities of their related businesses in other states to be treated as unitary with those in California. Indeed, it is the FTB view that the emergence of world-wide unitary combination resulted from the inclusion by some taxpayers of foreign operators in their combined reports, in order to reduce their assessment. The FTB can therefore not be blamed for applying the same treatment to others for whom the result was increased assessments.[11]

Whilst the mandatory application of the unitary principle and its extension to world-wide activities was beneficial to some, mainly US-owned, corporations, in the early 1970s it produced some rapid increases in liability to California tax of some other, mainly non-American, TNCs, resulting in a number of legal challenges. The US Supreme Court held in the Japan Line case that a state property tax based on formulary apportionment was unconstitutional under the commerce clause because it created a substantial risk of international multiple taxation and interfered with the Federal government's treaty power.[12] However, in the Container Corporation case the Court by majority upheld California's application of its corporate franchise tax on a world-wide unitary basis to a US TNC. Justice Brennan expressed the view that 'Allocating income among various tax jurisdictions bears some resemblance . . . to slicing a shadow. In the absence of a central co-ordinating authority, absolute consistency, even among tax authorities whose basic approach is quite similar, may just be too much to ask.'[13] Since geographical accounting based on the arm's length principle would be equally imperfect, and since no government *amicus curiae* brief had been filed to support the argument of interference with foreign relations, unconstitutionality had not been established.

In the meantime, a more generalized campaign developed to obtain a reversal of the trend towards unitary taxation. At first, the methods attempted were discreet: large corporations generally prefer to explain a reasonable case directly to a responsible official than to create a public row, which may be counter-productive. In this case, British TNCs found sympathetic ears in the British Treasury and the Board of Inland Revenue, and to some extent also in Washington, DC. As a result, the proposed new double tax treaty between the US and the UK published in 1975, included a clause 9(4) which prohibited the use of world-wide combined reporting by either Federal or state jurisdictions for TNCs based in the other treaty partner. However, state interests lobbied the US Senate, which in 1978 approved the treaty subject to the elimination of the restriction in clause 9(4) on state taxation powers. By this time, the unitary taxation issue had become a transnational row, in which British and European TNCs quickly obtained the support both of international business organizations (notably the International Chamber of Commerce, a veteran campaigner against double taxation of international business), as well as of most national governments and relevant inter-governmental organizations (notably the Fiscal Committee of the Organization for Economic Co-operation and Development (OECD), the most active body in the international tax field). Nevertheless, as state use of world-wide combined reporting continued to spread, the arguments of its advocates grew more stubborn. The US and UK Governments were obliged in 1980 to ratify their tax treaty subject to the Senate's modification. However, the British TNCs' Unitary Tax Campaign succeeded in obtaining approval in the House of Commons for a retaliatory amendment to the Finance Bill in 1983, providing for the withdrawal of rebates of Advanced Corporation Tax (ACT) from companies headquartered in unitary tax states.

In the meantime, the US Government was subjected to increasing international pressures. Extraterritorial jurisdiction was becoming a standing item on the agenda of international summit meetings, precipitating a major row among the Allies over the Siberian gas pipeline embargo in 1982–3. The Laker affair culminated in 1984 with the British Prime Minister making a fierce attack on the US Administration to ensure the dropping of the criminal antitrust suit against British Airways.[14] The Federal authorities pulled all available political strings to try to obtain changes in state taxation that might quell the storm over unitary taxation. The World-wide Unitary Taxation Working Group, set up by the President under Treasury Secretary Donald Regan, held lengthy hearings and negotiations in November–December 1983, but could not agree recommendations for President Reagan to report to the London Economic Summit of June 1984.

When the Regan report finally emerged in August, it contained agreement in principle on, but disagreement on the actual method for, the introduction by states of the option of water's edge unitary combination. This would allow both US and foreign TNCs to be taxed on the basis of unitary combination only for US business, although the world-wide combined approach could be used if separate accounting (between their US and foreign business) resulted in tax evasion, or failed clearly to reflect income, or if the company failed to comply with disclosure requirements. In exchange for moving away from WUT, the states obtained a promise of federal assistance with the taxation of corporations, especially TNCs. The Internal Revenue Service (IRS) agreed to put more resources into auditing international business, and to help states with disclosure from corporations, including making available to states information received from treaty partners under the information exchange arrangements of double tax treaties.[15]

Continued political pressure, as well as well-publicized threats by foreign TNCs to disinvest from unitary tax states, gradually led to a move towards the water's edge option. Finally, in September 1986,

California enacted an amendment offering corporate taxpayers a water's edge election, but on stiff conditions. Companies opting out of world-wide unitary taxation would be locked in to that choice for ten years ahead, would have to accept comprehensive disclosure, and to pay a fee into a special fund.[16] Although this was hailed as a victory for the anti-unitary taxation lobby, it was clear that it by no means heralded the death knell of world-wide combined formula apportionment. US TNCs objected to the inclusion of income received from abroad within water's edge income, arguing that it failed to meet the requirement of competitive fairness. The fee requirement was also criticized as 'a ransom'; nevertheless, the Reagan Administration withdrew the threat of Federal legislation, although litigation attempting to persuade the courts to outlaw WUT continued. California expected that only some 350 of the estimated 1,000 TNCs in the state would take the water's edge option, due to the fee and the ten-year requirement (although there were moves in the California legislature to reduce this to five). Nevertheless, it was clear that if corporate taxation based on separate US accounts were to be effective, it would require a significant increase in the enforcement effort. This entailed not only an increase of Federal examiners assigned to international tax returns, but assistance to the states and an expansion of the resources of the Multistate Tax Commission. The undertaking to supply states with information obtained from treaty partners would require modifications to tax treaties, which would be a slow process. More seriously, enforcement based on separate accounts not only requires more audit resources, it necessitates detailed regulations on various aspects of intrafirm pricing, which need both international co-ordination and frequent revision. The attack on the 'myth of arm's length' by advocates of WUT had achieved some effect: even the strongest advocates of separate accounting began to stress that the arm's length criterion is only a means of establishing true or fair accounts. In the view of some academic commentators, the unitary approach could have a continuing, and perhaps increasing, validity and usefulness.[17]

International Business Taxation

The dilemma between separate accounting and formula apportionment in the allocation of jurisdiction to tax international business has a long history. From the first emergence of direct taxation of business income or profits, jurisdiction to tax international business was an immediate issue. The switch to direct taxation took place in most developed countries after 1914, as the revenue demands of the modern welfare–warfare state led to general taxes on all incomes to replace the multiplicity of specific duties. This immediately brought home to business men the relative incidence of income taxes as a factor in their competitive position; and, to those involved in international business, the interaction of national taxes became an immediate issue.

This viewpoint was expressed by Sir William Vestey, the beef baron, one of the representatives of British international business who gave evidence to the British Royal Commission on Taxation in 1919.[18] The Vestey group had moved its headquarters to Argentina in 1915, to avoid high British wartime taxes on its world wide business. They would have preferred to be based in London, but called for equality in the conditions of competition, especially with the Chicago beef trust, which avoided all British taxes by consigning beef exports f.o.b. to the UK. Sir William called for a new approach to international business taxation:

> In a business of this nature you cannot say how much is made in one country and how much is made in another. You kill an animal and the product of that animal is sold in 50 different countries. You cannot say how much is made in England and how much is made abroad. That is why I suggest you should pay a turnover tax on what is brought into this country . . . It is not my object to escape the payment of tax. My object is to get equality of taxation with the foreigner, and nothing else.

The UK was distinctive, since it had a general income tax for much of the nineteenth century. From the start it applied to all income from any source of both individuals and bodies corporate resident in the UK. When incorporation began to be more widely used, after 1870, the question immediately arose of liability to British tax of companies whose activities took place abroad. In 1876, two cases were appealed involving companies incorporated and with a Board of Directors in England, but running operations abroad. C. B. Kelly was acutely aware that the cases involved 'the international law of the world'; but the statute clearly intended to tax all the earnings of British residents no matter where in the world they were earned; and in his view it was also clear that a company was 'resident' where the investment decisions were taken.[19] This view was confirmed and taken even further in 1909 by the House of Lords, when they held that De Beers, although a company formed in South Africa and operating mines there, was resident in London, since 'the directors meetings in London are the meetings where the real control is always exercised in practically all the important business of the company except the mining operations'.[20] The logic of the British approach flowed from the liberal principle of tax justice which required all British residents to be subject to the same tax regardless of the source of their income. The UK was by far the largest source of global investment funds prior to 1914, and so it was not surprising that the (perhaps inappropriately named) Inland Revenue, backed by the Courts, should apply the income tax to all businesses whose investment decisions were taken in London. However, it was bound eventually to come into conflict with other jurisdictions, those that were net importers of investment capital. As income tax rates in the UK began to rise (after Lloyd George's 'people's budget' of 1909), the UK's first TNCs began to take steps to reduce their tax liability, as well as raising the cry of unfair taxation. Hence Vestey's transfer of its headquarters to Argentina, and Sir William's appearance before the Royal Commission.

From 1916, the Treasury conceded relief in respect of Dominion tax paid, up to half the rate of British tax liability on the same income. The Revenue argued, however, that there was no political basis for negotiated arrangements with other countries, since there was not the same 'shared purpose' as within the Empire for what was regarded as revenue sharing. The Royal Commission supported this view, although it suggested that negotiations could be tried through the League of Nations.

After the First World War, the business campaign against international double taxation became more internationalized, articulated mainly through the newly founded International Chamber of Commerce (the ICC). The ICC set up a committee, which began with the simple faith that an evident wrong could be simply righted. As its chairman, Professor Suyling, in his report to the ICC in 1923 put it:

If only the principle that the same income should only be taxed once is

> recognised, the difficulty is solved, or very nearly so. It only remains then to decide what constitutes the right of one country to tax the income of a taxpayer in preference to any other country. It does not seem probable that there would be any serious difference on the matter.[21]

Unfortunately, serious differences quickly did arise. Not only were the tax systems of different developed countries based on different principles and traditions, but conflicting economic interests were soon apparent.

The UK was not the only country which had had to adjust its new income tax to limit its application to international business. In France, after several attempts, a general income tax was introduced in 1914, as a personal tax on the income of individuals; but in 1917 separate and parallel taxes on revenues were introduced, including commercial and industrial profits. This separation of the taxation of income from the so-called schedular taxes applied to specific types of revenue gave the former a 'personal' and the latter a 'real' character. Thus the tax on profits applied to any 'establishment' situated in France, whether owned by a French or a foreign company; and a French company was not liable to tax on profits from its establishments abroad. Only individual income tax was levied on the income of all those domiciled in France, regardless of its source. Thus in France, from the beginning, business profits were taxed at source, using the concept of the 'establishment'; though investment income would be liable to the personal income tax and taxed in the hands of the recipient.

In the United States, the ratification of the 16th Amendment in 1913 was followed by the introduction of a graduated individual income tax, and, in 1917, by a tax on corporations. Both were based on citizenship: US citizens, and corporations formed under US laws, were taxed on their income from all sources world-wide; foreign companies were liable on US-source income. However, this was mitigated by the introduction into US law of a credit against US tax for the tax paid to a foreign country in respect of business carried on there, on the basis that the foreign country had the prior right to tax income from activities taking place there.[22] To prevent US taxation from being pre-empted by other countries, however, it was quickly subject to a number of limitations, in particular that the foreign tax credited could not exceed the proportion of non-US to US income. However, the tax credit was extended to allow taxes paid by the foreign subsidiaries of US corporations to be credited against the taxes of the US parent on their profit remittances.

It can be seen that similar conditions in all these countries led to the emergence, at about the same time, of direct taxes on business income or profits. Each tax system had to be adapted in some way to the conditions of international trade and investment at the time and the relationship of each country to that world economy. There were certainly therefore divergences of economic interest and ideological standpoint which were embedded in the different regulatory principles that evolved in national tax systems. Nevertheless, the divergent regulatory approaches could be reconciled where conflicts of economic interest did not reinforce the regulatory divergence. Thus the principle quickly gained acceptance that shipping enterprises should be taxed only in their home country, and this was implemented through reciprocal agreements between the main trading nations in the 1920s.

The conflict between the source and residence principles in the taxation of international investment was harder to resolve. A group of economic experts reported to the League of Nations in 1923 that the encouragement of international investment required taxation of 'movable capital' by the creditor country; taxation by the debtor would increase the costs of borrowing. This point of view was rejected by both state and business representatives in capital-importing countries. Initially, the ICC favoured the US idea of the foreign tax credit. However, it soon became clear that this only helped businesses based in high-tax countries, and indeed provided an incentive to other countries to increase their tax rates. Although the unilateral tax credit meant that the United States had no immediate need to seek accommodation with other countries, after 1926 the US Government decided to participate actively in the newly established Fiscal Committee of the League. The Anglo-American aim, generally supported by big business, was to establish limits on taxation at source of foreign-owned business. US officials 'perceived that the United States could through tax treaties retain jurisdiction over the entire taxable income of its citizens and corporations, yet on a reciprocal basis prevail upon the other Contracting State to give up a part of its tax with a view to encouraging business and investments'.[23]

Principles of Allocation and Growth of the Network of Tax Treaties

For two decades the fiscal experts of the League, working closely with business representatives in the ICC, laboured to set up a comprehensive international tax scheme. An inter-governmental meeting in 1928 failed to agree on a uniform multilateral treaty, but did approve four drafts which, with variations, could provide the basis for states to negotiate appropriate bilateral treaties. Two basic principles were agreed: a foreign company could only be taxed at source if it operated through a *permanent establishment*, and on the business profits attributable to that establishment; the home country or country of residence of an enterprise was permitted to tax its total income (including that from foreign operations), but if it did so it should provide relief either by tax credit for foreign taxes paid or by exemption of the foreign source income already subjected to tax.

This left open the question of apportionment of profits between permanent establishments or related companies in different countries: for example where the same company manufactured in one country and sold in another or, even more problematically, where it brought components from its manufacturing operation for assembly and final sale in another country. The 1928 treaty drafts merely provided that the competent administrations of the states concerned should agree on the basis of apportionment between them. The Fiscal Committee therefore commissioned a detailed study of the taxation of transnational enterprises, funded by a $90,000 grant from the Rockefeller Foundation, which resulted in a report of over 1,200 pages, comprising parallel studies of the treatment of this problem in twenty-seven different tax systems.[24]

The studies were co-ordinated by Mitchell B. Carroll, the US expert on the Fiscal Committee, who summarized the issues in an analytical report. The nub of the problem was clearly identified. A tax official must start from the accounts (if any) of the local establishment, but:

> Tax collectors complain that sometimes enterprises take the rate of tax in various countries into consideration, and fix the transfer price from the factory to the selling establishment at so high a figure as to show little or no profit in the books of the sales branch.[25]

Three approaches were used in allocating the taxable income of transnational businesses: (*a*) separate accounting; (*b*) empirical methods (based on average profits in the industry or business); and (*c*) fractional apportionment. Each had advantages and disadvantages, and they were usually employed in combination by tax authorities. The UK report estimated that some 55 per cent of total cases were settled on the basis of separate accounts, usually after negotiation; but it emphasized that 'the fact that the revenue authorities have the alternative of basing profits on a percentage of turnover prevents the taxpayer taking up an unreasonable attitude'.[26]

In a small number of tax systems, however, fractional apportionment was the primary or only basis of allocation. In Spain, for example, any branch or affiliate forming a unity with a foreign business had its profits allocated not by principles laid down by law, but by criteria laid down by a 'jury', or committee of experts, subject to the taxpayer's right of appeal. Where separate accounts were maintained, the jury had regard to them in determining the criteria for allocation. The Spanish report argued strongly for this as the only equitable method, and one which maintained the liberty of the enterprise since it did not entail the control of hundreds of costs.

On the basis of the Carroll report the Fiscal Committee drew up a convention on the allocation of business income for tax purposes. It confirmed the permanent establishment principle laid down in the 1928 conventions, and provided that where a business had permanent establishments in more than one state, there should be attributed to each 'the net business income which it might be expected to derive if it were an independent enterprise engaged in the same or similar activities under the same or similar conditions'. This should in principle be done by establishing separate accounts, if necessary by rectifying 'to re-establish the prices or remunerations entered in the books at the value which would prevail between independent persons dealing at arm's length'. Failing this, the income of the establishment might be determined by applying a percentage to the turnover comparable to that of enterprises in a similar line of business. If both of these failed, the income might be computed by applying to the total income of the enterprise as a whole 'coefficients based on a comparison of gross receipts, assets, numbers of hours worked or other appropriate factors, provided such factors be so selected as to ensure results approaching as closely as possible to those which would be reflected by a separate accounting'.[27]

Although the draft treaties laid down a preference for separate accounting and the arm's length principle, those who advocated this approach were clearly well aware of its limitations, as was shown in the account of the British Inland Revenue's practice. The German report summed up by pointing out that the ideal would be a uniform assessment of enterprises on their global activities, and the allocation of that taxable profit on agreed principles. In other words, fractional apportionment would require agreement on (*a*) how to assess the total profit; and (*b*) the criteria for apportionment of that total. Short of this ideal, assessment could still be on a national basis, but this would require reciprocal assistance between tax authorities to provide information as well as establishing an agreed basis for allocations in the light of experience.[28]

The work done by the Fiscal Committee, and the drafts it produced, provided the basis for the first tax treaties. However, hopes that a comprehensive multilateral scheme would be set up to co-ordinate business taxation were far from realized. Although some sixty general tax treaties were concluded between 1920 and 1939, they were bilateral treaties, mostly between continental European states: the only multilateral tax treaty was that of 1931 exempting automobiles from tax if entering a country temporarily. Nevertheless, the work of the Fiscal Committee was considered one of the quiet successes of the League of Nations.[29] It certainly succeeded in establishing broad agreement in principle, as well as proposing specific practical measures, on a matter of considerable international political and economic concern. The nature of its achievement perhaps reflected its approach, which emphasized the technical and avoided the political aspects of the problem. The work of the two inter-war decades created considerable formal and informal international contacts of fiscal specialists, whether government officials, academics, or business representatives and advisers (and many combined more than one role, or moved from one to another). Significantly, the Committee itself was constituted as a committee of 'experts', so that members did not formally represent their government; this also enabled non-members of the League to participate, notably the United States which did so very actively.

Mitchell Carroll later practised as a lawyer with Coudert Brothers and in 1938 helped found the International Fiscal Association, of which he became the long-serving first President.

The period after 1945 saw the rapid growth of a network of bilateral double tax treaties, based directly on this pre-war work. The US Government took the lead in negotiating a treaty with the UK in 1944–5, which led to the enactment of a foreign tax credit scheme in British tax law in 1945, and to the renegotiation of arrangements within the Commonwealth along the lines of the new model treaty. Treaties were also negotiated between both the US and the UK and the main European states. Nevertheless, the coverage of the treaty network was far from complete (significantly, attempts to negotiate treaties with Latin American countries largely failed), and there were continued pressures from the business lobby for unilateral action by the home states of TNCs, to grant tax exemption for foreign-source income.[30]

The transition from the League to the United Nations Organization quickly showed that neither further progress nor a radical new approach was possible on the basic principles of international taxation. Its new Fiscal Commission, whose members were now state representatives rather than experts, quickly ran into multiple political disagreements. Developing countries, with the support of the Soviet bloc, fought for the principle that the burden for relief from double taxation for international investment should be borne by the home country. The development lobby (including significant elements of international business) argued for exemption from taxation of foreign source income. In reply, the US Treasury defended the foreign tax credit as establishing tax neutrality between home and foreign investment, and argued that exemption would lead to competition to lower taxes by capital-seeking countries and undermine a sound and equitable tax system. Since international financial matters were dealt with by the International Monetary Fund (IMF) and the World Bank (IBRD), and consensus on the main principles of the international tax system seemed impossible to attain, the Fiscal Commission ceased to meet after 1954, and the UN's main role in the tax field was in publishing a collection of tax treaties, and providing technical assistance to developing countries with their tax administrations.

The role of the League's Fiscal Committee was taken over by the Organization for European Economic Co-operation (OEEC, later the OECD), which set up a Fiscal Committee in 1956. It was clear, however, that there was no political basis, even within the relatively restricted OECD forum, for a uniform multilateral solution, and the OECD Fiscal Committee had to balance the needs for uniformity and universality. It therefore concentrated on negotiating an agreed text, based on the existing League drafts and actual treaties, to be published together with an authoritative commentary to assist uniform interpretation. Bilateral treaties based on the OECD model treaty of 1963 (or the revised version of 1977) rapidly covered all the main OECD states. When the UN revived its interest in the field and set up a group of experts in 1967, they were reduced to working in the slipstream of the OECD, and to suggesting amendments to the OECD model to try to make it more acceptable to developing countries. The number of bilateral tax treaties among OECD members is now estimated at 202, while the total number they have signed with other states amounts to some 550.[31] Nevertheless only a small proportion of these are with developing countries, who in general have signed few such treaties.

International Tax Avoidance and Mutual Assistance

In responding to the business campaign after 1918 to eliminate international double taxation, the League's fiscal experts took the view from the beginning that this should go together with equivalent provisions against international fiscal evasion.[32] Business opinion was more divided on fiscal evasion: while some thought the question should not be ducked, others thought that business circles should not advocate anti-evasion measures but should defend freedom of movement of investment funds and the need for secrecy in banking operations and confidentiality of business information.[33] The 1928 inter-governmental meeting agreed the texts of draft conventions on mutual assistance for both the assessment and collection of taxes, in addition to the double tax avoidance treaty drafts. However, few mutual assistance treaties were actually concluded, and they were mainly between neighbouring European countries.[34]

The question of administrative assistance between national tax authorities was unavoidable when it came to the allocation of the income of an international business. As we have seen, the 1935 model treaty provided that the accounts of transactions between permanent establishments of the same firm, or between affiliated companies, might require 'rectification' in accordance with the arm's length principle. Clearly, if such rectification were carried out unilaterally by one state, the result could be double taxation; to avoid this, some form of consultation and co-ordination was necessary. Business opinion stressed that such rectification must be by agreement, and that there should be a procedure for the settlement of disputes by a technical body. The 1935 treaty draft in fact provided for a dispute-settlement procedure before a technical body to be set up by the League.[35] However, national tax administrations were reluctant to cede their powers to assess the tax liability of their own taxpayers, and took the view that honest differences of view between tax authorities were possible, and such divergences did not necessarily amount to double taxation.[36] The League's Fiscal Committee continued to stress the interrelationship between the elimination of double taxation and provisions for mutual assistance between tax administrations, mainly in the exchange of information.[37] However, some governments, notably the British, were reluctant to modify their domestic legislation to comply with the needs of foreign administrations, or to ask their nationals for information not required for the purposes of national taxation.[38]

Even after 1945, no mutual assistance treaties were signed. Instead, provisions for mutual administrative assistance were included in the double tax avoidance treaties. The US IRS favoured comprehensive provisions for the exchange of information to combat tax evasion, as well as for assistance in collection. Within the British Government there was some fear that arrangements for the exchange of information, by threatening banker–client confidentiality, might lead to an outflow of money invested through the City.[39] Nevertheless, a limited clause was agreed in the US–UK treaty, for the exchange of information necessary for the operation of the agreement and subject to safeguards for confidentiality and the exclusion of information involving commercial secrets or national security. Although the UK refused arrangements for assistance in tax collection,[40] France and some other countries agreed treaties which included assistance in collection, as well as broader provisions for information exchange to combat tax evasion generally. Despite these variations, it seems that the US authorities supplied the same type of information to all treaty partners; no programme to combat international tax evasion was established until much later, and information exchange consisted mainly of supplying lists of recipients of dividend and other payments having an address in the other state.[41] Some work was done in the OECD committee to try to standardize the format for such lists.

In addition, the tax treaties made provision for 'corresponding adjustments' to deal with economic double taxation created by the 'rectification' of transfer prices unilaterally. This gave the individual taxpayer the right to lodge a claim with his own tax authority to recognize the effect of such a rectification by another; but it was left to the two 'competent authorities' to negotiate a corresponding adjustment, if they considered it appropriate. There was no obligation on the state authorities to resolve any overlapping taxation, the taxpayer was given no standing in the matter, and the procedure fell far short of the system of arbitration envisaged in 1935.[42]

The 'corresponding adjustment' procedure was part of a general power given to the 'competent authorities' to resolve by 'mutual agreement' any problems arising in the application of the convention. This mutual agreement provision is important in allowing the revenue authorities to make direct contact with each other to discuss and negotiate international tax issues falling within the general ambit of the treaty, without being required to go through diplomatic channels.[45] The legal character of this mutual agreement provision raises some fascinating issues, since it gives officials of different countries a discretionary power to reach accommodations which may have the effect of modifying national law, both in particular cases and in general.[44]

The growth of the tax treaty network clearly facilitated the expansion of international investment in the post-war period, and TNCs in particular were quick to set up the most advantageous international fiscal arrangements. These essentially involved the avoidance of tax on retained earnings, by routing intrafirm payments, via countries with favourable treaty arrangements, to be accumulated in intermediary companies in low-tax jurisdictions, or 'tax havens', ready for reinvestment. The Netherlands Antilles, which has long been one of the cornerstones of such arrangements, due to the extension of post-war Dutch tax treaties to it, announced low-tax rates specifically designed to attract holding companies as early as January 1953.[45] In the words of one tax specialist:

> Simply put, the game plan was, first to have the greatest possible amount of the multinational enterprise's income earned by foreign subsidiaries and, second, to have the greatest possible portion of the foreign subsidiaries' income earned in jurisdictions where the tax rates were low.[46]

This avoidance of tax on retained earnings was to some extent an accepted, although controversial, result of the tax policies of the TNCs' home countries. Under US law in particular, the earnings of foreign subsidiaries paid no US tax until remitted to the US; but once dividends were paid to the US parent, foreign taxes paid could be credited against the parent's US tax liability.

However, the TNCs' tax planning systems effectively undermined the aims of the international tax policies of the OECD countries, and the system of allocation developed and enshrined in the treaties, since they reduced the tax take of *both* the source country *and* the home country. Tax haven subsidiaries used for 'service' functions, such as making loans, licensing technology, organizing distribution, or arranging insurance, can make charges for these to the operating companies which are deductible from the latter's gross profits, thus reducing or even eliminating the business profits taxable at source; the treaty arrangements also restrict the withholding taxes that may be applied at source to any payments made by the operating companies in respect of such central service functions. Yet such payments, if they are accumulated in a tax haven, do not pay tax in the TNC's country of ultimate residence either, thus effectively avoiding all taxation. As we have seen, the treaty system embodied a compromise, which allocated business profits to be taxed where they were made (under the permanent establishment principle), while favouring taxation by the creditor countries of the returns on capital invested, to ensure tax neutrality between their home and overseas investments. But TNCs, by taking advantage of their financial centralization and of the differences between and interaction of national tax systems, have effectively managed to capitalize and allocate their central service or overhead costs so as to reduce the taxation of the business profits of their subsidiaries, while organizing their financial systems so as to eliminate taxation of retained earnings.[47]

Under domestic political pressures to ensure 'fair' taxation of profits from overseas investments, the tax administrations of the main capitalist countries, led by the United States, have been making desperate efforts to patch up the system. In the United States, a proposal by the Kennedy Administration to bring retained foreign earnings into tax resulted only in the relatively mild Subpart F provisions enacted in 1962. Although the abolition of deferral again figured in the original Reagan proposals for tax reform, it had disappeared by the time the reform was finalized in 1986.[48] In the meantime, other countries have also taken similar measures, which involve 'lifting the veil' of tax haven subsidiaries, defined in different ways as Controlled Foreign Corporations, and deeming their income to accrue to the parent and to be taxable in the home country. Such provisions have now been enacted by Canada, West Germany, France, Japan, and finally the UK, where proposals made in 1981 were much criticized by the City and weakened before enactment in 1984.[49] The generalization of such measures has weakened the cogency of the argument commonly made by TNCs at home, that such regulation might undermine their position in foreign markets *vis-à-vis* competitors. However, they have been on stronger ground in attacking the validity of the assertion of jurisdiction by their home country over their foreign profits. This has led to the limitation of such measures, by various complex technical devices, to try to avoid taxation of profits that could be said to be legitimately earned abroad; such limitations inevitably create further potential loopholes. Clearly, purely nationalistic political pressures that TNCs should bear their fair shares of national taxation are a poor basis for an adequate approach to international taxation.

The Problem of Transfer Pricing and the Growth of International Administrative Action

These measures against tax haven subsidiaries have attempted to reaffirm the jurisdiction of the creditor countries over investment profits. They have been paralleled by the efforts made to bring effectiveness to the existing system's other main principle, that of separate accounting for business profits, based on the arm's length rule. Most national tax systems have long included a provision requiring the accounts of related entities to be a fair reflection of normal trading principles.[50] From the late 1960s more active measures were taken to scrutinize inter-affiliate pricing and apply the arm's length rule. The IRS published detailed regulations under section 482 of the Tax Code in 1968; a commentator involved at the time as an official has described this as an attempt to 'bring order out of the chaos' of divergent applications of the rule by IRS field agents.[51] In the UK, the Inland Revenue in 1976 established a special central unit focusing on the pricing policies of TNCs, in the aftermath of the furore over the report of the Monopolies Commission on Hoffman-La Roche.[52]

The move towards the active policing of TNC transfer-pricing was co-ordinated through the OECD Fiscal Committee and its working parties: the well-known OECD report on *Transfer Pricing and Multinational Enterprises* of 1979 was followed by studies on specific aspects, notably the allocation of central management and service costs, the problem of thin capitalization, and foreign exchange gains and losses.[53] This work has concentrated very much on operationalizing the arm's length rule in a co-ordinated way, and has resulted in national administrative action in the main OECD countries.[54]

In addition to this co-ordinated national action, the past ten years have seen the growth of international administrative action in the taxation of TNCs. There has been significant growth of the procedures for negotiation by the 'competent authorities' of a 'corresponding adjustment' under the mutual agreement provision of tax treaties.[55] In 1970 the US IRS adopted regulations for invoking the competent authority procedure.[56] Although the numbers of such Competent Authority cases are relatively few, they involve large sums. Taxpayers complain of excessive delay and secrecy, and there is still pressure for an international quasi-judicial procedure and a right to a hearing.[57]

More directly aimed at combating tax avoidance has been the increased use of information exchange arrangements under tax treaties, especially information about specific taxpayers supplied on request. However, some tax authorities are wary of going too far: the Inland Revenue view in the UK is that information can be supplied only if it is already on file or if there is a UK tax interest—they do not wish to be thought to be making enquiries on behalf of foreign tax authorities.[58] There have also been the well-known difficulties in relation to bank secrecy, especially with Switzerland. The US authorities, who are the most persistent in requesting and the most willing to provide information, estimate that they handle an average of 150 requests in each direction for each country per year.[59] The IRS has permanent liaison officers stationed in several key US Embassies who act as contact points for information requests both directly to taxpayers and to the Competent Authority. The French tax administration also has five fiscal attachés in foreign embassies, whose role is essentially to facilitate information exchange with the local tax authorities; and West Germany is experimenting with an attaché in Washington, DC.

In addition, once again at the instigation of the United States, several countries have set up procedures for the *simultaneous examination* of related taxpayers, under semi-formal and secretive working arrangements.[60] These provide for the selection by mutual agreement of related taxpayers, whose assessment is then carried out according to an agreed timetable and with an exchange of information as it proceeds. The procedure is aimed particularly at related companies in treaty countries whose dealings are intermediated by tax haven affiliates. Since 1977 the US has established such arrangements with Canada, the UK, France, Italy, Norway, and West Germany, and others are under discussion. Although no more than a handful of company groups may be examined in this way each year, the aim is to establish accounting schemes that can be agreed between the revenue authorities and the company, which can merely be monitored in succeeding years.

The outstanding feature of these developments is that they involve purely administrative arrangements. In all the countries concerned, the legal authority for establishing the arrangements has been the existing tax treaties and national legislation embodying their provisions. Thus the regulations for the adjustment of transfer prices to the arm's length standard flow from a few lines in Articles 7 and 9 of the OECD model treaty. Similarly, the arrangements for information exchange, corresponding adjustments, and mutual agreement generally, as well as simultaneous examination, all derive from the treaty provisions based on Articles 25 and 26 of the OECD model.

The treaty provisions have also been used as the legal basis for the organization of regular meetings of tax administrators to co-ordinate action against international avoidance. In particular, France, West Germany, the UK, and the US have held regular meetings, at both policy-making level and in working groups of administrators, since about 1970, although even the existence of this group was officially admitted only in 1982. Those involved are very coy about discussing the work of the group, which is resented by outsiders who refer to it as the 'gang of four'. Its existence is formally justified by the reference in the mutual agreement article of the bilateral tax treaties to consultations over both the interpretation and application of the treaty provisions, as well as for the elimination of double taxation in cases not covered by the treaty.

A striking illustration of the reluctance to go outside the existing legal authority of the tax treaty network is provided by the failure of the European Commission to persuade the tax authorities of the EC states to make use of the Council's Directive on mutual assistance in direct taxation.[61] Although the actual formal provisions of this Directive are very similar to those of the tax treaties, the Commission's hope that the transnational nature of the Community would provide a basis for closer collaboration has been disappointed; its provisions have been little used, tax authorities preferring to operate under the bilateral tax treaty arrangements.[62] Equally, a proposed multilateral convention on mutual administrative assistance in tax matters, handled jointly by the OECD and the Council of Europe, was strongly opposed by the business lobby, creating political difficulties, especially in West Germany, which held up its approval, although its actual provisions are very similar to the League of Nation's drafts of 1935 on assistance in assessment and collection of taxes.[63]

The international arrangements have therefore taken a secretive, bureaucratic, and *ad hoc* form. In some respects, this may be an advantage to TNCs, since they have the resources and the authority to negotiate directly with the responsible national government officials, while their ability to plan globally far exceeds the degree of international co-ordination that tax officials have so far managed to achieve. The system may therefore be described as a bureaucratic–corporatist one, highly specialized and with a relatively small number of participants. The greater availability of resources to the business side also undermines efficient enforcement by the continual draining of skilled personnel: everywhere (with the possible exception of Japan) one finds that the key tax management consultants are former Tax or Treasury officials, usually those regarded as the best or most knowledgeable in the field.

However, in some respects the system is also disfunctional for the corporations. The administrators have a power of initiative which can be a significant threat to business planning. When propelled by pressures to take action against abuse, such administrative initiatives can prove very difficult to control or counter within the bureaucratic procedures described above. This seems to be the motive, for example, for the continued calls by business representatives for a more open and quasi-judicial framework for the 'corresponding adjustment' procedure via the Competent Authority. Similarly, the business opposition which held up the OECD/Council of Europe multilateral convention mentioned above, has been based on its lack of defined standards, inadequate rights of notice or provision for hearing, and so on.[64] Yet the business calls for a fairer procedure have been generally resisted by governments, since such changes are not easy to introduce into the technical, bureaucratic, and essentially *ad hoc* nature of the existing structure.

International Regulation and Legitimacy

The contradictions now facing the international tax system can be characterized in several respects as a legitimation crisis. I refer to legitimation not merely in an ideological sense, a deficiency of which could perhaps be remedied by the establishment of more open, even legal, and politically acceptable procedures. The problem of legitimacy goes deeper, indeed to the very roots of the regulatory system. The large transnational corporations embody concentrations of global economic power which, despite being subjected to a multiplicity of diverse and sometimes conflicting political direction, have largely escaped any effective social accountability and control. In the field of taxation, there is no real possibility of establishing 'fairness' in taxing TNCs, either in relation to individuals, national companies, or between TNCs in different industries or with different characteristics. The best that tax administrations can hope for is to establish an adequate levy, based on negotiation and bargaining. To be effective, such a system would require a great strengthening of international political authority and power, which would in turn undercut much of the economic foundations of international business concentration and centralization. This problem of legitimacy is therefore both national and international.

Since 1918, and especially since 1945, national income and profits taxes have been framed and co-ordinated to enable or facilitate direct foreign investment. Indeed, the globally integrated TNCs quickly found the means, after 1950, to ensure that their international investments bore a lower overall tax burden than would purely national investments. This undermined the existing processes for establishing tax equality both nationally and internationally. Nationally, the notion of equivalence between similarly situated taxpayers is very difficult or impossible to apply as between TNCs and domestic taxpayers, since the very reason for existence of a TNC is the advantage that integration of its activities gives it over firms operating the same businesses via the market. So, as we have seen, national pressures for TNCs to bear a fair share of tax, under the existing system, become demands for the claw-back of profits that could be said to be earned abroad.

At the international level also, the taxation of transnational business has been increasingly shown to rest upon an inadequate basis of legitimacy. The differences over the taxation of international investment resulted in a compromise between the residence and source principles, resulting in the double taxation treaty system. However, although there is some basis of reciprocity for this among developed countries, developing countries have generally been unable to accept it. They have consequently remained largely outside the network of administrative arrangements which have grown up to combat international tax avoidance and fraud.

Even between developed countries, as we have seen, the tax treaty system was undermined by the growth of globally integrated TNCs. Under domestic political pressure, the reaction of the regulators was to strengthen enforcement of the existing system, based on separate accounting and the arm's length rule. But the internationally integrated nature of the TNC has increasingly exposed the inadequacy of an inter-state allocation based on the market criterion of arm's length.[65] Studies of the operation of the arm's length rule, especially in the United States, have repeatedly shown the discretionary or even arbitrary nature of its operation in practice.[66]

This explains the heat generated by the controversy over Worldwide Unitary Taxation, which offers a radical alternative regulatory approach to international taxation. The validity of an alternative to separate accounting has indeed been understood from the beginning, as was shown by Sir William Vestey's remarks in 1919 quoted above. Even the technocrats who dominated the process by which the international tax arrangements emerged in the 1930s also recognized that global apportionment would provide a sounder basis for the system; but they shrank from the political challenge of advocating such a system. Nevertheless, as the German contribution to the Carroll report concluded, it might be that the process of administrative assistance could lead to 'the establishment of certain well-defined allocation percentages'.[67] It could be argued that this is what is now occurring through the bureaucratic–administrative allocation processes described above. Thus a technical, bureaucratic process of negotiated allocation is taking the place of a more overt political process to decide the principles which should be used.

Nevetheless, the clear lack of an adequate basis of legitimacy for the allocation process makes it very inefficient. The TNCs themselves complain about the lack of fairness of arbitrary allocations, as well as the secretiveness and delay, for example, of the Competent Authority procedure. Nevertheless, they generally defend the existing system, since their global tax planning enables them to take advantage of the interaction of national tax systems to minimize taxation of retained profits. The administrators, for their part, are not happy at the prospect of stirring up the hornet's nest of legitimacy. Nevertheless, they have been aware of symptoms of the weakness of the system (such as the imprecision of the 'permanent establishment' principle), and sensitive to criticisms of ineffective or arbitrary enforcement.

Even academics have generally been deterred by the complex technicalities of international tax arrangements from attempting analyses which go much beyond explanatory descriptions. A notable exception were the well-respected public finance specialists, Peggy B. and Richard A. Musgrave, who in two articles published in 1972 gave an insightful analysis from an economist's perspective of the problems of equity in the allocation of the international tax base.[68] Perhaps unsurprisingly, their view was that, for inter-nation equity, the principle of taxation by source was preferable to residence, while inter-taxpayer equity could be resolved in each country by allowing either credit or deduction of foreign taxes paid, depending on whether an international or national view is taken of equity. The source of profits is best defined, they argued, by a formula based on relevant economic factors reflecting *activity* rather than the formal legal criterion of an *establishment*. Above all, they showed that if the global activities of a TNC are interdependent, then separate accounting and arm's length pricing will always be inappropriate, since they cannot take into account the cost savings or monopoly profits produced by integration. This type of analysis went some way to explaining the practical difficulties experienced in administering the arm's length rule. The logic of the Musgraves' approach led to the need for multilateral agreement on a uniform corporation tax rate, which could be on a scale to allow for redistribution, related inversely to per capita income in the capital-importing country and directly to per capita income in the capital-exporting country. Further, some form of international tax administration would be desirable, to secure global reporting of balance sheet and income data, and for carrying out the apportionment of the tax base according to the agreed formula. Naturally, officials and TNC managers dismiss such talk as academic utopianism.

Nevertheless, WUT offers a perspective for radical reform of the regulatory system, although it is not a ready-made effective alternative basis for international taxation. Both business representatives and most administrators considered it a threat because its adoption would necessarily open up the questions of legitimation that have been largely concealed by the bureaucratic–corporatist system that has developed. Since WUT starts from global accounts, it poses squarely, at the international level, the key questions how the tax base should be calculated and how it should be apportioned. Hence the fears expressed by the business side, that each state would seek to maximize its own tax take by adopting the most advantageous definitions and formulae, which political conflicts would make it possible to reconcile. Yet the long history of international business taxation shows that it has never been a question of whether, but of how, national tax systems accommodate to the pressures of international investment. WUT would not require a globally agreed policy overriding national tax sovereignty. It needs only a definition of net income for allocation purposes, and agreed principles of allocation: each country would still be free to adopt its own definition of net taxable income and even its own tax rate if it wished. Plainly, also, the basis for the establishment of an international tax administration is already well under way, in the various arrangements described above.[69] Indeed, in many ways the international co-ordination developed over the past dozen years, although based on separate accounting and arm's length, has gone some way to laying the basis for a new approach.

Similar stories could perhaps be told in other fields of regulation of transnational business. Taxation certainly has its own special features, notably the long history of negotiation of a treaty system and the particular form of international bureaucratization that emerged from it. Nevertheless, a close examination of many areas of business regulation would show that national business regulation has never been compartmentalized, but was adapted to and interacted with other national systems within an international framework of some sort. A major characteristic of such regulatory systems, both internationally and nationally, has been their technical–bureaucratic nature. This has proved no hindrance to, and if anything has stimulated, the increasing international centralization and concentration of capital dominated by the TNC. Equally, the legitimation crisis created for those regulatory systems by that process of concentration is both international and national.

Notes

This chapter is part of a larger research project which has received generous financial assistance from The Nuffield Foundation and Warwick University. My thanks are due to the many officials and specialists who spared me some of their valuable time for interviews.

1. The classical discussions of these issues are R. O. Keohane and J. S. Nye (eds.), *Transnational Relations in World Politics* (Cambridge, Mass.: Harvard University Press, 1970); P. C. Jessup, *Transnational Law* (New Haven: Yale University Press, 1956).
2. C. P. Kindleberger, *American Business Abroad—Six Lectures on Direct Investment* (New Haven: Yale University Press, 1969); A. M. Rugman (ed.), *New Theories of the Multinational Enterprise* (London: Croom Helm, 1982); M. Casson (ed.), *The Growth of International Business* (London: George Allen & Unwin, 1983).
3. S. Hymer, 'The Multinational Corporation and the Law of Uneven Development', in C. Kindleberger (ed.), *The International Corporation* (Boston: MIT Press, 1970); E. Mandel, *Late Capitalism* (London: New Left Books, 1975), esp. ch. 3; E. A. Brett, *The World Economy Since the War—The Politics of Uneven Development* (London: Macmillan, 1985).
4. See S. Picciotto, 'Jurisdictional Conflicts, International Law and the

International State System', *International Journal of the Sociology of Law*, 11 (1983), 11–40; D. E. Rosenthal and W. M. Knighton, *National Laws and International Commerce* (London: Routledge & Kegan Paul for the Royal Institute of International Affairs, 1982); International Chamber of Commerce, *Report of the International Chamber of Commerce Committee on the Extraterritorial Application of National Laws* (Paris: ICC, 1986).

5. E. W. Hawley, *The New Deal and the Problem of Monopoly. A Study in Economic Ambivalence* (New Jersey: Princeton University Press, 1966).
6. See *In re Investigation of World Arrangements relating to Petroleum*, 13 (1952) FRD 280, extracts in 19 (1952) *International Law Reports*, 197; W. J. Reader, *ICI, A History*, vol. ii, *The First Quarter-Century, 1926–52* (London: Oxford University Press, 1975), esp. chs. 23, 24. PRO file FO 371/44589.
7. United Kingdom–United States: Memorandum of Understanding on Exchange of Information in Matters Relating to Securities and Futures, *International Legal Materials*, 25 (1986), 1431–8.
8. S. Picciotto, 'Political Economy and International Law', in S. Strange (ed.), *Paths to Political Economy* (London: George Allen & Unwin, 1984).
9. *State Railroad Tax Cases* (1875), 92 US 575, 601.
10. *Honolulu Oil Co.* v. *FTB* and *Superior Oil Co.* v. *FTB* (1963), 60 Cal 2d 406, 417.
11. B. F. Miller, 'Worldwide Unitary Combination: the California Practice', in C. E. McClure (ed.), *The State Corporation Income Tax. Issues in Worldwide Unitary Combination* (California: Hoover Institute Press, 1983).
12. *Japan Line* v. *County of Los Angeles* (1979), 441 US 434.
13. *Container Corporation* v. *Franchise Tax Board* (1983), 463 US 159, at p. 192.
14. D. Campbell-Smith, *The British Airways Story: Struggle for Take-Off* (London: Hodder & Stoughton, 1983), 194–6.
15. *The Final Report of the Worldwide Unitary Taxation Working Group. Chairman's Report and Supplemental Views* (Washington, DC: Treasury Department, 1984). R. N. Mattson, 'Setting Straight the Unitary Working Group Record', *Tax Notes*, 30 (1986), 57–61.
16. The fee would be thirty-thousandths of 1 per cent of its total of property, payroll, and sales in California; reducible, to a minimum of one-thousandth of 1 per cent by the amount spent in the state on new plant, facilities, or employment: Senate Bill No. 85; Cap. 660, s. 25115.
17. S. I. Langbein, 'The Unitary Method and the Myth of Arm's Length', *Tax Notes*, 30 (1986), 625–83. Report of the California Tax Policy Conference, *Tax Notes*, 33 (1986), 338–41.

18. Cmd. 615.
19. *Calcutta Jute Mills* v. *Nicholson; Cesena Sulphur* v. *Nicholson* (1876), 1, *Tax Cases*, 83, 88. See also *Sao Paulo Rly*. v. *Carter* (1895), 3, *Tax Cases*, 344, 407 (HL).
20. *De Beers Consolidated Mines* v. *Howe* [1906], AC 455 HL. See generally N. D. Booth, *Residence, Domicile and UK Taxation* (London: Butterworth, 1986), esp. ch. 6.
21. International Chamber of Commerce, *Double Taxation*, Report to the 2nd Congress, Rome (Paris: ICC, Brochure no. 25, 1923).
22. Revenue Act, 1918, ss. 222, 238.
23. M. B. Carroll, 'International Tax Law. Benefits for American Investors and Enterprises Abroad', *International Lawyer*, 2 (1965), 692–728.
24. *Taxation of Foreign and National Enterprises*, i–iv (Geneva: League of Nations, 1932–3).
25. Ibid. iv. 12.
26. Ibid. i. 191.
27. Draft Convention for the Allocation of Business Income Between States for the Purposes of Taxation, Annex 1 of the Report of the Fiscal Committee to the Council of the League of Nations (1935), II A 9. It should be noted that, although the 1935 draft treaty accepted fractional apportionment as an alternative method between branches of the same company, this did not apply to dealing between separate but related enterprises, for which only a narrow version of the arm's length rule was allowed.
28. *Taxation of Foreign and National Enterprises*, i. 122.
29. M. B. Carroll, 'International Double Taxation', in H. E. Davis, *Pioneers in World Order. An American Appraisal of the League of Nations* (New York: Columbia University Press, 1944).
30. See e.g. the Report of the ICC's Taxation Committee and statement of the ICC Council in Jan. 1951, in *Bulletin for International Fiscal Documentation*, 5 (1951), 113.
31. J. -L. Lienard, 'Present et avénir des modèles de convention de double imposition', *Journal de droit des affaires internationales*, 1 (1985), 91–102, at p. 94.
32. *Double Taxation and Fiscal Evasion*, Report of Committee of Technical Experts to Financial Committee of the League of Nations, 7 Feb. 1925, League of Nations doc. F212; cited in J. -L. Lienard, 'Resistances à l'impôt et co-operation internationale', *Revue Française de finances publiques*, 5 (1984), 113. Note that in the international context the word 'evasion' is frequently used in the French sense, which does not carry the connotation of illegality, for which the term 'fraud' is used. In what follows I will not distinguish between 'avoidance' and 'evasion', since 'fraud' is more appropriate when clear illegality is involved.

33. See e.g. discussion at the ICC's 3rd Congress, Brussels, 1925, Finance Group, ICC Brochure No. 43.
34. Especially France and Belgium with their immediate neighbours: see A. Piatier, *L'Évasion fiscale et l'assistance administrative entre états* (Paris: Sirey, 1938).
35. The comment of a British Treasury mandarin, Sir Richard Hopkins, on the draft 1935 convention, in a minute to the Chancellor, is of interest: 'There can be no harm and must be some advantage from the point of view of the Treasury, in going on with this, with the qualifications named. It is merely a proposal in favour of the adoption of reasonable business principles in the ascertainment of tax due. If it were generally adopted, which sounds an unlikely ending to a multilateral effort of the League—it might put the question of avoidance of double taxation to sleep for quite a long time.' Contained in Inland Revenue file in the Public Records Office: PRO file IR40/5703.
36. See notes of meeting of 22 June 1934 of Mr Slee and Sir I. Thompson with members of the British Committee of the International Chamber of Commerce, PRO file IR40/5703.
37. See memo by Carroll of 29 Sept. 1937 circulated to governments: League doc. F/Fiscal/99.
38. Summary typed at front of PRO file IR/40 5703.
39. See memo by Ministry of Information to Cabinet, WP(45) 216, in PRO file FO 371/44585; this was a last minute objection, overcome by confidential Bank of England discussions with the banks.
40. A limited provision for assistance in collection is included in the current treaty, Art. 26(2).
41. A. Joseph, 'International Tax Treaties—A Comparison of Basic Provisions', *Bulletin for International Fiscal Documentation*, 8 (1954), 8.
42. Although the Commentary to the OECD model treaty has since 1963 referred to the possibility of the OECD Fiscal Committee playing a role by giving opinions in such cases, no such development has taken place.
43. Offical channels are likely to prove especially tortuous since, in most countries, the Revenue comes under the Treasury, so that international contacts would involve inter-departmental discussions between the Treasury and Foreign Affairs ministries.
44. See J. F. Avery Jones *et al.*, 'The Legal Nature of the Mutual Agreement Procedure under the OECD Model Convention', *British Tax Review* (1979), 333–53, [1980], 13–27.
45. *Bulletin for International Fiscal Documentation*, 7 (1953).
46. D. R. Tillinghast, 'Taxing the Multinationals', *Harvard International Law Journal*, 20 (1979), 253–75, p. 257.
47. The Board of Inland Revenue's consultative paper on *Taxation of International Business* of Dec. 1982 referred to a survey carried out by

the Revenue of British-based multinational groups: in the 130 groups covered, over 200 non-resident companies were identified as 'carrying on activities which seemed likely to have as one of their main purposes the reduction of UK tax' (p. 15).

48. The deferral debate is discussed by Tillinghast, 'Taxing the Multinationals'.
49. For a comparison of the provisions in all 7 countries, see B. J. Arnold, 'The Taxation of Foreign Controlled Corporations: Defining and Designating Tax Havens', *British Tax Review* [1985], 286–385, pp. 362–76.
50. S. 482 of the US Tax Code originated in 1921. In the UK provisions date back to general rule 7 of the 1918 Income Tax Act. The modern version in s. 485 ICTA originated in 1951. Notably, although decisions under the US provisions are frequently litigated, in the UK there has been not a single case taken to either the Commissioners or the Courts, and even the power for the Board to issue a Direction is rarely formally used, tax inspectors preferring to negotiate 'under the umbrella' of the law (interview information).
51. Tillinghast, 'Taxing the Multinationals', p. 271.
52. Technical Division 2B deals with international tax matters in general, and the Board's 1984 report gave its staff as 25; the unit within TD2B dealing specifically with TNCs and transfer pricing was reported in 1983 as having 7 staff of whom 1 was a qualified accountant: Hansard (1983–4), 52, 222.
53. See *Transfer Pricing and Multinational Enterprises. Three Taxation Issues* (Paris: OECD, 1984); Committee on Fiscal Affairs, *Current Activities* (Paris: OECD, 1985); *Issues in International Taxation No.1, International Tax Avoidance and Evasion* (Paris, OECD, 1987).
54. e.g. the Administrative Principles passed in West Germany in 1983: see H. D. Hoeppner, 'German Regulations on Transfer Pricing: A Tax Administrator's Point of View', *Intertax*, 6–7 (1983), 208–23; also the Special Taxation Measures Law of Japan s. 66–5, submitted by the Ministry of Finance to the National Diet on 30 Jan. 1986.
55. Note that many if not most transfer pricing adjustments will involve claw-back of tax from a tax haven and not a high-tax or treaty country, so no question of adjustment would arise. Some tax authorities indeed take the view that there is little point in expending effort investigating pricing between high-tax jurisdictions.
56. Revenue Procedure 70–18. From 1970 to 1985 a total of 951 applications were made under this procedure; of these 601 were for a negotiated allocation, of which 66% resulted in full double taxation relief and 8% partial relief: figures supplied by the IRS. See also M. Abrutyn and C. Halphen *Income Tax Treaties—Administrative and Competent Authority Aspects* (Washington, DC: Tax Management,

1984), and Avery Jones *et al.*, 'The Legal Nature of the Mutual Agreement Procedure'. About half the US Competent Authority cases are with Canada, negotiated at quarterly meetings; cases with other countries are usually dealt with by correspondence.

57. Such a proposal is embodied in a draft EEC Directive put forward in 1976 (OJ C 301/4) which has made little progress due to lack of support from national tax administrations.
58. Interview information.
59. Interview information.
60. Although the British authorities consider it confidential, the text of the UK–US Working Arrangement has in fact been published, in J. Newman, *US/UK Double Tax Treaty on Income and Gains* (London: Butterworth, 1980), 103.
61. 77/799 of Dec. 1977.
62. See *Community Action to Combat International Tax Evasion and Avoidance*, Communication from the Commission to the Council and the European Parliament, 28 Nov. 1984, COM(84) 603, esp. para. 8.
63. See the report on *Co-operation in Tax Matters* prepared by the Committee of Experts in Tax Law, adopted by the European Committee on Legal Co-operation, Dec. 1985, Addendum to CDCJ (85) 78. The background to this initiative is explained in the papers given at a Colloquy on *International Tax Evasion and Avoidance* held in Strasbourg in 1980 (Amsterdam: Bureau for International Fiscal Documentation, 1981).
64. See comments by W. Ritter, Chairman of the ICC's Taxation Committee and head of the Legal Department of BASF to *Die Welt*, 18 Aug. 1986, and *Handelsblatt*, 14 May 1986.
65. Discussed in the paper's assembled in R. Murray, *Multinationals Beyond the Market* (Brighton: Harvester Press, 1981), esp. R. Murray's own article, 'Transfer Pricing and its Control: Alternative Approaches'.
66. Despite a revamping of the enforcement procedures in 1973, the IRS was stung by a subsequent study by the General Accounting Office, *IRS Could Better Protect US Tax Interests in Determining the Income of Multinational Corporations* (Report to the Chairman, House Committee on Ways and Means, 30 Sept. 1981), which showed that only 3% (12 of 403) adjustments, in all categories, were based on a 'true arm's length price' (i.e. the comparable uncontrolled price method). A more detailed study published by the IRS in 1984, *Study of International Cases Involving s. 482 of the Internal Revenue Code*, sought to defend IRS enforcement of s. 482, but even so showed a rate of 21.2% (225 of 1,062) for use of the 'comparable uncontrolled price' method. This study also reveals that, even in the US, where there is much more ready resort to the appeals process (and there is incentive

to appeal, since the average adjustment involves nearly $2m.), 58% of adjustments were negotiated.

67. *Taxation of Foreign and National Enterprises*, i. 122.

68. R. A. Musgrave and P. B. Musgrave, 'Inter-nation equity', in R. A. Bird and J. G. Head (eds.), *Modern Fiscal Issues* (Toronto: University of Toronto Press, 1972); P. B. Musgrave, 'International Tax Base Division and the Multinational Corporation', *Public Finance*, 27 (1972), 394–413. See also S. S. Surrey, 'Reflections on the Allocation of Income and Expenses among National Tax Jurisdictions', *Law & Policy in International Business*, 10 (1978), 409.

69. Both these points are made by G. J. Harley, in *International Division of the Income Tax Base of the Multinational Enterprise* (Boulder, Colorado: Multistate Tax Commission, 1981), 416–17, 420–2. Harley also argues that the disadvantage to developing countries of an allocation formula based on the monetary value of turnover, property, and payroll could be overcome by using 'real' quantities of units sold, square metres of space, and employees. This nevertheless confirms that uniformity cannot be achieved even under the formula approach by applying a general principle of allocation, but requires specific criteria, judgements, or negotiation for individual industries or even firms, and therefore depends on either a central administration or close co-ordination of regulators.

3

Investor Protection and the Culture of Capitalism

Michael Moran

Honesty, Tradition, and the Culture of Capitalism

Behind every great fortune, said Balzac, lies a great crime. The remark typifies a tradition of cynicism about wealth, especially about wealth embodied in the business enterprise. This tradition was given new life in the 1970s by the rediscovery of 'crime in the suites': by the particular revelations of Watergate; by the general realization of the scope of white-collar crime; and by a spate of cases involving criminal and immoral acts by some large corporations.[1]

Revelations of wrongdoing by businessmen have both a policy significance and an analytical significance. In the policy sphere, crime and immorality destroy public confidence in the market system and create demands for tighter regulation of business. For instance in the United States in 1975, after Watergate, 80 per cent of a sample of public opinion described big business as 'greedy and selfish' if left uncontrolled.[2] Scandals in the City of London have had a similarly destructive effect on confidence and are one of the reasons for the great changes in regulation introduced in the 1980s. These changes include the passage of the first comprehensive law governing financial regulation (the Financial Services Act) and the foundation of a semi-public regulatory body, the Securities and Investments Board.[3]

The policy implications are given added weight by more analytical concerns. Business venality is not simply due to Original Sin. It is also the result of one of the great dilemmas of capitalism: how to reconcile the competitive urge and the desire for gain with the preservation of an effectively regulated moral order. Venal conduct in markets amounts to competition by means which happen to be illegal or subject to some cultural proscription. Yet from Smith to Habermas social theorists of capitalism have argued that the effective functioning of competitive markets depends on the creation of a moral order capable of disciplining and restraining the capitalist appetite.[4] What is more, the conviction that this moral order is a legacy of pre-capitalist culture has led some of the most influential modern writers to conclude that the culture of capitalism has progressively destroyed these pre-capitalist moral foundations. Hirsch's famous picture of capitalism in moral decay is a synthesis of this large literature.[5] Writing in a different ideological tradition Habermas has offered a remarkably similar analysis: 'Motivational structures necessary for bourgeois society are only incompletely reflected in bourgeois ideologies. Capitalist societies were always dependent on cultural boundary conditions that they could not themselves reproduce; they fed parasitically on the remains of tradition.'[6]

One of the remarkable features of these academic analyses is the extent to which they are echoed in 'common-sense' explanations of moral crises in the business community. Thus the dominant explanation offered by practitioners in the London financial markets for the numerous recent scandals is a variant on the 'moral decay' thesis—to wit, that intensified competition has eroded traditional 'gentlemanly' restraints on unacceptable behaviour.[7]

The view that capitalist development involves cultural corrosion and moral decay is, however, challenged by an alternative account. In his great essay on the culture of the market, Max Weber, while stressing the calculating character of capitalism, also emphasized the restraints imposed by capitalist rationality on unrestrained acquisitiveness.

> The impulse to acquisition has in itself nothing to do with capitalism . . . Capitalism may even be identical with the restraint, or at least a rational tempering, of this irrational impulse . . . The universal reign of absolute unscrupulousness in the pursuit of selfish interests has been a specific characteristic of precisely those countries whose bourgeois–capitalistic development . . . has remained backward.[8]

We thus possess two different accounts of the evolution of the culture of high capitalism—as a descent into unrestrained opportunism or an ascent from unscrupulousness. The debate necessarily involves evidence about the character of past culture: thus the notion that there was indeed once a stable moral order bequeathed by traditional society has been variously challenged, for instance by Gray.[9] But the argument also plainly turns on evidence about the present. If the 'moral decay' hypothesis is correct it should follow that in those sectors of the economy where the institutions of the market are most advanced—are most competitive, rational, and calculating—moral restraints should be most thoroughly eroded.

The purpose of this chapter is to use evidence about investor protection in American and British financial markets to contribute to this debate. The choice of evidence is dictated by a number of policy concerns, and by an overwhelming analytical consideration. The regulation of investor protection has been a major agent of policy debate and policy change on both sides of the Atlantic for over fifty years. Failure to provide protection damages market performance, whether measured in the conventional language of liquidity and information efficiency, or in terms of the contribution made by financial markets to the supply of funds for investment in the wider 'productive' economy. In Britain, the subject has a particular topicality because of the twin revolutions in trading practices and regulation now sweeping through the markets.[10]

These policy concerns are allied to an analytical consideration. Financial markets in Britain and the United States are, by any conceivable measure, among the most highly developed institutions of market capitalism. Their capacity for innovation; their experience of revolutionary structural change; the ferocity with which they practice competition; their increasingly global organization; the extent to which they apply rational calculation and high technology: all these show them to be the social vanguard of the market order.[11] If moral decay is taking place, here is where corruption and the associated crisis of regulation should be most advanced.

In the following pages I organize the evidence as follows. The next section sketches the grosser frauds on investors, and tries to estimate how far their incidence, detection, and prevention are growing more difficult. The section on insider trading might strictly speaking have been incorporated into a discussion of fraud, but the practice illuminates so many important themes that a separate discussion is warranted. 'Chinese Walls and the Culture of Capitalism', which deals with the regulation of conflicts of interest, examines how far institutions capable of enforcing codes of behaviour can be developed at the level of the enterprise. The two last sections examine some of the wider concerns raised by this volume.

Fraud and the Culture of Capitalism

Fraud dramatizes the problem faced by market economies in setting acceptable limits to competition. Market exchanges rest on trust; fraud succeeds by abusing that trust, and in succeeding destroys the cultural conditions in which trust can be fostered.

The recent history of fraud on both sides of the Atlantic at first glance suggests that it is a major policy problem in market economies, and ample demonstration of the proposition that competition destroys cultural restraints on unscrupulous behaviour. In the United States, for instance, it was estimated in the late 1970s that 30 per cent of all corporate liquidations were due to fraud.[12] American investors have been victims in recent years of a series of brazen frauds stretching from the Great Salad Oil Swindle to the Equity Funding affair. (The latter was particularly grotesque: Equity Funding, a concern which never earned an honest cent, became a highly rated stock on Wall Street; involved fraud committed by over fifty people, stretching for more than a decade; and engaged in a series of extraordinary deceptions—for instance, insuring fictitious lives, 'killing off' the insured and collecting the premiums—which went entirely undetected by the seven separate institutions responsible for supervision.)[13]

In Britain, the problem has seemed even more acute. By the mid-1980s there existed a fraud crisis in London. A series of financial scandals led to heated debates in Parliament, the City, and the press. The agencies of enforcement seemed overwhelmed by their task. In 1984, for instance, over fifty firms in the commodities markets were under official investigation, and it was commonly alleged that London was becoming the world capital for commodity fraud.[14] The speed with which the fraud crisis developed was astonishing. In 1983 the Commissioner of the Metropolitan Police reported that his officers were investigating frauds totalling £264 million; in 1984 the reported figure had risen to £617 million; by the end of 1985 it was reckoned to top £1,000 million.[15] The magnitude of the problem has in turn created a sense of crisis in the agencies of detection and prosecution. In 1984 the authorities were forced to form a special Fraud Investigation Group (FIG) to co-ordinate enforcement and prosecution; yet the group, with a staff numbering only twenty-one, has already been overwhelmed by the volume and complexity of cases.[16] Perhaps the most serious consequence of the fraud crisis has been to produce an associated crisis in the jury system. Between the 1930s and the beginning of the 1980s the average length of a fraud trial at the Old Bailey quadrupled.[17] This in turn reflected the increased complexity of the whole business of detection and prosecution. The evidence to the Roskill Committee's inquiry into fraud trials was dominated by calls from City interests for the abolition of the jury system on fraud cases. The Committee's own report supported these calls, though the proposal is unlikely to be implemented.[18]

One of the remarkable features of the debate prompted by this crisis is how far the explanations offered by actors in the markets echo the reasoning of social theorists who picture capitalism in moral decay. In London there exists a powerful oral tradition which explains the change as follows. In the past the markets were dominated by 'gentlemen'—in other words, by a socially and culturally homogeneous élite drawn from aristocratic circles. This élite curbed competition and enforced high ethical standards. But the competitive revolution of recent years destroyed these restraints and introduced into the City all sorts of unscrupulous characters—foreigners, people without a good public school education, and similar. A decline in standards of honesty is thus, so the argument goes, linked to a decline in the influence of traditional élites and traditional values.

When practitioners and social theorists offer the same diagnosis the argument plainly deserves a respectful hearing. Yet as soon as we reflect on this picture of historical decay some obvious objections occur. Four merit mention.

The first is that even the most casual historical observation suggests that fraud was endemic in traditional cultures. To take a single instance: Gower shows how the South Sea Bubble was part of a vast structure of swindling whose effects retarded the development of English company law for a century.[19] To take a second instance: the central place of fraud in the culture of early capitalism is attested by the astonishing number of great nineteenth-century novels using fraud as an engine of plot. Consider Bulstrode in *Middlemarch*; the skein of City fraud unravelled in *The Way We Live Now*; the gallery of swindlers in Dickens—Merdl in *Little*

Dorrit, Tom Gradgrind in *Hard Times*, Carker in *Dombey and Son*. Fraud in retail banking—the stuff of so many nineteenth-century novels—only disappeared towards the end of the century with the domination of retail banking by a few large capitalist concerns.

The second difficulty is more restricted, but is nevertheless illuminating: some important kinds of modern fraud are explicable by particular circumstances which have little to do with the broader evolution of market culture. Ellen and Campbell's analysis of international maritime fraud—the species which has proved most lucrative in recent years—explains its growth in terms of a number of particular factors, such as the entry into markets of naïve or corrupt Third World governments, and the invention of particular fraud techniques. (Thus the most spectacular frauds are, according to Ellen and Campbell, patterned on Savundra's great Costa Rican Coffee Swindle of 1959.)[20]

A third difficulty is more central to the argument. If the fraud crisis is due—to use everyday language—to the ascendancy of 'players' over 'gentlemen', why are so many of the crooks also gentlemen? To put the point more analytically: the history of financial fraud is in part a history of scandals within traditional élites. Think of Richard Whitney, the leader of the old Guard on the New York Stock Exchange, jailed for embezzlement in 1938; of Sir Denys Lowson, former Lord Mayor of London, who expired while the Fraud Squad were, so to speak, knocking on his front door; of Sir Trevor Dawson, the old Harrovian baronet who committed suicide to escape the consequences of dishonesty; of the scandals at Lloyds, which have touched the élite of the market.[21]

The spectacle of so many dishonest gentlemen should make us wonder about the ethical content of traditionalism. Doubt is increased by a fourth, final, consideration. If fierce competition and the continuing development of a culture of high capitalism explain the fraud crisis, we should find that the most advanced capitalist institutions are the most fraudulent. The reverse is true: the great investment banks, commercial banks, and brokerage houses are least likely to be convicted of fraud. Shapiro's study of investor fraud in the United States shows the characteristic fraud to be small scale, short lived, and the work of tiny operators.[22] It is conceivable, of course, that giant corporations are not more honest than others, but are simply more powerful and therefore better equipped to escape detection and prosecution. This argument is, however, untenable because it cannot explain why powerful traditional élites have been publicly implicated in fraud scandals.

The observation that traditional élites have commonly perpetuated fraud, and that the most advanced capitalist institutions are characteristically honest, now gives us a glimmer of a solution to the nature of the fraud crisis. It is common to picture the traditional values of pre-industrial capitalism as a restraining influence on competitive unscrupulousness. Yet there are some obvious ways in which the values of traditionalism are in truth a massive incitement to dishonesty. One of the distinguishing features of traditionalism is a stunted notion of the public sphere: an absence of any clearly regulated distinction between private rights and public obligations; a lack of any developed mechanisms of accountability in economic and political affairs; and a preference for informality and secrecy in decision-making.

Crises of traditionalism occur when institutions dominated by traditional élites and traditional cultures encounter more modern conceptions of honesty and accountability. Thus the crisis of traditionalism in the political sphere in Britain came in the nineteenth century from the challenge of ideologies of bureaucratic competence and democratic control. The crisis produced an assault on corruption, a cleansing of public life, and the decline of traditional (aristocratic) élites. The crisis of traditionalism was delayed in the financial markets—until the 1930s in the United States, and until the last decade in Britain.

We can illustrate the American case by the well-documented history of its greatest securities market, the New York Stock Exchange. The history of the NYSE before the 1930s is a story of legendary unscrupulousness. This culminated in the scandalous practices of the great bull market of the 1920s. If, says Sobel in the history of the market, a 'rascality index' could be devised, the 1920s would mark a peak.[23] The aftermath is by now well known: the Great Crash; the scandals revealed by Congressional investigation; the enforced separation of investment from commercial banking; the imposition of regulation in the form of the 1933 and 1934 Securities Acts; and the setting up of an instrument of regulation in the form of the Securities and Exchange Commission.[24]

These externally imposed reforms accompanied a struggle inside the Exchange. The NYSE was dominated by the Old Guard, a patrician élite drawn from the floor traders and specialists. Floor traders and specialists did not deal with the public; they traded inside the exchange, living off their (often considerably dishonest) wits. Throughout the 1930s they were opposed by a reform wing led by the commission house brokers, large firms with retail networks dealing with the public. The houses were, because of their retail business, anxious to cleanse the Exchange in order to restore public confidence. The struggle within the Exchange was thus a struggle between the traditional and the bureaucratic, modernizing, wings of capitalism. The divide between traditionalism and bureaucratic modernization was reflected in the terms of argument: the reformers wanted to replace the secrecy and informality of NYSE government by a full-time paid President (in effect a Chief Executive) supported by his own staff. In short, they wished to bureaucratize the Exchange, a wish supported by the Securities and Exchange Commission. The Great Crash discredited but did not dislodge the Old Guard; its power was only finally destroyed by the conviction for fraud in 1938 of Richard Whitney, the Exchange President. Whitney's disgrace was followed by the ascendancy of the reformers, by changes in internal government, and by the reform of trading practices.[25] The Morganization of American capitalism—to misquote Sobel's phrase—was thus succeeded by its bureaucratization; and with bureaucratization went the decline of a culture of fraudulent manipulation.

The change is nicely illustrated by the history of a single dynasty, the Kennedys. Joseph Kennedy made a vast fortune from unscrupulous stock exchange manipulation in the 1920s. By luck or foresight he sold out at the top of the market. He then opportunistically allied himself with Roosevelt's campaign to subject capitalism to bureaucratic regulation, and finally achieved a semblance of respectability as the first Chairman of the Securities and Exchange Commission.[26] His sons, with the unscrupulously acquired Kennedy fortune honestly invested and bureaucratically managed, made careers by continuing the Roosevelt tradition of running a bureaucratically regulated capitalism.

At the risk of repetition: the history of the control of fraud in the American Securities industry is a history of rising standards of behaviour, enforced by the least socially traditional, and most economically advanced, wing of the industry.

The present fraud crisis in London is explicable in similar terms. In the last couple of decades City markets have been increasingly dominated by the characteristic institutions of bureaucratic capitalism—by corporations with elaborate hierarchies and complex structures, run by professionally trained élites attached to rule-governed behaviour. The fraud crisis has occurred, not because standards have fallen but because, as markets have been subjected to bureaucratic modernization, moral expectations have become more exacting. The more traditional the institution—the more secretive its culture, the more formal its rules, and the more patrician its élite—the more intense has been its fraud crisis. Hence Lloyd's is now a byword for scandal because the traditional codes of behaviour in the market have become anachronistic through structural and cultural change. The political and journalistic concern with fraud itself reflects this change in cultural sensitivities, as does the increasing administrative effort put into detection and prosecution. The panic about fraud in London does not reflect a decline in standards; it reflects the growing extent to which traditional practices have been exposed and found wanting.

Fraud is one of the most culturally relative of transgressions. Behaviour which in one generation is 'gentlemanly', in the next can become improper, and in the next can become a crime. That, in a sentence, also sums up the history of insider trading, to which I now turn.

Insider Trading and the Culture of Capitalism

The attempt to regulate or to prohibit insider trading—dealing in securities using non-published, price sensitive information—has been called 'the unwinnable war',[27] on the grounds that a practice so elusive makes detection virtually impossible. Some of the most intellectually influential monetary economists indeed argue that prohibition is not only pointless but is positively harmful. Stigler suggests that since in efficient markets 'almost every event casts a shadow before it', the advantages conveyed by possession of non-public information are trivial because markets rapidly discount the special information available to insiders.[28] More ingeniously, Manne has argued in a famous study that insider trading is vital to the efficient functioning of the modern capitalist enterprise. Healthy capitalism, he suggests, requires entrepreneurs with a direct stake in the profitability of their business. The separation of ownership from control in the modern corporation breaks the direct link between personal reward and corporate success; but the link is reforged by insider trading, since it allows corporate insiders to profit from advance information about the performance of their firm. To this thesis Manne adds the argument that, since there is an obvious and powerful demand for inside information, attempts to regulate or prohibit its flows are a waste of resources.[29]

These views are open to dispute, but they plainly offer an intellectually powerful means of legitimizing a policy of minimal control. Yet the striking feature of insider trading regulation on both sides of the Atlantic is that this opportunity to legitimize inaction has been rejected. The story of recent decades is a tale of the imposition of increasingly strict ethical standards. What is more, standards are most demanding, and sanctions most punitive, in the more advanced American markets. The notorious failures to punish insider trading in Britain are traceable to the comparative stunting of capitalist development in London and to the lingering influence of traditionalism.

I substantiate these assertions by examining the American and British experience in turn.

There exists scarcely any American legislation directly concerned with the regulation of insider trading. This in turn reflects a tradition of indifference in the common law. In the words of a standard commentary: 'early common law cases held that in a faceless market insiders had no duty to refrain from trading in their corporation's stock when armed with material inside information.'[30] The Securities Acts of 1933 and 1934—the foundation of the regulatory system—make only brief reference to the practice. Yet, in the 1980s, regulation of insider trading is the centrepiece of the Securities and Exchange Commission's enforcement programme, there is a huge and hotly contested body of case-law on the subject, Congress has (in 1984) passed legislation imposing heavy sanctions on those convicted of insider trading, and there is continuing pressure to strengthen this legislation.

This journey from moral indifference was prompted partly by a series of court decisions dating from the 1940s, but largely by administrative actions and court cases brought by the SEC between the early 1960s and the mid-1970s. In these years the Commission succeeded in criminalizing the practice and in expanding the definition of what constituted insider trading. Three steps were crucial in this process. First, the SEC was able to persuade the Courts to define certain kinds of insider trading as fraud, and thus a legitimate subject for regulation under the anti-fraud provisions of the securities laws.[31] Secondly, the Commission used the principle of full and fair disclosure which is the heart of the American securities legislation to impose obligations to disclose dealings on selected categories of insiders. More generally, it evolved the 'disclose or abstain' rule, by which insiders are obliged either to abstain from dealings in a corporation's stock or to reveal to the market the full information on which their trading is conducted.[32] Finally, the Commission was able to refashion the doctrine of fiduciary obligation to impose duties not to trade for profit on an increasingly wide range of 'insiders'.[33]

The analytical significance of these developments should be plain: they suggest that key actors in the markets have been increasingly constrained by legal and ethical obligations. The expanded role of fiduciary duty is especially significant, because the conception of a fiduciary obligation transforms the low trust relations between actors in impersonal markets into something much more morally demanding. In Cardozo's often quoted words, 'a trustee is held to something stricter than the morals of the marketplace'.[34]

It is tempting to conclude that the American history of regulating insider trading points unambiguously to the growth of restraints on unscrupulous acquisitiveness. But this conclusion has to be qualified by three developments: by the evolution of judicial doctrine since the mid-1970s; by the detection and enforcement problems involved in the implementation of insider trading rules; and by the spectacular insider trading scandals uncovered in 1986, involving some of the leading figures on Wall Street.

Until 1975 court rulings on insider trading were consistently expansionist; that is, they tended to widen the definition of an 'insider' and to work with a generous notion of the scope of fiduciary obligation. Since then, a series of landmark decisions (*Chiarella* v. *US*; *Dirks* v. *SEC*) have been much more restrictive in character.[35] In addition, in 1983 a series of court judgements placed quite unexpected restrictions on the powers available to SEC officers investigating suspected cases of insider trading.[36]

The most important court judgement, both substantively and

analytically, concerned the Chiarella case.[37] Chiarella was a printer employed to set up and produce details of offers in intended take-overs. He used the advance information thus gained profitably to invest in stock before the public announcement of an offer. The Courts held that, while he was undoubtedly in possession of privileged information, he was not a corporate insider and was therefore exempt from a fiduciary obligation to refrain from profiting on the basis of information acquired in a position of trust. The substantive significance of the judgement is that it set off a search for an agreed definition of an 'insider'. The analytical significance of the case lies in the way it marks a retreat from the previously expansive conceptions of trust and duty imposed on actors in markets.

The second qualification concerns the effectiveness of the SEC's campaign against insider trading. The practice is notoriously elusive. The standard detection technique is market surveillance, the extensive statistical analysis of price movements to monitor unusual changes in advance of key announcements like take-over offers or company results. Shapiro's exhaustive study of SEC enforcement systematically establishes what is intuitively apparent—that market surveillance techniques of this kind are poor instruments of detection, and that the information which regulators thus uncover is fortuitous and haphazard.[38] To take a single example: privileged inside information may be used to guide inaction as commonly as it is used to guide action, as when an insider refrains from trading in the knowledge that impending results will depress prices.

Not only is insider trading difficult to detect; there is also evidence that market conditions in the 1980s made it especially lucrative. The scandals uncovered in 1986 involving figures such as Ivan Boesky showed that, in an era of hostile take-overs, astonishing profits could be made by those possessing inside information.

The recent evolution of more restrictive judicial doctrines; the practical problems involved in detection; the revelation in the 1980s of the huge profits made from insider trading: all these are necessary qualifications to the view that its regulatory history is a simple tale of the imposition of more exacting ethical standards. Nevertheless, the total weight of evidence forces the conclusion that the markets now have to work in a more demanding moral climate than was the case in the historical past. The Chiarella judgement, though it narrows the range of those obliged to act as fiduciaries, leaves intact the notion that insiders must conform to something more demanding than 'the morals of the market-place'. The 'awakening of the common law'—to use Hazen's phrase—itself reflects a wider cultural change hostile to insider dealing.

The change can also be seen in the enforcement activities of the SEC, even in the Reaganite 1980s. Action against insiders now dominates enforcement policies: between 1949 and 1977 only fifty enforcement actions were brought; between 1978–81 alone, forty were brought; and in 1983 alone, twenty-four were filed.[39] In 1984 Congress passed, under intensive SEC lobbying, the Insider Trading Sanctions Act which considerably stiffened the penalties for those convicted of insider trading.[40] The SEC has also put increased pressure on foreign regulators—notably the secretive Swiss—to allow the pursuit beyond American borders of those guilty of insider trading.[41] Indeed, the revelations in the insider trading scandals of 1986 were made possible because of new and more effective disclosure procedures negotiated between the Securities and Exchange Commission and foreign authorities.

I have looked at some length at American regulation because the rules are complex and because the rise of controls over insider trading has some analytical significance. Impersonal dealing in 'faceless' markets has not only been compatible with, but has actually in some degree forced, higher ethical standards. The more primitive evolution of regulation in Britain is due precisely to the greater traditionalism of British markets.

Anecdotal evidence suggests that until well into the 1950s insider dealing was culturally acceptable in British financial markets.[42] These anecdotal recollections are supported by the silence of the statute book, the indifference of bodies like the Stock Exchange, and the lack of a clear pattern in the pronouncements of the Courts.[43] The first serious attempts at control were prompted by the revelations about dealing accompanying the take-over wave of the 1950s. Throughout the 1960s the Stock Exchange and, later, the Panel on Take-overs and Mergers, struggled in vain to regulate the practice.[44] So unsuccessful were these efforts that in 1973 the main City bodies agreed with the Conservative Government that legislation was needed. The admission that the criminal law was necessary to regulate a City practice was extraordinary at a time when the City was still clinging to the notion that self-regulation was the appropriate way to conduct its affairs.

Bills containing legislation controlling insider trading were lost in the 1970s by the fall of governments, and it was thus not until 1980 that legislation was enacted. The 1980 Companies Act prohibits directors and senior employees from dealing or tipping on the basis of unpublished, price sensitive information.[45] Implementation relies on market surveillance by the Stock Exchange, which reports suspect price movements to the Department of Trade and Industry, which in turn investigates and decides whether prosecution is to be advised.

The law against insider trading is a notorious example of ineffective enforcement. In a typical year (for instance, fiscal 1983) the Stock Exchange examined over 13,000 price movements, investigated just under 500 cases in detail, and passed only twenty to the D.o.T. for further scrutiny.[46] In the years 1980–5, eighty cases in all were passed to the Department, resulting in five, trivial, prosecutions. There can be few more striking instances where an acknowledged and common evil has produced such a supine policy response. Small wonder that Leigh has remarked that 'if ever a topic afforded material for an abusive Marxist thesis, insider trading does'.[47]

The British history of insider trading prohibitions is commonly thought to signify declining standards of conduct. In truth, the reverse is the case. The clue to all this can be put in one, familiar, word: traditionalism. The weight of anecdotal evidence overwhelmingly supports the view that in the recent past insider trading was widely practised and was culturally acceptable. This attitude was challenged from the late 1950s, when the traditional City élite was penetrated by new institutions, new people, and new ideas. The search for more stringent moral standards was, in other words, a consequence of the decline of traditionalism. The cultural shift was also—in a manner reminiscent of the United States—signalled by the increasing insistence of the Courts on more stringent standards of open and fair dealing in share transactions.[48]

The rise of British regulation on insider trading is due to the decline of traditionalism; but comparatively lax enforcement is due to the residual persistence of traditionalism in London. As Rider has remarked, the practical problems of detecting insider trading have been intensified by the 'single capacity' system, especially by the special role of jobbers. Only now, with the abolition of single capacity, is London building a detailed 'audit trail' capable of allowing the reconstruction of transactions necessary to detect insider trading.[49] In other words, enforcement has been hindered by an anti-competitive practice characteristic of British traditionalism. Detection and punishment in London have also been hampered by the stress on informality in regulation, and by the residual normative and social solidarity of the City élite. The best way to detect insider trading is through informers; but cultural prohibitions on 'sneaking' have been a powerful deterrent to informing.

Chinese Walls and the Culture of Capitalism

Insider trading is a special case of a wider problem encountered in all market exchanges: to wit, the scope offered to abuse privileged position or privileged information for purposes of personal or corporate gain. This problem is crystallized in the notion of 'conflicts of interest'. When individuals or institutions act as agents of others—for instance, by the provision of brokerage services, investment advice, or fund management—numerous potential conflicts of interest are created. The most immediate of these concerns the pricing of services—the interest of the client being to minimize, that of the provider of the service to maximize, charges. More subtly, agents may be forced to make choices between serving the interests of different clients; it is commonly alleged, for instance, that rich customers who generate large incomes are persistently favoured at the expense of smaller customers.

The most serious conflicts of all occur when an institution or individual acts in a variety of roles. A typical financial conglomerate—of the kind common in the United States and becoming common in Britain—will deal for its own profit in a stock, underwrite issues, act in an agency role as a broker, provide investment advice to clients, and act as the discretionary manager of investment funds on behalf of individuals or institutions. The possible abuses range from the fraudulent (appropriating clients' funds for self-dealing) to the unethical (slanting investment advice to favour stock in which the adviser has an interest).

Containing potential conflicts of interest raises policy problems and analytical issues. Changes in markets have made the policy problems acute on both sides of the Atlantic. In the cartelized markets common until recently, some serious conflicts of interest were contained by the anti-competitive segregation of functions. The most persistent structural development in recent years on both sides of the Atlantic has involved the erosion of many barriers and the creation of financial conglomerates fulfilling a variety of potentially conflicting roles. The present structural changes in London, for instance, are creating firms combining banking, underwriting, investment management, and market making. In such circumstances, as one fund manager put it, 'the scope for conflicts of interest multiplies like amoeba'.[50] The most distinguished critic of the 'City revolution' has persistently argued that the new arrangement will destroy trust: 'The conflicts of interest within the firms that have been swallowed up . . . are absolutely tremendous . . . The private investor will be ill-advised to deal with any firm which doesn't deal for him solely as an agent.'[51] The most advanced financial institutions thus face a familiar dilemma: how to reconcile competition with the creation of a stable moral order.

In examining solutions we should begin with the United States, because it is there that structural changes and fierce competition are most advanced. The most significant attempt to contain conflicts of interest has involved constructing Chinese Walls. A 'Chinese Wall of Silence' (Franklin Roosevelt seems to have originated the phrase's application to financial regulation) refers to institutional arrangements inside firms designed to restrict the internal flow of information between parts of the firm performing different, and potentially conflicting, functions. In merchant banking, for instance, this involves separating divisions responsible for corporate finance from divisions responsible for discretionary management of clients' funds. Without this separation, there exists an obvious temptation to invest funds in stock which the institution has to place, and a converse temptation for fund managers profitably to exploit the inside information available to the corporate finance division.

The language of Chinese Walls is now so common as to be unavoidable. The phrase is nevertheless in some respects misleading, suggesting, as it does, the universal existence of physical barriers inside firms. Some large corporations do indeed practise physical segregation, but the phrase is better understood as a reference to a range of procedures, varying in formality, designed to foster a corporate culture sensitive to the management of conflicts of interest. The 'Wall' may amount to no more than an informal agreement restricting, for instance, the degree to which officers responsible for different functions can consult each other's files. At the other extreme, in some of the largest American institutions, it involves the total physical separation of divisions, the creation of distinct career hierarchies in those divisions, the fostering of a distinct corporate culture by periodic circulation of rules governing the management of conflicts of interest, and the 'policing' of the Chinese Wall by a 'compliance office' headed by a senior executive.[52] These arrangements are now being replicated in London by the new conglomerates.

Chinese Walls have a twofold significance. They have an immediate relevance to the problem of regulation in the markets, because rule enforcement is most likely to be effective when it is underpinned by a supporting culture at the level of the firm. But they have a wider significance in the debate about the morality of market institutions because—if effective—they demonstrate a capacity for restraint, and for the creation of codes of conduct, which the 'depleting moral legacy' hypothesis would not lead us to expect.

The crucial phrase here, of course, is 'if effective'. British observers have been sceptical of the efficacy of Chinese Walls, a scepticism summed up in Gower's often quoted remark: 'I have never met a Chinese Wall that did not have a grapevine trailing over it.'[53] Scepticism in London is, indeed, entirely understandable. Chinese Walls have been less effective in Britain than in the United States; but they have been less effective because of the comparatively backward character of capitalism in Britain's financial markets. By contrast, it is precisely the advanced character of commercial culture across the Atlantic which explains their rise.

Three connected forces have been at work in the United States. The first is scale. The most effective Chinese Walls—physical barriers typically policed by compliance officers—exist in the most advanced capitalist institutions: in the conglomerates formed around the biggest investment banks, commercial banks, and brokerage houses. The reason is in part elementary: only large institutions can afford the expense of physical separation and policing. A more fundamental reason is quintessentially Weberian. The biggest capitalist institutions are highly bureaucratic. They exhibit a complex internal division of labour, extended organizational hierarchies, and detailed systems of rules. In short, they have a culture and social structure eminently hospitable to the construction and policing of Chinese Walls.

The second force is even more closely connected to the development of capitalism, and can be described in one word: competition. The point is well illustrated by Hermann's study of the long-term growth in the autonomy of commercial bank trust departments. Hermann shows that historically trust departments were small, poorly staffed, and were typically the creatures of more powerful divisions in their banks. The expansion of trust business, and growing competition for the custom of increasingly discriminating trust clients, has forced banks to demonstrate to the market the independence of their trust departments.[54]

The third and final force compelling the more sensitive management of conflicts of interest in the American financial community is the law. American business works in a ferociously litigious environment. Lawsuits are used routinely and opportunistically to acquire business advantage. Firms—especially large firms—run the constant risk of civil suits designed to milk them of assets. In addition they run the constant risk of prosecution from regulators administering a complex and often uncertain body of rules. In this predatory environment firms have a powerful incentive to develop Chinese Walls as a sign that they are sensitive to the reconciliation of conflicts of interest. Woolfson has described how these pressures have contributed to the construction of elaborate forms of Chinese Walls in investment banking.[55] More generally, Herzel and Colling have shown that in the last twenty years Chinese Walls have spread widely through financial institutions because courts and regulators have been ready to accept the existence of an effectively policed Wall as 'an important evidentiary aid in lawsuits', making more credible a defence against charges of insider trading.[56]

The construction of Chinese Walls is an important sign of a more general cultural change in the American financial community—of growing sensitivity to the problem of managing conflicts of interest and the growing salience of a sense of fiduciary obligation. In the United States now, Chinese Walls are advertised as a mark of probity; before the landmark insider trading cases of the 1960s their absence was advertised to attract business.[57] Scale and the bureaucratization associated with scale; growing competition; the need to provide protection in an atmosphere of predatory litigation: all these forces have contributed to change.

We can see immediately that the greater traditionalism of London inhibited such developments in Britain. The aristocratically dominated merchant banking community, for instance, exhibited quintessentially traditional cultural traits: hostility to 'bureaucracy'; small-scale organization; informality and secrecy.[58] In such conditions, rules for the management of conflicts of interest were inevitably exiguous and were enforced only by implicit and fragmentary cultural norms. As London becomes more closely integrated with the advanced American markets we should expect these practices to be displaced. This, of course, is precisely what is taking place—even to the point of imitating characteristic American inventions like compliance officers.

Legitimacy and the Culture of Capitalism

'Let the buyer beware; that covers the whole business' (Henry Havermeyer, President, American Sugar Company, 1899).[59]

> My work [at the Securities and Exchange Commission] brought me into frequent contact with white collar criminals. Most of them were confidence men, but some of them struck me as oddly decent and engaging. I also had frequent contacts with defrauded investors. While some of them seemed to need and deserve the special protection of the government, others struck me as victims of their own greed. (Roberta Karmel, 1982)[60]

'Legitimacy', Habermas rightly remarks, 'is a contestable validity claim' because it refers to 'a political order's worthiness to be recognised'.[61] The 'motivation crisis' of the culture of advanced capitalism arises from many forces not examined in this chapter: the secularization of popular values; the declining capacity of élites to exercise power by ideological mystification; the weakening of traditional modes of cultural control—all central themes in, for instance, Habermas's analysis of how cultural decay creates legitimation crises. Yet evidence about the behaviour of the most advanced capitalist institutions, and the most highly developed markets, is plainly central to any account of the changing culture of high capitalism. The account offered in this chapter is unexpected in its policy implications and in its analytical content.

In the policy sphere, the structural changes now taking place in

London are characteristically viewed as a source of regulatory problems and as a danger to traditionally high standards of ethical conduct. If the evidence of the preceding pages is convincing, the opposite is the case: the increasing domination of London by large financial conglomerates will raise, not lower, standards of business morality. The moral panic which has recently coloured policy argument and journalistic coverage of the City is in one sense quite unjustified, based as it is on the assumption that standards—in respect of gross fraud, insider trading, or the more subtle abuse of conflicts of interest—have fallen. On the contrary: the obsession with these problems is itself an index of how far standards have risen and moral sensitivities become more acute.

The reasons for this cultural change can be compressed into a single phrase: democracy and bureaucracy. On both sides of the Atlantic there has been a long-term increase—limited, halting, uneven, but inexorable—in the degree to which secretive and autonomous traditional élites in financial markets have been subjected to regulation by elected politicians and their agencies. Scandal has been one of the most important instruments of change, causing recurrent crises of traditional élites—in the 1930s in New York and in London in the 1980s. The anatomy of scandals in traditional financial élites is remarkably similar: a single spectacular incident—a gross fraud, a corporate bankruptcy—subjects the élite to external political scrutiny and journalistic investigation; a wide variety of traditional market practices are publicized and pronounced unacceptable; rapid changes in standards are forced on the market, leaving some less adaptable and slow witted operators to be stigmatized for swindling or unethical conduct.

The extension of public regulation is greatly helped by the character of structural change in the markets. Everywhere, bureaucratically organized corporations are in the ascendant at the expense of more traditional kinds of ownership: the partnership is giving way to incorporation; the single-industry, single-country concern to the multinational financial conglomerate. In culture and organization the great bureaucratic corporations of the private sector are eminently congruent with the regulatory institutions of the public sector. The bureaucratization of ownership means that markets are dominated by rule-governed institutions permeated by professional ideologies. The scale which accompanies bureaucratization also acts as an independent check on unscrupulousness.

Gross fraud is rarely committed by large corporations because fraud is characteristically a solitary vice, or one committed by a few consenting adults in secrecy. The routinized, dispersed, and formal modes of decision-making in bureaucracies are a serious obstacle to concealment. More diffusely, the domination of financial markets by sophisticated institutions provides a strong incentive to display, and to practise, high standards of conduct.

The argument summarized here may seem Panglossian in its complacency. This is far from the case: the bureaucratization of financial markets, by its impact on standards of conduct, causes recurrent crises. Three sources of crisis merit description.

First, large corporations are themselves periodically exposed as corrupt. The examples range from the great corporate bribery scandals revealed by the Watergate investigations to the offences committed in 1985 by E. F. Hutton, one of Wall Street's great securities houses.[62] The characteristic feature of misconduct by a large corporation is that it is bureaucratically enacted. In other words, it is rarely the result of private excess by one individual, but is embedded in the standard operating procedures of the institution. Thus the process of cleansing can be immensely difficult because it involves not just removing individuals but also changing those standard operating procedures. Bureaucratization, while it raises standards, thus also routinizes corrupt conduct in a way that makes difficult its recognition and reform. In some cases this rigidity can institutionalize a culture of corruption in a whole industry—a state of affairs vividly described by Braithwaite in his study of pharmaceutical companies.[63]

A second kind of crisis is created by the decline of traditional élites. The great bureaucratic corporations are bounded by traditional institutions marked by secrecy, low standards, and periodic moral scandals. Scandals besmirch the whole business community. The problem is intensified by the social and cultural insularity of traditional élites, which makes them slow to adapt to challenges to their customary privileges and practices. From Richard Whitney's description of the New York Stock Exchange in 1933 as 'a perfect institution',[64] to the extraordinary behaviour of the Council of Lloyd's in the 1980s, the public face of traditional élites has been the same: arrogant, decadent, and stupid.

If on the one side the corporations are bounded by venal, declining élites, on the other they face an even more insidious menace—the venality of the financial fringe. The systematic evidence confirms what is intuitively apparent—fraud and gross exploitation of conflicts of interest are disproportionately found among small entrepreneurs. The reasons are twofold: there are serious problems of surveillance at the fringe of financial markets; and there is often a fierce struggle for survival among economically marginal small operators. The great corporations have an ambivalent relationship with the fringe. They commonly deplore its venality, especially at times of scandal, and support its closer regulation. Yet they do business with fringe operators, and absorb the more dynamic and successful fringe firms into bureaucratic capitalism, thus continually renewing the vigour of the system.

Capitalism, Culture, and Financial Regulation

Some of the most important social forces identified in this chapter are characteristic of the financial markets in all advanced capitalist economies. The increasing domination of markets by multinational conglomerates and the destruction of barriers to competition are almost universally observable. To that degree the Anglo-American experiences of regulation is some guide to the evolution of regulation elsewhere. Yet it is also plainly the case that the aspects of the national setting identified in the conclusion to this volume—the economic setting, the political culture, and the legal culture—work their own unique effects. The politics of investor protection in London and Washington has been investigated in some detail; but investigation of the two other focal points of the global securities market—West Germany and Japan—has hardly begun. Britain and the United States have a similar history—varied only by the economic backwardness and cultural traditionalism of British markets. This resemblance is not surprising: investor protection in the two countries takes place in financial systems, and in societies, with common political and legal inheritances. Differences exist—but they result in variations on common themes. In future investigations pushing the analysis beyond the Anglo-American arena to Japan and West Germany we must expect three obvious distinctive influences to reveal themselves: the comparative unimportance of securities markets, by contrast with their central position in Anglo-American financial systems; the early emergence of the state as a major actor, by contrast with its more recent arrival in the United States and—particularly—in Britain; and the existence, especially in the West German case, of a highly legalistic culture of regulation. Explaining the tensions in the field of investor protection between the universal features of the culture of capitalism, and the particular features of individual national capitalisms, thus involves looking beyond the Anglo-American arena.

Notes

Work for this chapter was funded by the Economic and Social Research Council as part of its 'Corporatism and Accountability' initiative (Grant No. E. 0425 0010). I have benefited from the comments of Ursula Vogel, Michael Clarke, and participants in seminars at the Political Studies Association Annual Conference, 1986, and at the Department of Economics, University of Manchester.

1. For some examples: D. Boulton, *The Lockheed Papers* (London: Cape, 1978); T. Hadden, 'Fraud in the City', *The Company Lawyer*, 1 (1980), 9–13; E. P. Ellinger, 'Fraud in Documentary Credit Transactions', *Journal of Business Law* (1981), 258–70.
2. M. Clinard, *Corporate Ethics and Crime* (London: Sage, 1983), 15.
3. For the background see G. Pimlott, 'The Reform of Investor Protection in the U.K.', *Journal of Comparative and Capital Market Law*, 7 (1985), 141–72.
4. These themes have been widely examined: see e.g. the essays in A. Ellis and K. Kumar (eds.), *Dilemmas of Liberal Democracy* (London: Tavistock, 1983).
5. F. Hirsch, *Social Limits to Growth* (London: Routledge & Kegan Paul, 1977).
6. J. Habermas, *Legitimation Crisis* (London: Heinemann, 1976, trans. T. McCarthy), 76. I rely heavily on R. Plant, 'Hirsch, Hayek and Habermas: Dilemmas of Distribution', in Ellis and Kumar, *Dilemmas of Liberal Democracy*, pp. 45–64.
7. This paragraph is based on interviews with market participants and regulators carried out in the summer and autumn of 1985.
8. M. Weber, *The Protestant Ethic and the Spirit of Capitalism* (London: Unwin, 1985, trans. T. Parsons), 17, 57. (I have run together quotations from separate pages.)
9. J. Gray, 'Classical Liberalism, Positional Goods and the Politicisation of Poverty', in Ellis and Kumar, *Dilemmas of Liberal Democracy*, pp. 174–84.
10. *Financial Services In The United Kingdom: A New Framework For Investor Protection*, Cmnd. 9432, 1985.

11. There are summaries of these developments in e.g. L. Goldberg and L. White (eds.), *The Deregulation of the Banking and Securities Industries* (Lexington: Lexington Books, 1979).
12. M. Comer, *Corporate Fraud* (London: McGraw Hill, 1977), 3–4.
13. On the Salad Oil Swindle see N. Miller, *The Great Salad Oil Swindle* (London: Gollancz, 1966). The Equity Funding fraud has produced a large literature. The best source is L. Seidler, F. Andrews, and M. Epstein, *The Equity Funding Papers: The Anatomy of a Fraud* (New York: Wiley, 1977), esp. pp. 1–19.
14. The figure is from L. C. B. Gower, *Investor Protection, Report*, Part 1, Cmnd. 9125, 1984, 27 n. 5.
15. *Report of the Commissioner of Police for the Metropolis for year to end 1984*, Cmnd. 9541, 1985, 99.
16. On the origins and functions of the FIG see L. H. Leigh, 'Detection and Prosecution of Commercial Fraud: An English Perspective', *Business Law Review*, Feb. 1985, 57–61.
17. M. Levi, *The Phantom Capitalists: The Organisation and Control of Long Firm Fraud* (London: Heinemann, 1981), 290.
18. See e.g. the submission to Roskill given by the Council for the Securities Industry, in *Annual Report*, 1985 (London: CSI, 1985), Appendix A.
19. L. Gower, J. Cronin, A. Easson, and K. Wedderburn, *Gower's Principles of Modern Company Law* (London: Stevens, 1979), 28–32.
20. E. Ellen and D. Campbell, *International Maritime Fraud* (London: Sweet and Maxwell, 1981), 1, 21.
21. J. Brooks, *Once in Golconda: A True Drama of Wall Street 1920–1938* (New York, Harper and Row, 1969); M. Clarke, *Fallen Idols: Elites and the Search for the Acceptable Face of Capitalism* (London: Junction Books, 1981), 59 ff.
22. S. Shapiro, *Wayward Capitalists: Target of the Securities and Exchange Commission* (New Haven: Yale University Press, 1984), 26–43; S. Shapiro, 'The Road Not Taken: The Elusive Path To Criminal Prosecution For White-Collar Offenders', *Law and Society Review*, 19 (1985), 179–217.
23. R. Sobel, *The Big Board: A History Of The New York Stock Market* (London: Collier Macmillan, 1965), 235.
24. The authoritative account is J. Seligman, *The Transformation of Wall Street: A History of the Securities and Exchange Commission and Modern Corporate Finance* (Boston: Houghton Mifflin, 1982), chs. 1–6.
25. This relies on Seligman, *Transformation of Wall Street*, pp. 156–212. The phrase in the next sentence misquotes Sobel's Morganization of America, pp. 147–73 of *The Big Board*.
26. For Kennedy's extraordinary and unscrupulous early career see R.

Whalen, *The Founding Father: The Story of Joseph P. Kennedy* (New York: New American Library, 1964), 3–161.

27. A. Lewis, 'The Unwinnable War on Insider Trading', *Fortune*, 13 July 1978.
28. G. Stigler, 'Public Regulation of the Securities Market', *in his The Citizen and the State: Essays on Regulation* (Chicago: University of Chicago Press, 1975), 98.
29. H. Manne, *Insider Trading and the Stock Market* (New York: Free Press, 1966), 131–45. These arguments are still very much alive. For examples couched in lawyer's language: M. Dooley, 'Enforcement Of Insider Trading Restrictions', *Virginia Law Review*, 66 (1980), 1–83; D. Carlton and D. Fischel, 'The Regulation of Insider Trading', *Stanford Law Review*, 35 (1982–3), 875–96.
30. T. Hazen, 'Corporate Insider Trading: Reawakening The Common Law', *Washington and Lee Law Review*, 39 (1982), 845–60. (The quotation is on p. 847.)
31. This relies on M. Karsch, 'The Insider Trading Sanctions Act: Incorporating a Market Information Definition', *Journal of Comparative Business and Capital Market Law*, 6 (1984), 283–305.
32. G. Wang, 'Dirks v. Securities and Exchange Commission: An Outsider's Guide to Insider Trading Liability Under Rule 106–5', *American Business Law Journal*, 22 (1985), 569–82.
33. D. Karjala, 'Statutory Regulation of Insider Trading In Impersonal Markets', *Duke Law Journal*, 5 (1982), 627–49, is one of many summaries in the legal literature.
34. Quoted, R. Schotland, 'Introduction', to Twentieth Century Fund, *Abuse on Wall Street: Conflicts of Interest in the Securities Markets* (London: Quorum, 1980), 4–22 (p. 3).
35. Wang, 'Dirks v. Securities and Exchange Commission'.
36. 'Annual Review of Federal Securities Regulation II', *The Business Lawyer*, 40 (Nov. 1984), 159–218.
37. The significance of the Chiarella case is well described in Karsch, 'The Insider Trading Sanctions Act'.
38. Shapiro, *Wayward Capitalists*, pp. 98–134.
39. A. F. Matthews and D. Becker, 'The SEC's Enforcement Program', *New York Law Journal*, 31 (1984), 8–19.
40. D. Langevoort, 'The Insider Trading Sanctions Act of 1984 and its Effects on Existing Law', *Securities Law Review 1985* (New York: Boardman, 1985), 187–212.
41. J. Siegel, 'United States Insider Trading Prohibition in Conflict with Swiss Bank Secrecy', *Journal of Comparative Corporate Law and Securities Regulation*, 4 (1983), 353–76.
42. This is based on interviews with market actors and regulators carried out in the summer and autumn of 1985.

43. The traditional state of affairs is summarized in B. A. K. Rider and H. L. Ffrench, *The Regulation of Insider Trading* (London: Macmillan, 1979), 146 ff.
44. This is based on Committee To Review The Functioning Of Financial Institutions, *Second Stage Evidence* (London, 1979), 3–22; B. A. K. Rider, 'Self-Regulation: The British Approach To Policing Conduct In The Securities Business', *Journal of Comparative Law and Securities Regulation*, 1 (1978), 319–48; T. P. Lee, 'Law And Practice with Respect to Insider Trading and Trading on Market Information in the United Kingdom', *Journal of Comparative Law and Securities Regulation*, 4 (1982), 379–87.
45. There is a summary and review in P. Mitchel, 'Insider Dealing—Two Years On', *Business Law Review*, 3 (Nov. 1982), 343–4.
46. Stock Exchange, *Report And Accounts 1984* (London, 1984), 8.
47. L. H. Leigh, *The Control of Commercial Fraud* (London: Heinemann, 1982), 11.
48. Leigh, *Control of Fraud*, 3–4.
49. Rider, 'Self-Regulation: The British Approach'.
50. M. Newmarch, 'The Fund Managers' Guide to the City's Brave New World', *The Times*, 12 Feb. 1985. The author is chief executive of Prudential Portfolio Managers.
51. S. Das, 'The Cassandra of the City Revolution' (an interview with David Hopkinson), *Investors Chronicle*, 5 Apr. 1985, 10–11. For a more elaborate outline of Mr Hopkinson's views see D. Hopkinson, 'The Coming Changes in Stock Markets', *The Treasurer*, 11 (1984), 37–8.
52. I. Herzel and D. Colling, 'The Chinese Wall and Conflict of Interest in Banking', *The Business Lawyer*, 34 (1978), 73–116.
53. L. C. B. Gower, *Review of Investor Protection, Report: Part II* (London, 1985), 28.
54. E. Hermann, 'Commercial Bank Trust Departments', in *Abuse On Wall Street*, pp. 23–157.
55. N. Woolfson, 'Investment Banking', in *Abuse On Wall Street*, pp. 365–432.
56. L. Herzel and D. Colling, 'The "Chinese Wall" Revisited', *The Company Lawyer*, 4 (1983), 14–19 (p. 15).
57. Herzel and Colling, 'The Chinese Wall and Conflict of Interest in Banking'.
58. For a graphic illustration of the culture of traditionalism in the merchant banking community before the era of change, and for the ethical problems thus created, see *Proceedings* of the Tribunal appointed to Inquire into allegations that information about the raising of the Bank Rate was improperly disclosed (London, mimeo minutes of evidence, 1957), 98 ff.

59. Quoted, T. McGraw, *Prophets of Regulation* (Cambridge, Mass.: Harvard University Press, 1984), 166.
60. R. Karmel, *Regulation by Prosecution: The Securities and Exchange Commission vs. Corporate America* (New York: Simon and Schuster, 1982), 27.
61. J. Habermas, *Communication and the Evolution of Society* (London: Heinemann, 1979), 178. (I have reversed the order of the remarks.)
62. There is a useful summary of this case and its aftermath in 'The Hutton Investigation', *Business Week*, 23 Sept. 1985.
63. J. Braithwaite, *Corporate Crime in the Pharmaceutical Industry* (London: Routledge & Kegan Paul, 1984). The point is emphasized more generally by C. Stone, *Where The Law Ends: The Social Control Of Corporate Behaviour* (New York: Harper and Row, 1975).
64. Quoted, Seligman, *Transformation Of Wall Street*, p. 73.

PART 2

Sectoral Regulation

4

Regulating Drug Prices: The West German and British Experience

Leigh Hancher

Introduction

This chapter aims to explore and compare the role of law in the process of policy initiation and implementation in the Federal Republic of Germany and the United Kingdom, two countries with distinctive constitutional and legal traditions. The West German penchant for legalism in general and the centrality of the administrative court system (*Verwaltungsgerichtbarkeit*) has already attracted the attention of comparative policy analysts.[1] This tendency towards legal formalism, together with the extreme fragmentation of the West Germany policy-making process are recognized as important determinants of the fate of policy objectives.[2] There has been little attempt, however, to identify the impact of similar or surrogate institutional constraints on British policy makers, so that the analysis of the role of law in the policy process remains largely uncharted territory.[3] That said the reader should be warned that what follows represents only a tentative exploration, and that the chosen subject-matter, recent attempts by each state to reduce the share of prescription drugs products in their respective health bills, is not necessarily offered as a representative sample of the institutional landscape. And yet the eventual fate of national initiatives provides evidence of striking differences in terrain.

Health care is now the second largest social programme after pensions, and one of the largest single overall expenditure costs in all OECD countries.[4] Changing demographic structures as well as advances in medical technology have continued to exert pressure on spending levels despite a slow-down in the rate of growth since the oil crisis of 1973. Although patterns and levels of drug consumption vary from country to country,[5] the need to rationalize, and indeed ration, access to and payment for prescription drug products has become an important policy objective as successive governments in each country seek ways of reducing the burden of reimbursement costs borne by public funds. At the same time governments of different political complexion in each country have been concerned to safeguard the export strength and foreign exchange earning capacity of an industry which has become increasingly multinational in its organization and in its marketing strategies. A change in the political climate of the host state may encourage footloose firms to threaten to seek more temperate zones for all or part of their operations, confronting governments with the complex task of reconciling public expenditure ambitions with industry's profit-related aspirations.

Nevertheless a number of what may be collectively termed 'cost containment' measures, aimed at reducing the volume of demand for prescription products on the one hand and controlling their selling prices on the other, have been introduced in the last decade. Both will adversely affect the profitability of the drug companies, but the introduction of demand-related controls will depend in part on their acceptability to the medical profession and in part on the capacity of industry to resist more directly intrusive or legally sanctioned forms of profit or cost control. The institutional positions of the industry and the medical profession, in conjunction with the availability of legal remedies, may allow the former to resist direct controls on its own profitability and shift the burden of cost containment on to the latter. Alternatively both may unite in their attempts to resist governmental control and intervention, frustrating cost containment in its entirety. In seeking to impose cost containment measures governments are, to a certain extent, attempting to offset the absence of competition, or at least the absence of price-based competition,[6] in a market where the normal rules of supply and demand are displaced when the not so invisible hand which writes the prescription is not the one which proffers payment or pops the pills.

Although most European governments can rely on the general mechanisms of competition law to check abusive pricing, the peculiarities of the market for pharmaceuticals have caused them to seek additional methods of control. Few companies can be said to dominate the entire market in medicine but many enjoy a monopoly position in respect of specific, self-contained therapeutic sub-markets.[7] Hoffman-La Roche, as we shall see, was found to hold a dominant position in the market for tranquillizers, although its share of the total market for prescription products in the UK was relatively small. In addition, as long as a product is in patent, companies are usually sufficiently immunized from competition to set prices at high levels, which could not necessarily be described as 'abusive' in a technical sense. Governments can intervene to compensate for this lack of competition either by controlling the price of supplies or by improving the quality of the demand. Strategies designed to achieve the latter usually aim to improve market transparency, that is, to encourage doctors to select the medicine which represents the best value for money and which is the most effective in treating a patient. Although transparency measures are a less intrusive method of controlling overall costs, they are resented by the firms and the health professionals alike. Industry is anxious to resist any encroachment on its economic freedom while the medical profession are equally concerned to protect their professional autonomy in prescribing matters. Again each party will try to take advantage of institutional and legal factors to avoid unwanted interference in their affairs.

A further source of institutional constraint is of course the organization of the health care delivery system and the structure of cost reimbursement. The West German and British systems diverge considerably, generating distinctive sets of problems, pressures, and priorities. These divergent structures in turn impose their own restrictions on the perceptions of policy makers, on the range of available options, and on the realization of cost containment measures.

In this chapter I examine the way in which legal factors in particular constrain the process of policy initiation and implementation. An adequate understanding of this process requires a 'two-dimensional' analysis of the role of law; not only an appreciation of the legal rights and powers of the various policy actors but furthermore an awareness of the strategic or operational advantages and disadvantages of legal challenge. Hayward's observation that 'the norms of a particular polity will prescribe which matters of public policy are or are not negotiable'[8] may be extended to embrace the importance of those same norms in determining acceptable modes of negotiation and bargaining. Both the British and West German Governments have preferred bargaining over costs, as well as consensually oriented methods of self-regulation, as opposed to 'adversarial' modes of cost control. Why the predominantly co-operative reaction on the part of British industry has not been replicated in West Germany is a question which this chapter seeks to answer. The availability and widespread use of legal challenge in West Germany is surely an important factor in explaining not only the industry's successful subversion, and displacement of cost containment measures, but also the lack of incentive to be drawn into an institutionalized negotiating framework.

Institutional arrangements are said to 'evolve in response to crisis and opportunity'.[9] British industry faced its particular crisis some twenty years earlier than its West German counterpart, but the former exploited the available 'opportunities' to erect a complex, self-regulatory system of cost control. This precocious start to self-regulation has equipped the industry with ways of deflecting the more recent threats of interventionism, allowing it to exploit the 'corporatist bias' that is the legacy of the institutional arrangements of the 1950s.[10] Armed with a set of cast-iron constitutional guarantees, West German industry has successfully beaten off similar interventionist threats, and thus followed a very different institutional path. The divergent legal cultures, that is, the different legal rights and remedies available under each legal system as well as different attitudes to their mobilization, are central to an explanation of the varying strategies adopted by the industry.

The concluding section of the chapter deals with a final problem—the end product of the divergent strategies adopted by industry. At a superficial level we could point to the difference in price structures and consumption levels as prima-facie testimony to the success of the West German style of bargaining over policy goals and methods of control.[11] It is not without reason that the West German market is known as the 'golden market' to manufacturers. That British prices have, until recently, remained at the lower end of the European spectrum would suggest that governmental effort has met with more success.[12] I will argue, however, that the consensual approach to cost control has imposed its own limitations on policy initiatives and that certain legal mechanisms, although not in the form of constitutionally recognized rights, have served equally well to strengthen industry's negotiating position in the United Kingdom.

The Organization of Health Care and Reimbursement

Health care in the United Kingdom is the responsibility of a single, albeit sprawling, central government department—the Department of Health and Social Security (DHSS). This department, in consultation with the Treasury, determines the capital and current budgets of the regional health authorities who in turn distribute funds to district health authorities to finance hospital and community services. Family practitioner services are currently financed directly by the DHSS. Responsibility for purchasing equipment or drugs has never been fully centralized, but the DHSS exercises broad control over staff numbers.[13] The cost of prescription drugs is borne for the most part by the National Health Service (NHS) which is in turn funded by taxation and national insurance contributions. A charge is levied on each prescription item, representing approximately 40 per cent of the average cost of the drug. Until April 1985, and the introduction of the 'Selective List', all prescription drugs were reimbursable.

In West Germany, the picture is one of fragmentation of responsibility and control at both Federal and *Länder* levels.[14] Several ministries participate in the general supervision of various aspects of health care. While the Ministry of Labour and Social Affairs is responsible for social and health insurance, the Ministry of Youth, Family, and Health is concerned with safety and consumer protection measures as well as with the regulation of the professions. The professions are organized on a regional basis and a doctor must be registered with one of eighteen regional Associations of Registered Physicians (KV) and accredited by the legally independent Sickness Funds (Kassen), as a *Kassenarzt*, in order to obtain reimbursement from them. There is no legal relationship between the doctor and the Sickness Funds or between the doctor and the state.[15] Attempts by the Kassen to restrict the number of registered doctors were frustrated by a series of actions in the Constitutional Court,[16] so that it is now virtually impossible for a Kasse to refuse to accredit a qualified doctor. Recent proposals by the Minister of Labour and Social Affairs to limit the number of registered doctors per head of population were thought to be of dubious constitutionality and have been abandoned.

Under West German social security law,[17] the cost of perscription drugs is generally reimbursable by the National Health Insurance

Fund (GKV), to which virtually all employed persons must belong and to which employers and employees must contribute.[18] About 90 per cent of the population is insured under the GKV, which accounts for almost half the total national expenditure on health.[19] The GKV is administered by the Sickness Funds which are organized on a tripartite basis, with the National Federation of Sickness Funds at the apex, *Länder* Federations of Sickness Funds in the middle, and some 1,200 Local Sickness Funds. Each fund administers an essentially similar health insurance reimbursement scheme, being legally obliged to offer a minimum range of services but competition over the package of benefits on offer is considerable and this has had a significant impact on cost containment measures. The KV collect the fees due to their members from the Kassen and distribute them according to guidelines laid down by a complex series of agreements.

West German doctors are reimbursed on a 'fee for service basis', itself an incentive to prescribe. In addition the structure of fees is such that doctors profit substantially by using high technology equipment.[20] Whereas in the United Kingdom fees for services and reimbursement rates for pharmaceutical products are centrally negotiated by the DHSS and the professional associations, the West German Federal Government has persistently failed in its efforts to create a Uniform Valuation Standard (EBM) for the multiplicity of fee schedules currently negotiated between the Kassen and the KV. The Kassen have no effective means of controlling the quantity and quality of these services.

The very structure of the West German system creates pressures on the cost of health care which have no counterpart in the British per capitation based fee structure and the decentralized nature of much of the decision-making on health care expenditure has frustrated effective Federal direction.[21]

Relations between Government and Industry

The United Kingdom

Prescription drug prices in the United Kingdom are currently controlled under the pharmaceutical price regulation scheme (PPRS). Despite its name the PPRS is concerned with manufacturers' *profits* as opposed to prices of individual products and it is essentially a voluntary, non-binding agreement. Its present structure and operation as an instrument of cost containment can only be understood in terms of the origin of its predecessor, the voluntary price regulation scheme (VPRS) which established a particular pattern of relations between government and British-based industry.

The optimism displayed by the architects of the NHS, who were content to leave the responsibility for the supply of medicine to private industry, was founded on the belief that health costs would remain static or even decline as general health levels improved.[22] The rising cost of the 'cascade of medicines pouring down British throats',[23] especially branded medicines, prompted an early re-assessment. The Ministry of Health, already compromised by its guarantee of doctors' freedom to prescribe the medicine of their choice,[24] could only rely on mere persuasion and exhortation. Following the Committee on Prescribing's recommendation that some sort of price control over branded products should be introduced the Minister proposed to align the allowable rate of return on sales to the industry on its sales to the NHS to that of other government contractors.[25] The industry association, the ABPI, was quick to stress the unique position of the drugs industry in its dealings with government; it was not guaranteed a stable, predetermined market, and it needed a higher level of return in order to finance high risk research. Fearing the potential use of the power at the disposal of the NHS, its principal customer, the ABPI accepted the need for some system of price control and proposed its own scheme, which, albeit in modified form, was to provide the basis for the first VPRS, officially adopted in 1957.

Negotiations on the VPRS had in fact coincided with the first official inquiry into the costs of the NHS, which declined to investigate the cost of prescription drugs when the Ministry and the manufacturers were already involved in drafting a price regulation scheme. In consequence the Ministry's only source of information on pricing structures and price formation in the industry was the ABPI itself.

It is perhaps not surprising that few were impressed by the final version of a scheme which was of limited coverage and which relied heavily on the so-called 'export criterion', i.e. the product's selling price on foreign markets. Little evidence was adduced to substantiate the basic assumption that world prices reflected greater competitiveness than British prices,[26] and to appease Treasury officials, the Ministry of Health sought a *voluntary undertaking* from the ABPI that current prices would not be increased except where the increase was justified in terms of costs. The Association, being a voluntary organization and having no real power to secure compliance, could only give a written undertaking of its good intentions. The extent to which a firm's profit estimates could be adequately checked by the Ministry was a source of further concern, given the complete absence of reliable, independent data. Any comparison of home and export prices was more a matter of guesswork than good accounting practice, a problem which could only be aggravated by the absence of adequate expertise at the disposal of the Ministry.[27]

Although the VPRS did not produce spectacular savings for the Health Departments, in retrospect it is not difficult to understand the enthusiasm with which it was greeted. The Ministry itself was weak, being something of a political backwater and its officials were 'shell-shocked survivors of encounters with the medical profession in the 1940's'.[28] The idea of a price control scheme, conceived under a Labour Government, came to fruition under a Tory Government committed to 'making a bonfire of controls'.[29] As a major earner, the pharmaceutical industry could not fail to wield substantial influence at a time when balance of payments problems were a national preoccupation.[30]

Two features of this version of the scheme have endured despite five renegotiations; the lack of any real or formal investigative powers for DHSS officials and the almost complete absence of enforcement powers, should a company refuse to supply information or fail to negotiate. Powers to require information and to set prices, initially enacted in the Emergency Powers Act, 1934, have subsequently been incorporated into the National Health Service Act, 1977, but these powers may only be enacted by the tortuously slow process of Order in Council.

It is the continued commitment to mutual trust and confidence which has made the British approach to price control so distinctive. This state of affairs cannot, however, be attributed to a general level of satisfaction with the scheme. Average rates of return remained persistently high throughout the first decade of its operation, with wide variations in the earnings of American and

Swiss companies. The Government continued to rely on industry's own profit data and it was only as a result of the American Senator Kefauver's inquiries into the industry's activities that the scandalous level of profits on antibiotic sales to the NHS was uncovered.[31] The Minister chose to rely on indirect powers, namely Section 46 of the Patents Act, 1949, which empowered him to work a patent in the services of the Crown as a way of forcing down prices for hospital supplies.[32] The substance of the VPRS remained unaltered.

Following the election of a Labour Government whose leader had a reputation as a formidable critic not only of the industry but also of the VPRS, a Committee of Inquiry, chaired by Lord Sainsbury, was appointed in 1965, to report on the relationship of the pharmaceutical industry with the National Health Service.[33] Despite its fairly rounded criticism of the VPRS, Sainsbury subscribed to the general belief in the merits of a voluntary agreement and recommended strengthening the Ministry's negotiation hand through improved information retrieval and accounting practices. Extended powers to impose prices or require information were envisaged only if voluntary compliance proved unattainable, but indirect powers, including the power to award compulsory patents, were to be extended to cover drugs used by general practitioners as well as hospitals.[34] Although a system of independently audited Annual Financial Returns (AFR) which allowed the Ministry to monitor and influence profit, but not prices as Sainsbury had recommended, was introduced it was only a last minute amendment to the Health Services and Public Health Bill, 1968, by Labour backbenchers which secured the extension of Section 46 to include doctors.[35] Legal sanctions remained otherwise supplementary to the VPRS and its successor the PPRS, while participation in it meant exemption from general regimes of price control.[36]

The British system of profit control, based on essentially subjective criteria of 'reasonableness' and voluntary compliance, is perhaps the best method of accommodating the Department of Health's conflicting roles of official sponsor and regulator of the drugs industry. When introducing the most recent version of the PPRS, the Minister commented that the Government's task was to strike a balance between providing an acceptable profit to the industry while at the same time providing value for money to the

NHS and the taxpayer.[37] The informal nature of the scheme has allowed the Government to make several short-term adjustments to compensate for excessive shifts of this balance in industry's favour. In 1983, acting on Treasury instructions to cut drug expenditure, the DHSS forced the industry to accept a one-year price freeze and an average 2.5 per cent reduction in prices of some 1,500 individual products.[38] A further price freeze was imposed in the following year, but in 1985 the sudden introduction of the Selective List dealt an unprecedented blow to the time-honoured tradition of extensive prior consultation and negotiation with interested parties.[39] The 'Limited List', to give it its popular name, is intended to yield savings of some £75 million for the NHS. It restricted reimbursement for seven therapeutic categories of drugs to the cheapest available products. As most of the products in question were long out of patent, the List was seen as introducing generic prescribing by the back door.[40] The ABPI and the British Medical Association both sought legal advice on the compatibility of the List with European law but the European Commission has informed complainants that unless and until proof of discrimination against imports can be produced, the terms on which the List is compiled appear to comply with the jurisprudence of the Court of Justice.[41]

In the summer of 1986 a West German company, Schering Chemicals, brought a High Court action against the Government's refusal to list its product Noctamid by its brand name as opposed to its non-proprietary name on the list of reimbursable products. Schering complained that it had been deprived of the benefit of its trademark and that its imports had subsequently suffered. The judge found no evidence of intention to discriminate against imported medicinal preparations.[42] He also noted that 'it would plainly be difficult if not impossible to mount an attack upon the Secretary of State's in terms of [its] unreasonableness or upon any of the traditional grounds upon which judicial review is available'.[43] Legal challenge appears to be of little value in resisting abrupt changes in policy.

Industry has been more successful in deflecting long-term change. In 1983 the Government announced its proposed revisions to the PPRS. These included a reduction in the target rate of profit and stricter controls over the allowable level of promotional expenditure which could be offset against NHS sales. In addition the DHSS proposed to introduce stricter methods of assessing the reasonableness of prices for raw materials charged by overseas parent companies to their British affiliates. Three years of protracted negotiations later, the Government backed down on its more radical, interventionist revisions to the scheme.[44] Prices are now set to allow £250 million to be spent on pharmaceutical R. & D. And yet when asked what information he had about the principal areas of research carried out by the industry in the last five years the Minister had to admit that he had none.[45] Mutual trust and co-operation remain the twin pillars on which the British system of profit control rests.

The Federal Republic

The West German experience of cost control reflects an entirely different approach to and style of regulation. In the first place direct price control of any product has been confined by an early judgement of the Federal Supreme Court to times of relative emergency, when 'defensive pricing' is permissible,[46] and secondly the fragmented and decentralized nature of the West German health system makes for a very different political and legal environment.

Under conditions of economic growth West German health care expenditure expanded rapidly as the range of services and the extent of coverage increased. During the period 1960–80 the average contribution per member of the GKV increased from 292 DM to 2,530 DM per person, an increase which fell on both employers and employees.[47] Increased drug costs and hospital fees were identified as the two main culprits. Freed from the twin threats of formal price control and monopolistic uses of purchasing power, the West German pharmaceutical industry lacked the incentive to enter into formal arrangements with either the Government or the Kassen. The Federal Government, deprived of the important 'stick' of direct price control and lacking a centrally directed apparatus with which to tackle the cost explosion in health care in general and drug costs in particular, was forced to find alternative methods of control in the 1977 Federal Law on Cost Containment.[48]

The actual form and eventual fate of the measures adopted under this Act has been determined in part by the constraints inherent in the German Federal policy-making process and in part by legal factors. While it would appear that there was all-party consensus on the need to act on health costs, there was 'an almost unspoken agreement that the measures to be taken . . . should be sought within the existing institutional framework' and that the level of services should be maintained.[49] There was considerable disagreement, however, both within the ruling SDP/FDP coalition, and between the latter and the opposition parties who were in a majority in the Bundesrat, over the degree of state intervention necessary to limit costs. The final version of the Act represented a compromise thrashed out in the parliamentary conciliation committee to which it had been referred. Most of the SDP's original proposals to strengthen the hand of the Kassen in their dealings with industry and the doctors' powers were lost.

Instead the Act erected a complex structure of consensual, non-binding agreements between the various parties, the terms of which would be guided by a Federal steering mechanism, the Concerted Action Committee (KAG).[50] This Committee, chaired by the Minister of Labour and comprised of representatives from industry, the health professions, the hospital boards, the Kassen, and local and Länder government representatives was to meet twice yearly to determine expenditure and to review standards of efficiency in health care provision. Whereas the level of contributions to the GKV had previously been determined by the amount expended by the Kassen, the 1977 Act effectively inverted this principle and introduced an income related expenditure approach. Maximum ceilings on expenditure for ambulatory care only[51] were to be calculated on the basis of the forecast increase in the basic wage (*Grundlohnsumme*), pharmaceutical prices, and the number of patients treated. The KAG could be described as a tentative and cumbersome experiment in global budgeting which failed. It attempted to superimpose centrally determined costings onto a fragmented system of health care delivery,[52] and failed to equip the Kassen with the necessary sanctions to ensure observance of the voluntary agreements on prescribing with the doctors.

In an effort to introduce greater economies on prescribing the 1977 Act entrusted the Federal joint committee of doctors and Kassen to compile a 'negative list' of minor drug products which could be excluded from reimbursement, and secondly to produce prescribing guidelines, enabling doctors to make comparisons between the usefulness of products. In addition, the Transparency

Commission, an advisory body to the Minister of Health, set up by the 1976 Medicines Act, and comprising representatives from industry, the Kassen, and the health professions, was given the task of publishing transparency lists which would compare different drugs with similar indications on the basis of safety, efficacy, and treatment costs.[53] It was hoped that this would lead to more cost effective prescribing. Representatives of the medical profession and of industry, as well as dissenting politicians, have displayed a propensity to raise legal objections to any attempt to reduce the volume of demand for drugs so that actual as well as potential legal challenge has delayed and undermined the effectiveness of all three initiatives. In determining which products were candidates for inclusion on the negative list as well as the comparability of one drug with another for the purposes of transparency lists and prescribing guidelines, each committee was forced to make its decision on criteria based on the efficacy of a product. Under the 1976 Medicines Act the task of establishing product efficacy falls to an entirely separate government institution—the BGA.[54] Considerable doubt as to the legal capacity of the joint committees to touch on such matters in their prescribing guidelines, published in accordance with the 1977 Cost Containment Act, both delayed the publication and restricted the final scope of the guidelines. Similar problems attended the work of the Transparency Commission whose lists were substantially amended to accommodate industry objections to the use of certain comparative criteria.[55] The compilation of the 'negative list' was shelved when the responsible committee found that it was impossible to come up with a legally watertight definition of a 'trivial ailment'.[56]

The work of the Transparency Commission was finally undermined by a judgement of the Federal Supreme Court in 1985 on its powers to request the submission of data on quality. The Court, ruling on an appeal brought by a small drugs company, held that the publication of a transparency list was an infringement of Article 12 of the Basic Law which protects entrepreneurial activity, including the right to compete on equal terms. Irrespective of their indirect nature, the purpose of the lists was to alter the basic conditions of competition and as such could only be effected by an Act of Parliament.[57] The Transparency Commission had been created by a ministerial order and it required an amendment to the Medicines Act in 1986 to provide the Commission with a statutory basis.[58] An earlier amendment to the 1977 Act had allowed the Labour Ministry to assume responsibility for the compilation of the negative list.[59]

These attempted restrictions on global expenditure and on the volume of demand for drugs would appear to have been a signal failure in the Federal Republic. So far the Minister of Labour's only response to the failure of the 1984 KAG procedure to arrive at an agreement on expenditure ceilings has been the introduction of new, detailed price comparison lists for doctors, based on a threefold system of product classification.[60] These lists are intended to include the so-called 'combination' products which occupy a lucrative share of the West German market. As legal responsibility for the compilation of the Transparency Lists rests with the Minister of Health it is probably unconstitutional to combine them with the Ministry of Labour's new Price Lists, so doctors will be sent two partial sets of guidelines instead of a single informative document.[61] Protracted doubts as to whether the Price Lists offended the constitutional principles of clear and precise standards and of equal treatment prevented their publication until the autumn of 1986. The method of their compilation has already been the subject of several unsuccessful challenges in the lower courts.[62] As long as the various actors on the health care scene could rely upon their legal rights as an effective means of safeguarding their respective interests, the corporatist institutions created by the 1977 Act had little to offer and, in contrast to the British situation, there was little incentive for industry to comply with voluntary controls whose legal basis could so easily be eroded. Given the enormous political obstacles which any legislative programme must overcome in West Germany, there is little prospect that these weak measures will be replaced by interventionist controls, despite ministerial threats of a post-election overhaul of the entire system of health insurance.[63]

The British system of profit control rests on mutual trust and confidence. It has enjoyed some success in holding 'average' prices for pharmaceuticals at a low level. But what happens when a company refuses to play by the existing rules of the game? Are the British authorities any less constrained than their West German counterparts?

The Price of Corporatism?

We have seen that in the United Kingdom the voluntary arrangements for profit regulation are underpinned by the existence of indirect legal controls, including the provisions of patent law. In the Federal Republic the commitment to the social market economy as well as constitutionally imposed restrictions on the use of price controls might suggest that the provisions of general competition law could be applied to guarantee effective competition in the pharmaceutical market, offering an alternative means of checking abusive pricing practices. A survey of the number of pharmaceutical pricing cases reviewed in the Annual Reports of the Cartel Office, the principal competition authority, confirms this view, although the majority are concerned with relatively minor pricing adjustments. The relationship between these controls on prices and the forms of regulation previously described is the subject of this section.

The West German competition law, Gesetz gegen Wettbewerbbeschränkungen (GWB), 1958, as amended, invests the Cartel Authorities and in particular the Federal Cartel Office (FCO) with substantial powers of investigation and enforcement, always provided that these are exercised within strict legal limits. Whereas British competition law is characterized by the extensive discretionary powers attributed to the Director-General of Fair Trading and the Secretary of State for Trade and Industry, the role of the Monopolies and Mergers Commission (MMC) being purely advisory, West German competition law is both legally formalistic and complex and this is particularly true of Section 22 GWB which deals, *inter alia*, with abusive pricing practices. Section 22 has been the subject of four amendments, each of which has added to the complexity of the definition of such key terms as 'market dominance' and 'abusive conduct'.[64] The British system, which relies predominantly on the voluntary 'undertakings' given by companies following the threat of a reference or an adverse report, has not found much favour with the competition authorities in West Germany.[65] The following review of attempts in West Germany and the UK to recoup the alleged monopoly profits earned by Hoffman-La Roche offers further illustration of national divergences to problems of price control, divergences attributable to the legacy of the controls discussed earlier as well as to the different legal cultures informing the application of competition law in each country.

Hoffman-La Roche is a Swiss-based multinational with extensive operations throughout the world. In 1957 it discovered the compound which was to form the basis of its two leading tranquillizers, Librium and Valium. A carefully constructed international web of patent rights allowed Hoffman-La Roche to retain almost complete monopolistic control over the manufacture of the active ingredients which were supplied in bulk form to various national subsidiaries at inflated costs. This practice, known as transfer pricing, minimized the subsidiaries' tax liability. The Achilles' heel of this marketing strategy was Italy, where patent protection on medicines was unavailable until 1978. This allowed independent companies to manufacture the active ingredients of Valium and Librium at a fraction of the costs charged by Hoffman-La Roche.[66]

The company's persistent refusal to participate in the British VPRS forced the Government to refer the company's pricing practices to the MMC in 1971 while differences in West German and Italian selling prices prompted the FCO to commence investigations in 1973. The final outcome of each case offers an illustration of the impact of legal factors on the strategic implications of different methods of dispute settlement.

In the following discussion patent law is subsumed under the general heading of competition policy, it being generally acknowledged that there is a 'grey area' where the concerns of competition law and patent law overlap, if not conflict. The limited period of legal monopoly enjoyed by a patent holder can be an important determinant of a company's economic strength on a particular therapeutic sub-market.[67] An abuse of patent privileges may attract the sanction of either competition law or patent law, but it is relatively rare for a competition authority to define a 'relevant market' for the purposes of competition law in terms of the market share of any single patented product, and although both West German and British legislation provides its competition authorities with powers to award compulsory licences,[68] or impose fines,[69] these have rarely been used.[70] It is generally agreed that there are far fewer restrictions on the manner in which a West German as opposed to a British patent holder may manufacture, sell, or licence his or her products.[71]

Official ambivalence over the granting of monopoly privileges for pharmaceuticals delayed the availability of all product patents in West Germany until 1968. Patents on drugs, although introduced in the UK in 1949, were originally subject to a compulsory licensing procedure. Section 41 of the 1949 Act empowered the Comptroller of Patents to grant a licence on food or drug products to a competitor, and to determine the royalties payable to the patent holder. In arriving at this sum he was to endeavour to secure that goods were available at the lowest price consistent with the original patentee deriving reasonable advantage from their patent rights. These licences were abolished in 1977.

The Dispute in the United Kingdom

Hoffman-La Roche's refusal to enter into negotiations on its Valium prices under the second VPRS in 1964 prompted officials at the Ministry of Health to take a closer look at the group profit element in the price charged by the Basle-based parent company to its British subsidiary for imported bulk materials. Hoffman-La Roche was informed that in the Ministry's estimation at least 20 per cent of these so-called costs represented profit. Hoffman-La Roche justified its refusal to participate in the VPRS on the basis that its products were now subject to competition from compulsory licence holders who were importing their products from Italy, and so there was no need for further control over its profits on them. In fact Hoffman-La Roche succeeded in delaying the issue of the licences up until 1969.[72] Its recalcitrance over the VPRS was initially not countered with legal sanctions, but was resolved through a compromise settlement. Between 1967 and 1969 Hoffman-La Roche made a series of one-off cash repayments to the Ministry and supplied its products free of charge to hospitals and to the Army.

This strategy of negotiation suited the company well. In determining the royalty rate payable to Hoffman-La Roche by DDSA, the first private company to be awarded a Section 41 licence, the Comptroller based his calculations on Hoffman-La Roche's current selling prices. Although he acknowledged this to be a monopoly price, he wrongly assumed it to have been subject to VPRS procedures and took it to be reasonable.[73] In any event Roche refused to supply any further details on its costs. DDSA who could buy their basic produce for some £20 per tonne on the Italian market were forced to pay a further £140 per tonne in royalties, making the final price of their product much less competitive. Hoffman-La Roche then proceeded to use its trademark rights to undermine DDSA's sales campaign, successfully challenging the company's rights to sell the product in the same 'get up', i.e. in green and black oblong capsules.[74]

The free supply of its product to NHS and Army hospitals also had the advantage of forestalling a possible use of the Crown's right to work its patents under Section 46, while familiarizing junior house doctors with Hoffman-La Roche brands. Pressure on retail chemists to take Hoffman-La Roche brands placed small competitors at a further disadvantage. Pharmaceutical products are only included on the Ministry of Health's Drug Tariff, and on the DHSS's comparative cost charts, if chemists stock them. As doctors could not rely on chemists keeping stocks of DDSA brands and had not been alerted to the price differentials, they were reluctant to prescribe them.[75]

The peculiarities of the British reimbursement system enabled Hoffman-La Roche to undermine the competitiveness of its rivals, and neutralize the impact of compulsory licences, while using their very existence as a reason for its continued refusal to participate in the Fourth VPRS in 1970. In the meantime the Minister used his legal powers to obtain sufficient information on Hoffman-La Roche's costings to calculate that, even allowing for the free supplies to hospitals and the cash repayments, the profits on Valium and Librium were exorbitant.[76] In the face of continued recalcitrance the case was referred to the MMC.[77] Hoffman-La Roche remained firm, however, in its resolve to supply only minimal information to government authorities, and dismissed the discrepancies between Italian and British prices as 'mere differences'. The company only agreed to supply fuller information if the MMC accepted that additional information on cost calculations would be based on world prices and average costs as opposed to national figures.[78] The MMC declined to do so and found that Hoffman-La Roche had made grossly excessive profits at the expense of the NHS between 1969 and 1972. It recommended that these profits should be *recouped* by way of the imposition of price ceilings on *current* prices, effectively circumventing the absence of any power under British competition law to impose fines on errant companies.[79]

Hoffman-La Roche, being reluctant to forgo high profits while patents on Valium and Librium remained extant, refused to give a voluntary undertaking to the Secretary of State, so that the MMC's recommendations were implemented by the more formal and rarely used Order procedure.[80] Despite extensive lobbying on the part of the company,[81] the Order was finally approved by both Houses three months later. Hoffman-La Roche then sought a declaration in the Courts that the MMC had failed to observe the rules of natural justice in its assessment of the transfer pricing issue, rendering its report and the subsequent Statutory Order void.[82] The Secretary of State retaliated with an injunction to prevent Hoffman-La Roche from exceeding the prices stipulated in the Order but Hoffman-La Roche counter-claimed that it would only comply with the Order on the condition that the Crown gave financial guarantee of compensation should the company's earlier case succeed. These legal issues were resolved in the following year,[83] but in the meantime Hoffman-La Roche finally conceded defeat, produced the data originally requested by the MMC, and resumed supplying hospitals free of charge.

The Government was also suffering from this four-year war of attrition. Hoffman-La Roche was still refusing to come back into the VPRS to negotiate prices on its other products and it was beginning to make threatening noises about the future of its British-based investments. Finally a compromise agreement was announced in the House of Commons: Hoffman-La Roche would repay £3.25 million instead of the original £13 million recommended by the MMC, so that increases allowable under normal VPRS guidelines would be taken into account. The prices of Librium and Valium were halved and the company agreed to withdraw all legal action against the Government.[84] The latter appeared to have won a minor victory. In the longer term, however, it would appear that Hoffman-La Roche won the war, even if it lost the battle. By the time the settlement was announced the patent on Librium had expired. The Government persistently refused to disclose what the price of Valium would have been under normal VPRS rules, and in any event the price was allowed to rise by some 45 per cent in the following year.[85] Furthermore the final sum was only repaid in late 1975, by which time the company had had five years to reap the benefits of its excess profits and to take advantage of a 30 per cent depreciation in sterling.[86] To ensure the completion of the company's Scottish vitamin plant, the Labour Government made available subsidies in the region of £46 million under the Industry Act,[87] and an additional £1.2 million to meet half the cost of a railway siding was paid in 1977.[88] If further subsidies for development work from the Scottish Development Agency (SDA) are included, some £100 million of the total cost of £140 million was contributed by the Government. This corresponded to assistance approaching £300,000 per job created.[89]

In terms of the effectiveness of indirect controls over the operations of the pharmaceutical industry, two aspects of the Hoffman-La Roche affair deserve further comment. First, not one of the government bodies was able to compel a reluctant Hoffman-La Roche to produce detailed information on its profit calculations, so that the successive investigations by the civil servants at the DHSS, the Comptroller of Patents, and the MMC depended upon the scant findings of a past inquiry. Lack of information on manufacturing and R. & D. costs caused the MMC to concentrate excessively on promotional expenditure, exposing themselves to Hoffman-La Roche's charge that there had been a failure to observe the rules of natural justice, as the company was not in a position to answer the case against it fully. Secondly, the informality of approach inherent in the VPRS has a 'knock on' effect on the value of indirect controls. The agreement between Hoffman-La Roche and the Ministry of Health was not apparent to the Comptroller who assumed prices to have been negotiated under the VPRS and, as such, were reasonable. The resulting royalty rates severely undermined the competitiveness of the smaller rivals, casting the compulsory licensing procedure into general disrepute.[90]

It is perhaps ironic that despite the DHSS's unique position as the major customer of the pharmaceutical industry, together with the control which it exercises over every stage of the distribution and retail of prescription products, it was unable to co-ordinate action taken under VPRS with attempts to stimulate competition by opening up patents. And yet Hoffman-La Roche could justify its refusal to comply with direct profit controls by its alleged compliance with the provisions of these indirect controls, effectively turning the tables on the DHSS. Far from supplementing direct controls, the Government's attempts to make use of its indirect powers in effect frustrated the efficient exercise of the former, seriously threatening the fragile basis of consensus on which the

VPRS rested. The adversarial situation provoked by the use of formal legal sanctions was in the long run resolved by tried and true methods of voluntary co-operation.

The Dispute in the Federal Republic

The Hoffman-La Roche saga reveals the enforcement of British competition policy to be suffused with a mixture of discretion and pragmatism. Has the formalistic West German approach proved more effective as a method of indirect price control? West German competition law places considerable emphasis on the *regulation of conduct*: 'Establishment of an abuse is a complex attempt to advance from an analysis of market conduct, market structure and market result tests to specific cases of misconduct.'[91]

The FCO commences its investigation of alleged abuses by analysing a company's position on its relevant product market. Product markets are determined according to the functional interchangeability of different products and cross-elasticity of their prices. The GWB gives little guidance on the meaning of such key concepts as 'dominance' and 'abuse'. There is a rebuttable presumption of market dominance in the case of a market share of more than one-third, but the final decision will turn on qualitative criteria. In its investigations into the Hoffman-La Roche case, the FCO tried to break down the market for tranquillizers as far as possible, ruling that Valium and Librium competed with only five other products. This finding was successfully contested by Hoffman-La Roche and the relevant market redefined to include a further three products so that Hoffman-La Roche's position was taken to be more akin to that of an oligopolist.[92]

Having established relative dominance, the FCO must then show that there has been abusive conduct in the relevant market. Section 22(4) stipulates that an abuse exists if a market-dominating enterprise demands prices or terms of business which deviate from those which would have been agreed upon in all probability if effective competition had prevailed. The Courts in their interpretation of Section 22 have laid considerable stress on techniques of market reconstruction, requiring extensive comparison of prices in different geographical markets, as well as examination of past pricing practices and the profit levels currently earned by the company. In the Valium case the FCO ordered Hoffman-La Roche to decrease its prices for Valium and Librium to 60 per cent and 65 per cent respectively, taking the difference between Italian and West German prices of Valium as evidence of an abuse.[93] The ensuing court proceedings lasted six years. The FCO's order was upheld in its essential parts by the Kammergericht (KG), although it accepted Hoffman-La Roche's contention that price differentials could be attributed to the absence of patent protection for pharmaceutical products in Italy, adding that the purpose of anti-trust law was not to undermine patent protection. The Court instead compared the West German price with that prevailing for *patented* products on the Dutch market and recommended a 28 per cent reduction in Hoffman-La Roche's prices.[94]

On appeal, the Federal Supreme Court[95] held that, in principle, a finding of abusive conduct may be based on a comparison between the prices prevailing in comparable geographic markets, provided the differences between those markets and the price calculations of the companies engaged in such markets are duly taken into account. The case was referred back to the KG for a reconsideration in the light of this new, strict interpretation of Section 22.[96] The KG again upheld the FCO's order, but in 1980 the Federal Supreme Court finally reversed the order, holding that the volume of the corresponding Dutch market was too small to afford a reasonable basis for comparison with the West German market and that a finding of abusive conduct must be based on an examination of the pricing structure which should have prevailed on the West German market if *substantial* competition existed.[97] Limited price reductions were enforced in 1978, but this was after the expiry of Hoffman-La Roche's patent, and, as the FCO concluded, 'the groups on which abusively high prices can be challenged have been so stringently defined, and the time scale involved in implementing these procedures has become so long, that legal challenge has certainly proved a worthwhile course for a company to follow, even if it eventually loses the case'.[98]

More recently the FCO enjoyed some success in a case involving West Germany's leading drug, Euglucon, jointly manufactured by the multinationals, Hoechst and Boehringer Mannheim. In the course of separate proceedings against a generic manufacturer for patent infringement, it was revealed that while production costs averaged 4 DM per pack, the drug sold for 75 DM per pack, earning sales revenue of 75 DM million for each company in 1984.

The FCO, erring on the side of caution, allowed generous margins for R. & D., quality control, and so on, and estimated a reasonable selling price to be 13 DM. The case only went as far as the Kammergericht, which upheld the FCO's order, enabling it to negotiate substantial price reductions with the companies.[99] It might be noted that the FCO's request for this modest price reduction came *after* the patent had expired and a number of generic producers had already entered the market. Although Section 22 of the GWB has undergone two further amendments since the Valium litigation was begun in 1973, leading one commentator to compare the GWB with a novel,[100] the FCO has consistently maintained that it is of little use in controlling abusive pricing practices, especially in oligopolistic markets.[101] Its reluctance is demonstrated by its recent refusal to open proceedings against the manufacturer of the tranquillizer, Tavor, despite allegations of large discrepancies between the West German and other European selling prices.[102] It may be concluded that the Courts, by requiring the FCO to demonstrate price levels under conditions of 'substantial competition', have added the formidable test of 'market result' to the statutory tests of market share and market conduct, effectively preventing the FCO from exercising effective control over prices.

Conclusion

The British attempts to control prices have been based on a series of non-binding agreements which, despite modification, have retained their essentially consensual character. Although it is often argued that the continued participation of the drug companies in later, more onerous, versions of the schemes has been secured by the threat of increased indirect sanctions, we have tried to argue that the effectiveness of these sanctions is in reality conditional on a continued commitment by all parties concerned to the principal, voluntaristic method of price control. The Labour Government's attempt to use sanctions against Hoffman-La Roche proved an exercise in futility. It would seem that if the 'rules of the game' of price restraint are to work, both sides must retain a commitment to the consensual approach. Where a company steadfastly refuses to participate, governments have been forced to revert to the tried and trusted methods of control by persuasion.

If consensus has provided the foundation of the British system of price control, signs of strain from both within and outside the system suggest that it will not always provide the blueprint for the future.[103] West German companies have threatened to test the legality of the PPRS under European law should the DHSS insist too strongly on an extensive R. & D. commitment and investment in the UK.[104] At first such threats were dismissed by officials as just another bargaining counter which, if the players remain the same, can be traded for another concession. There are, however, signs that there may be a different set of players at the table: the European Commission is presently questioning the compatibility of the Italian and Belgian price controls with the Treaty of Rome. Its continued, though tacit, approval of a British scheme which appears to hinder free movement of goods may well be questioned by one of those Member States, if not by an individual firm.

The historical combination of a fragmented health care system, the constitutional ban on direct price control, as well as the obstacles to legislative reform, have all conspired to ensure that price restraint was a relative latecomer to the West German scene, by which time both industry and the professions had found other ways of safeguarding their vested interests. Although voluntary controls on the demand for drugs have been introduced, their potential impact has been minimized by legal action or threats of legal challenge. The suspicion surrounding voluntary, private undertakings or a discretionary approach to anti-trust law,[105] combined with the formal complexity of GWB, has allowed companies to exploit a series of legal issues, delaying and diluting the FCO's potential impact on prices. Nor do West German companies have anything to fear by using adversarial techniques in challenging government initiatives. Whereas excessive legalism on the part of British-based companies might be interpreted as a fundamental departure from the 'rules of the game', forcing the government itself to adopt a more interventionist style of cost containment, West German companies are compelled to rely on legal challenge—they cannot threaten to withdraw their co-operation from institutional arrangements such as the KAG, which are, in reality no more than paper tigers.

The respective legal cultures of each country have played an important part not only in determining what is negotiable between government and industry but also the manner and style in which negotiations are conducted. These factors are not without influence on the actual success of policy initiatives in practice. The United Kingdom had built a relatively successful policy of price restraint but on a fragile basis of legitimacy. While prices did remain comparatively low by world standards, the system could not withstand serious challenge by an individual firm. Moreover, the 'corporatist bias' which was built into the early versions of the scheme has operated as a bulwark against the introduction of a more rigorous system of controls in the late 1980s when average prices have steadily increased. The British regulator is caught in a vicious circle: to tighten existing controls would alienate the industry whose continued co-operation is a condition of the system's operative efficiency, but the price of consensus is fairly loose control. Governments are forced to adjust policies not to suit their own priorities but to reflect industry's own definition of its needs. As Vogel has commented 'the effectiveness of British regulatory policy and the failure of British industrial policy are related. The very style of policy-making that improves the effectiveness of the former diminishes the effectiveness of the latter.'[106]

The German legal tradition has not bequeathed the West German regulators a much happier legacy. Undoubtedly potential legislative reforms offer scope for incremental change. Whereas the bureaucratization of policy problems in the UK hinders regulatory progress it is the inevitability of their politicization in West Germany that condemns so many initiatives to failure. Such institutional factors as an almost pathological commitment to legalism are an important factor in that process of politicization. Neither scenario promises dramatic improvement in the near future.

Notes

Work for this chapter was funded by the Economic and Social Research Council as part of its 'Government and Industry' initiative (Grant No. E. 0525 0005). I would like to thank M. Ruete for his help on earlier drafts.

1. For a rare example see D. Nelkin and M. Pollack, *The Atom Besieged. Antinuclear Movements in France and Germany* (Cambridge, Mass.: MIT Press, 1981).

2. K. von Beyme, 'Policy Making in the Federal Republic: A Systematic Introduction', in K. von Beyme and M. Schmidt (eds.), *Policy and Politics in the Federal Republic of Germany* (Aldershot: Gower, 1985).
3. See, however, A. C. Page 'Public Law and Economic Policy: The UK experience', *Journal of Law and Society*, 9 (1982), 225–52.
4. OECD, *Trends in Health Care Expenditure* (Paris: OECD, 1985).
5. B. O'Brien, *Patterns of European Diagnoses and Prescribing* (London: OHE, 1984).
6. G. Sermeus and G. Andrianssens, *The Consumer and Pharmaceutical Products in the European Economic Community* (Brussels: EC Commission, 1985).
7. See generally M. L. Burstall, *The Community's Pharmaceutical Industry* (Luxemburg: European Communities, 1984).
8. J. E. S. Hayward, 'Mobilising Private Interests in the Service of Public Ambitions', in J. Richardson and G. Jordan (eds.), *Policy Styles in Western Europe* (London: George Allen & Unwin, 1982).
9. C. Maier, ' "Fictitious Bonds . . . of Wealth and Law": On the Theory and Practice of Interest Representation', in S. Berger (ed.), *Organising Interests in Western Europe* (Cambridge: Cambridge University Press, 1981), p. 28.
10. The phrase has been used by a number of commentators on the British style of intervention, and most recently by Keith Middlemas, *Power, Competition and the State* (London: Macmillan, 1986).
11. Sermeus and Andrianssens, *The Consumer and Pharmaceutical Products*.
12. R. Klein, *The Politics of the NHS* (London: Longmans, 1983).
13. OECD, *Trends in Health Care Expenditure*.
14. A. Murswieck, 'Health Policy Making', in von Beyme and Schmidt, *Policy and Politics in the Federal Republic*, pp. 82–106.
15. F. E. Munnich, 'The Economics of Medical Care: West German Problems', *Zeitschrift für die Gesamte Staatswissenschaft*, 138 (1982), 1–18.
16. Decision of the Constitutional Court, B. Verf. GE 8,274; 21,292.
17. Reichversicherungsordnung (RVO) of 1911 as amended. For a commentary on the law, see D. Krauskopf, *Soziale Krankenversicherung* (Munich: Stand, 1981).
18. About 90% of the population is insured through the public health system. The remaining 10% comprises civil servants who are insured under their own scheme. Welfare recipients have the same rights to health services as those insured in the GKV. Between 0.2–0.4% have no public or private insurance cover.
19. Murswieck, 'Health Policy Making', p. 102.
20. Munnich, 'The Economics of Medical Care'.

21. Murswieck, 'Health Policy Making'.
22. Klein, *The Politics of the NHS.*
23. A. Bevan, quoted in Klein, *The Politics of the NHS*, at p. 47.
24. Ministry of Health, *A National Health Service*, Cmd. 6502 (London: HMSO, 1944).
25. See R. Lang, *The Politics of Drugs* (Farnborough: Saxon House, 1974).
26. Committee of Public Accounts, Session 1956–7, *Third Report from the Committee on Public Accounts*, HC 243 (London: HMSO, 1954).
27. Ministry of Health, *Annual Report for Year Ending 1955*, Part 1, Cmd. 9564 (London: HMSO, 1956).
28. Klein, *The Politics of the NHS*, p. 48.
29. R. K. Middlemas, *Industry, Unions and Government: Twenty one yers of the NEDC* (London: Macmillan, 1983).
30. See generally Committee of Public Accounts, Session 1956–7, *Special Report and First, Second and Third Reports of the Committee on Public Accounts*, HC 75, 93, 190, and 243 (London: HMSO, 1957).
31. J. Braithwaite, *Corporate Crime and the Pharmaceutical Industry* (London: Routledge & Kegan Paul, 1984), provides a useful account of these hearings.
32. For an assessment of their economic impact, see C. T. Taylor and I. A. Silberston, *The Economic Impact of the Patent System* (Cambridge: Cambridge University Press, 1974), 231–63.
33. Cmnd. 3397, 1967 (London: HMSO, 1967).
34. In the case of *Pfizer Corpn.* v. *Ministry of Health* [1965], AC 512, the House of Lords had ruled that Section 46 could only be applied to Crown services. This was interpreted narrowly to exclude the Family Practitioner Service.
35. Lang, *The Politics of Drugs.*
36. Prices and Incomes Acts, 1966–9, and, more specifically, Counter-Inflation (Prices and Pay Code), 1973, S.I. no. 658, 1973 and Counter Inflation (Notification of Increases in Prices and Charges) Order, 1973, Sched. 2, Clause 17.
37. Parl. Deb., 5 July 1986, Vol. 100 Cols. 65–6.
38. Committee on Public Accounts, Session 1984–5, *Twenty-Third Report: NHS Supplies and the PPRS*, HC 280, 1985.
39. Committee on Public Accounts, Session 1984–5.
40. K. Macmillan and I. Turner, 'The Cost Containment Issue', in S. Wilks and M. Wright, *Comparative Government–Industry Relations: Western Europe, the United States, and Japan* (Oxford: Clarendon Press, 1987), 117–47.
41. European Parliament, Written Question: M. de Ferranti, O. J. C.214/18, 15 May 1986.

42. *R.* v. *Secretary of State for Social Services, ex parte Schering Chemicals PLC*, 10 July 1986, not yet reported.
43. Ibid.
44. Department of Health and Social Security, *The Pharmaceutical Price Regulation Scheme* (London: DHSS, 1986).
45. HC Debates, Session 1985–6, vol. 100, col. 66.
46. H. F. Zacker, *Rapport sur le droit économique en RFA* (Brussels: EC Commission, 1973), 107.
47. Murswieck, 'Health Policy Making', p. 120.
48. Krankenversicherungskostendämpfungsgesetz (KVKG).
49. Murswieck, 'Health Policy Making', p. 115.
50. Konzentierte Aktion und Gesundheitswesen.
51. Hospital costs were not included in the 1977 Act.
52. Article 328f RVO allowed the individual parties to determine voluntary ceilings.
53. See generally Scrip, *The Pharmaceutical Market in West Germany* (Richmond: PJB Publications, 1982).
54. The Federal Drugs Agency (Bundesgesundheitsamt).
55. Scrip, *The Pharmaceutical Market in West Germany*.
56. R. Coppock, 'The West German Pharmaceutical Market' (unpublished, 1984).
57. Bundesverwaltungsgericht: judgement of 18 Apr. 1985.
58. Zweites Gesetz zur Anderung des Arzneimittelgesetzes, 1986, 39.
59. KVKG, 1981.
60. E. D. Schenider, 'Die Preisvergleichsliste', *Pharmazeutische Industrie*, 48(8) (1986), 896–8.
61. Scrip no. 1022, 23 July 1986, 5.
62. Scrip no. 1154, 12 Nov. 1986, 4. Two companies—Bristol-Myers and Pfizer—were refused temporary injunctions to prevent publication of price lists which included their products.
63. Scrip no. 1021, 13 July 1986, 5.
64. R. Mueller, M. Heidenhain, and H. Schneider, *German Anti-Trust Law* (Frankfurt: F. Knapp Verlag, 1982).
65. K. Markert, 'The FCO's Experience in Negotiations', *Journal of Consumer Law*, 7 (1984), 262–5.
66. Full product, as opposed to process, patents were available from 1978.
67. See generally Burstall, *The Community's Pharmaceutical Industry*.
68. Section 20 of the GWB and Sections 46, 57, and 53 of the Patents Act, 1977.
69. Section 38(1) of the GWB.
70. Cmnd. 9117, 1983, and Mueller *et al.*, *German Anti-Trust Law*, p. 41.
71. Ibid. 40.

72. A series of legal actions over the question whether a compulsory licence could be extended to *imported* products as well as products manufactured by the applicant delayed the award of the licence for 5 years.
73. *Hoffman La-Roche's Patent* [1969], RPC 504 at 517.
74. *Hoffman La-Roche* v. *DDSA* [1972], RPC 1.
75. Monopolies and Mergers Commission, *Chlorodiazepoxide*, HC 197, 1972–3 (London: HMSO, 1973).
76. Ibid.
77. Under Section 1 of the Monopolies and Restrictive Practices Act, 1948.
78. Monopolies and Mergers Commission, HC 197.
79. See generally R. Whish, *Competition Law* (London: Butterworth, 1985).
80. Regulation of Prices (Tranquillizing Drugs No. 1), Order S. 1 193.
81. The company's tactics were criticized as 'aggressive' in the House of Lords.
82. *Hoffman-La Roche* v. *Secretary of State for Trade* [1974], 2 A11 ER 1128.
83. The only question before the Court related to the natural justice issue.
84. HC Debates, 1974–5, vol. 889, cols. 1543–8.
85. *Financial Times*, 17 Apr. 1976.
86. W. P. Reekie and M. H. Weber, *Profits, Politics and Drugs* (London: Macmillan, 1978).
87. Sections 7 and 8 of the Industry Act, 1972.
88. Railways Act, 1974, HC Debs., Session 1977–8, vol. 975, col. 658.
89. See *Scottish Sunday Standard*, 16 Jan. 1983, referred to by M. Sharp and M. Brech, *Inward Investment*, (London: Routledge & Kegan Paul, 1984).
90. The abolition of Section 41 licences was advocated by the Banks Commission in 1970. The Sainsbury Committee had also found Section 41 licences to be of little value.
91. K. A. Hopt, *Restrictive Practices: A Comparative Study* (Florence: European University Institute, 1984).
92. Kammergericht, Wuf Wfe OLG 2053 (Decision of 24 Aug. 1978), 1974, 68 f.
93. Wu W/E BkartA 1526, Decision of 16 Oct. 1974.
94. Kammergericht, Wu/W/G OLG 1645, Decision of 5 Jan. 1976.
95. Wu/W/E BGH 1678, Decision of 12 Feb. 1980.
96. WU W/E OLG 2053, Decision of 24 Aug. 1978.
97. Wu W/E BHG 1678, Decision of 12 Feb. 1980.
98. Federal Cartel Office Annual Report (*Tätigkeitsbericht*), 1978, 27.
99. Kammergericht, Decision of 23 Dec. 1982.

100. Hopt, *Restrictive Practices.*
101. K. Hopt, 'Merger Control in the FRG', in K. Hopt (ed.), *The Legal Control of Multinational Companies*, (Berlin: de Gruyter, 1982), i. 71.
102. Scrip no. 1021, 13 July 1985.
103. The phrase 'the blueprint for the future' is borrowed from Klein, *Politics of NHS.*
104. For the new rules on capital R. and D. allowances see DHSS, *The Pharmaceutical Price Regulation Scheme.*
105. For a recent criticism see Monopolkommission Hauptgutachten, 1980/81, Fortschrift bei der Konzentrationserfussing (1982).
106. D. Vogel, *National Styles of Regulation* (Cornell: Cornell University Press, 1986).

5

Governments, Markets, and Regulation in the West European Consumer Electronics Industry

Alan Cawson, Geoffrey Shepherd, and Douglas Webber

Introduction: The European Consumer Electronics Industry

This chapter examines the relationships between government and industry in the consumer electronics sectors of Britain, France, and West Germany. It traces the role of government in the structural changes which have occurred in the industry over the last fifteen years, largely as a response to intensified competition, first from Japanese and later from other Far Eastern producers. In the most recent period industrial restructuring has acquired a pronounced European dimension, and the debate on trade policy has increasingly shifted towards the EEC level.

Consumer electronics production in Europe is largely concentrated on colour television (which accounted for nearly 70 per cent of output value in 1982) and, more recently, video. Gradual contractions in output and some major withdrawals have led to a progressively more limited audio industry, with the major market share captured by Far Eastern producers.

Overall employment is declining and real output is relatively stagnant as labour is displaced through technical change in manufacturing processes and output growth is restricted by the loss of market share to Far Eastern producers. The protection afforded to a large part of the European industry by the patents arising from the dominant European television technology Phase Alternate Line (PAL) has largely disappeared as these patents have expired, and the European producers were relatively slow in responding to the shifts in demand towards smaller screen sizes which accompanied the growth of the market in second sets.

The European industry has become more concentrated through

acquisition and merger, and two groups—Philips and Thomson—have emerged as major players in the world market, occupying positions one and two respectively in terms of world colour television production.[1] While both these companies maintain relatively broad product ranges, the remaining companies tend to concentrate on television and are beginning video cassette recorder (VCR) assembly. Most major Japanese companies have set up European manufacturing operations through greenfield investments, acquisitions, and joint ventures although these remain relatively small scale by the standards of their parents. The main motive appears to be a bid to circumvent threatened trade restrictions, although reduced shipment costs are also important. In 1982 Far Eastern investments accounted for 8 per cent of total EEC colour television (CTV) production and 16 per cent of video recorder output, but by 1986 their share had risen to 14 per cent and 43 per cent respectively.

Britain, France, and West Germany all have a trade deficit in consumer electronics, amounting in 1985 to $1316 million, $750 million, and $188 million respectively. There is thus considerable pressure for protection, particularly in the expanding field of video products, which culminated in the Voluntary Export Restraint agreement between the EEC and Japan in 1983 (see below).

Table 1 compares the production of major consumer electronics products in Britain, France, and West Germany in 1985, and shows that the West German industry is by far the largest, exceeding the combined total of Britain and France. It should be noted, however,

Table 1. Consumer Electronics Production in Britain, France, and West Germany, 1985 ($m.)

	Britain	France	West Germany
Colour television	629	500	986
Monochrome television	13	23	—
Video tape recorders	187	19	538
TV games	—	11	—
Audio products	70	137	450
Other*	26	126	204
TOTAL	925	805	2178

* including electronic watches, but excluding home computers

Source: Mackintosh Yearbook of West European Electronics Data, 1987 (London: Benn Publications, 1986).

that, particularly through its acquisitions of Telefunken, Nordmende, and Thorn-EMI-Ferguson, the French Thomson group accounts for a significant share of current West German and British production.

The European industry has not, with the exception of Philips, developed a presence in the new and emergent technologies of video and compact disc, and with its staple product colour television rapidly approaching maturity, European producers are becoming increasingly vulnerable to competition from the Far East. Increasingly severe competitive conditions are likely to lead to further rationalization and concentration in the industry in the next few years.

Interventionism and Restructuring in Britain

In 1976 there were eleven companies manufacturing colour televisions in Britain. In 1987 there were eleven companies manufacturing colour televisions in Britain. But there the similarity ends, because in the last decade the industry has undergone a substantial upheaval which has left it barely recognizable. In 1976 eight of the eleven companies were British owned, and they accounted for two-thirds of production; in 1987 two of the eleven companies were British owned, and they accounted for only 6 per cent of production, with 48 per cent produced by Japanese firms which have entered the industry in the last twelve years, and the remainder by Philips and Thomson. Moreover, one-quarter of the British consumer electronics market in 1985 consisted of video tape recorders, two-thirds by value of the British industry's staple product, colour television.[2] In VCRs British firms have no technological capability, and only Amstrad now has a tiny share of production in a joint venture with a Japanese firm.

The colour television industry developed in a cushioned domestic market in the late 1960s. A combination of the protection offered by PAL licences and the domination of the market by rental companies, in turn linked to the major British manufacturers, ensured a comfortable climate which offered good returns without the need to develop an export trade. In the peak year of 1973 just over two million sets were produced, of which only 2 per cent were exported.[3]

There was little effective resistance to the contraction in audio products, but pressures from imports in the colour television market in the mid-1970s did produce a response from industry and government. In 1971 the Conservative Government reduced purchase tax and relaxed hire purchase controls which led to a sudden spurt in consumer demand. The British market in consumer electronics trebled in the space of three years. The industry was totally unprepared for this, and there remains much bitterness within the industry that demand management was not phased to its supply capacity. Domestic production was unable to meet demand, and import penetration reached 25 per cent in 1973.[4] With the demise of the 'Barber boom' in 1974, domestic demand collapsed, and excess capacity quickly developed, particularly as imports remained at around the 20 per cent level, climbing to nearly 30 per cent by the end of the decade.

Until the 1970s there were no specific government measures towards the industry, and, apart from the effects of competition and price policy in the rental sector, the main impact of government was confined to general macroeconomic policy. In 1976, however, a Sector Working Party (SWP) was set up for the industry as part of a major extension of NEDO's role in spearheading the Labour Government's industrial strategy. It consisted of representatives from the major British manufacturers (and Philips, and later a representative of the Japanese firms), trade unions, and the Department of Industry, and was charged with the task of evaluating the problems and prospects for the industry, establishing targets and suggesting action to be taken by industry and government to meet these targets. After a successful campaign of opposition to a plan by Hitachi to follow Sony and Matsushita by establishing a greenfield factory in 1977, the stance taken by the SWP on inward investment was to try to encourage the Japanese or other Far Easern producers to take over existing plants which British-based firms (including Philips and ITT) could not run profitably.

The SWP diagnosed the structural problems of the industry in 1977 as principally the level of excess capacity, which it believed should be trimmed by 20–30 per cent, exacerbated by a high degree of fragmentation, which it believed should be countered by rationalization, and the level of import penetration. It was widely believed that British producers had lost market share to the Japanese through unfair competition, and in 1978 the SWP commissioned the Boston Consulting Group to examine the performance of the consumer electronics industries in Japan, South Korea, and West Germany.

The report had a profound and cathartic effect on the British industry. Whilst British products were broadly competitive with those of West Germany, the report silenced all the complaints about dumping by showing in great detail how the Japanese managed to achieve a substantial cost advantage (of up to 25 per cent despite lower wages in Britain) through superior production technology, better set design using fewer and more reliable components, and producing at much higher volumes than British plants. The report was kept secret for fear that its contents would adversely affect the sales of British products if it were to circulate within the retail trade.

The SWP devised a detailed strategy aimed at halting the industry's decline and improving its export performance. It argued that the British average annual production of 100,000 sets per plant should be increased to 500,000 through a programme of plant closures and rationalization, a planned reduction of sixteen plants to six. The existing high volume producers, Thorn and Philips, could be joined by Far Eastern producers, alone or in joint ventures, as long as they utilized existing plants. In addition the SWP saw an important role for inward investment in broadening the product range of the British industry, especially into video recorders, developing exports where the British industry was traditionally weak, and providing support for the British components industry.[5] A second phase of the strategy was very successful in improving the quality and supply of components by adopting Japanese 'parts per million' approach to failure rates, and encouraging closer links between manufacturers and components suppliers.

The active support for the strategy from the D.o.I. representatives, in the context of the Labour Goverment's interventionist industrial policy, appeared to be pushing government–industry relations to a new and active phase, which can be seen both as a change in the nature of regulatory activity and in the criteria for determining how decisions should be made. The SWP recognized that government support was crucial on three levels. First, financial support would be necessary to encourage reinvestment in new products and processes. Secondly, the D.o.I. would need to ensure that inward investment was in accordance with the SWP's guidelines. Thirdly, the Government would need to continue to back the industry's continuing efforts to reach agreement with Far Eastern producers to restrain their exports to Britain.

In March 1979 the Government accepted the SWP's strategy, and promised substantial financial assistance. The SWP had been hopeful of agreement to a special industry scheme involving the allocation of some £80 million, but was advised that the inevitable delay in launching such a scheme, including reference to the European Commission, might take it beyond the next election and the possibility of a Conservative Government which would be hostile to intervention on such a scale. It was therefore decided to encourage applications for selective assistance under Section 8 of the Industry Act, 1972, and D.o.I. officials were active in soliciting applications.

The major response came from Thorn, which in 1979 embarked on 'Project 1982' which aimed to modernize its plants around a new range of chassis by 1982. It had closed its tube plant in Skelmersdale in 1977 with the loss of 1,400 jobs, and its two television factories in Bradford the following year with 2,500 redundancies. Production was concentrated on two remaining factories at Gosport and Enfield, involving a total investment of £13 million of which £2.8 million was paid in government grants for R. &. D. and specific capital projects. Its new range of TX portable televisions launched in 1983 contained 25 per cent fewer components than earlier models, and 84 per cent of them were inserted automatically. The time taken to produce, test, and pack the sets had been reduced from 3.5 to 1.4 hours. These changes made Thorn's production broadly comparable with the Japanese companies examined in the Boston report, but because component costs are some 20 per cent higher in Britain than in Japan, Thorn's sets (and those of the British Japanese producers) can only compete with Japanese imports under the protection of a 14 per cent tariff and lower transport costs. Even after a further round of restructuring costing some £30 million in 1985–6, Thorn was increasingly vulnerable as a national competitor in a global market, and decided to sell its television and video division to Thomson in July 1987.

Apart from Philips, none of the other British-based manufacturers was able or willing to reinvest on the scale necessary. Two of them, Rank and GEC, went into partnership with Toshiba and Hitachi respectively, but then left the industry, as did Tandberg, Rediffusion, ITT, and Decca, all of whom sold plants to Japanese firms, or in the case of Decca to the Taiwanese company, Tatung. These investments have taken place under the guidelines which were prepared by the SWP and adopted by the D.o.I. Although some of these firms have started to broaden the product range by producing video recorders, this has been a direct result of the 1983 European voluntary restraint agreement and fears of even greater protectionism rather than an adoption of the spirit of the guidelines. Further, no Japanese company has invested in R.& D. facilities in Britain, and their export performance has been sluggish, although there are exceptions such as Sony and Panasonic, with the latter exporting 50 per cent of its British production which is more than any of the British industry has managed. The Japanese companies have also benefited in the last three years from a more favourable industrial relations climate which has in part developed as a consequence of the active pursuit of single-union and no-strike agreements by the Electricians' Union (the EETPU).

The 'regulatory space' being created by the NEDO initiative in 1979 contracted sharply after the election of the Thatcher Government in 1979 as grants were reduced, and the industry was largely left alone to adjust to the continuing threat of international competition. The intense diplomatic pressure which helped the industry's trade association to negotiate restraint agreements in the Far East slackened, and, in negotiation with the South Koreans in 1984–5, the British negotiators realized their threats of government action were hollow. Leading firms report satisfaction with the non-interventionist pattern of government–industry relations, but are reliant on international trade politics to keep import pressure at tolerable levels. Although Thorn-EMI did hold discussions with potential partners in Europe, notably Thomson and Siemens, there proved to be little enthusiasm for collaborative solutions, and Thorn's management preferred to abandon consumer electronics production altogether, concentrating on its rental and retail interests.

France: Problems of a State-led Strategy

The consumer electronics sector has constituted one of the test cases of the capacity of France's Socialist Government to direct the course of industry. In a particularly intense period of government–industry relations in 1982–3, the Government sought to further its sectoral objectives through the newly nationalized firm Thomson. If the Government appeared to fail to get what it wanted,[6] this failure should be set against a long history of intervention going back to the early 1960s, a history where the government–Thomson relationship is central.

The protection afforded to France by its adoption of an independent colour television transmission system (SECAM)[7] and French policy favouring the emergence of 'national champions' helped Thomson to become a dominant firm in consumer electronics by the end of the 1960s. French fiscal and subsidy policies generally favoured the merger process by which Thomson grew in the 1960s, but it was additionally to be groomed as one of two leading French electronics firms—the other being CGE. The key interventions occurred with the 'electronics Yalta' of 1969, when the Government helped engineer a division of electronic labour between the two firms in which Thomson became the flagship for military and consumer electronics and semiconductors.[8] After substantial success in the 1970s, the firm was driven to near bankruptcy, largely because of problems it encountered after the Government had encouraged it to enter the market for telecommunications equipment in 1976.[9] From 1981 Thomson was making losses, not returning to profit until 1985. The Thomson empire was a sprawling one, with very uneven strengths. The firm was highly dependent on the markets and subsidies the state provided and it was, in the form in which it emerged, in many ways the creation of the state.

By the late 1970s Thomson's growth strategy in consumer electronics was becoming more 'commercial' (and less based on technological capability and innovation). One strand of this was to take over foreign—particularly West German—capacity in order to gain market share. By 1982 it had acquired a 19 per cent share in the West German TV market. In the late 1970s Thomson started sourcing some of its products from its own factory in Singapore and it started importing video equipment from Japan Victor Company (JVC) in Japan. These links with JVC were to develop to the point where, in May 1981, Thomson agreed in principle a European joint venture—J3T—with JVC, Thorn-EMI, and Telefunken to assemble video products. This 'commercial' strategy reflected several problems. First, Thomson had failed to keep up in product innovation. Secondly, it had paid insufficient attention to rationalizing the rather fragmented TV production facilities it had acquired. To add to these problems, the French consumer electronics market stagnated from 1982 onwards. In 1983 Thomson made its first ever losses in consumer electronics and this division continued to be unprofitable until 1986.[10]

As Thomson's weaknesses in consumer electronics became apparent in the late 1970s, the stirrings of a more interventionist industrial policy became evident; worries were expressed about the implications of weaknesses in consumer electronics for the rest of the electronics *filière* and pressure for the repatriation of offshore jobs in Asia began to be felt. Thus the concerns of the new Socialist Government of 1981 showed some continuity.

The new Government's first major act in consumer electronics was to veto Thomson's participation in J3T in November 1981, in the interest of a more national, or European, solution. A French subsidiary of Philips has long been the second pole of the French consumer electronics industry (though with more distant relations to the Government than Thomson), and, at this time, elements in Thomson suggested that Philips was interested in such a veto.[11] It may or may not be coincidence that Philips undertook to start producing VCRs in France in 1981 (this eventually happened from November 1982, though Philips later gave up production).

After completing the nationalization of Thomson and appointing a new Chairman, Alain Gomez, the Government sought to persuade Thomson to follow a strategy in consumer electronics that the Government had evolved. Thomson also negotiated a *contrat de plan* with the Ministry of Industry which Thomson was able to keep very vague so that it be constrained as little as possible.

In early to mid 1982 there was a degree of consensus between the Ministry of Industry and the President's office on objectives for Thomson. There was first a general objective of European co-operation in consumer electronics (which was urged in a report of the Mission de la filière électronique in the spring of 1982, authored by Abel Farnoux who was employed in Thomson until early 1981 and was until then the principal architect of Thomson's technology-acquisition, as opposed to commercial, strategy). Secondly, there were specific objectives of Thomson becoming a producer, in France, of VCRs and audio equipment. In fact, the Government supported the strategy of Thomson taking over Grundig (which had been looking for European partners since 1981). Grundig, 24.5 per cent owned by Philips, had co-developed with Philips the latter's V2000 VCR and now produced it in West Germany. Taking over Grundig would make Thomson both a producer of VCRs and a partner of Philips.

In the aftermath of nationalization, Thomson's own objectives were less clear; its recent actions had been dominated by a commercial, pro-Japanese policy, but Thomson may have been prepared to explore two alternative strategies, one European and one Japanese. According to Philips-France, Philips and Thomson had first broached the subject of co-operation in 1977 and Philips reports it had 'let' Thomson acquire capacity in West Germany.[12] In May 1982, after several months of talks about a Thomson take-over of Telefunken, negotiations were abruptly broken off.[13] Given Telefunken's participation in J2T—the JVC, Thorn-EMI, Telefunken joint venture that went ahead without Thomson—these negotiations could be seen as Thomson's way of continuing to pursue a relationship with JVC through the back door, a relationship inconsistent with Thomson's instructions to seek co-operation with Philips and Grundig. Following the break-off of these negotiations, Grundig courted Telefunken and, on 26 July 1982, the two firms agreed that Grundig would later take control (see below). The prospect of Thomson acquiring Telefunken along with Grundig must have appealed to Thomson as keeping alive its alternative Philips and JVC strategies.

After Thomson began talks with Grundig and Philips, the remarkable Poitiers incident erupted. In October France suddenly routed all VCR imports through this one obscure customs post, thus creating a large informal barrier to trade (to which Japan strenuously objected). Officially, the measure was to prevent last minute buyers from getting under the net before a new tax on VCRs was introduced at the beginning of 1983.[14] But this may be doubted for several reasons.[15] France had experienced a record balance-of-payments deficit in September and Poitiers, along with the introduction of new requirements for labelling of origins in the same month, may be seen as a panic reaction by a government that had undertaken to 'reconquer the domestic market'. After the fact, at least, several observers, as well as the French Government itself, interpreted Poitiers as having a more protective intent. It was credited by Trade Minister Jobert with a decisive role in getting the Japanese to agree to 'export moderation' to the EEC as a whole in early 1983 (see below). Poitiers, which caused much concern among France's European partners, applied pressure on them to provide a more 'legal' form of import control. By November, Philips was producing VCRs in France and, since most VCR imports were purchases by Thomson from JVC, it is not inconceivable that Poitiers may also have served as a warning to Thomson about its Japanese links.

Having anticipated a decision against the proposed merger with Grundig by the West German Cartel Office, Thomson announced an agreed take-over of Telefunken only three days after the decision in early March 1983. This was followed at the end of April by a wide-ranging technical co-operation agreement between JVC and Thomson which would, *inter alia*, make Thomson the first licensee to produce VHS components outside Japan. This appears to have been a better deal for Thomson than it would have got under the defunct May 1981 agreement.[16] The Poitiers restrictions were lifted almost immediately after the Thomson–JVC agreement.[17]

The French Government may have been able to acquiesce in the specific outcome for Thomson for several reasons. First, Thomson ended up as the fully fledged VCR producer that the Government wanted (even if the VCR was Japanese). Secondly, the atmosphere within government, and its view of nationalized industries, had changed in important ways since 1982: the initial phase of expansionary macroeconomic policies had proven calamitous and the austerity package of deflationary measures introduced in the spring of 1983 signalled the end of the Socialist 'dash for growth'. At the same time the Government also scaled down its grander interventionist ambitions for nationalized industries in favour of emphasizing a return to financial profitability. This change was personified in the March 1983 switch of Industry Ministers from Chevènement to Fabius who was strongly committed to maintaining the managerial autonomy of the nationalized firms.[18]

Thomson's nurturing as a national champion, and the support given by the French state for its acquisitions in West Germany, have allowed Thomson to escape the fate suffered by the British firms. Its take-overs of Thorn-EMI-Ferguson and General Electric-RCA in 1987 signal the emergence of Thomson as a global producer, now significantly free from the earlier government pressures which restricted its freedom to locate some production in the Far East.

The Federal Republic of Germany: Holding the Ring?

For more than thirty years after the Second World War, consumer electronics in West Germany, as elsewhere, was a growth industry. Output growth in the industry was sustained by buoyant consumer demand for successive generations of new or modified products, such as radios (which had already begun to be manufactured, of course, before the Second World War), black-and-white and then colour television sets, hi-fi equipment.[19] Among the largest West European states, West Germany had by far the strongest industry. Even as recently as 1982, West Germany accounted for 60 per cent of the consumer electronics production in the four biggest EEC states. The West German industry developed a strong export orientation—in the early 1980s as much as 60 per cent of West German production was exported, and West Germany held a larger share of the world market than any other national industry apart from the Japanese. It was also technologically extremely innovative—the first tape recorders, the PAL colour television technology, and the technology which later permitted the development of the video cassette recorder all originated in West Germany.

The standard-bearers of the West German consumer electronics industry were the owner-managed firm, Grundig, and Telefunken, which belonged to the electrical engineering conglomerate, AEG-Telefunken. The technological innovations for which the West German industry became famous all stemmed from the laboratories of Telefunken, which, in the 1960s, still constituted one of AEG's most profitable divisions. Telefunken and Grundig together probably accounted for around one-third of employment in the German industry in the mid-1970s. Both had extensive foreign production facilities. At the same time, compared with the other EEC states, there was still a relatively large number of small and medium-sized consumer electronics firms in Germany. Besides Grundig and Telefunken, the biggest were Blaupunkt, a subsidiary of Bosch, the automobile components manufacturer, Siemens, and the subsidiaries of the ITT-owned firm, SEL. Up until the late 1970s, there was relatively little foreign-owned manufacturing capacity in the West German consumer electronics industry.

During the 1970s, this picture of a strong West German consumer electronics industry began slowly to change and, by the end of the 1970s, colour television manufacture no longer offered a guarantee for the continued prosperity or even survival of the German industry. The market for colour television sets was increasingly saturated—by 1978 56 per cent of all households in West Germany had a colour television set and 93 per cent of all households possessed a television set of some kind.[20] From 1978 onwards, the West German market for colour television sets began to contract. Moreover, the PAL patents began to expire around 1980 and the West German firms then became exposed to more intense competition on the (declining) domestic market.

The West German firms' best chances for maintaining or expanding output and profitability lay in their transition to the manufacture of a new generation of consumer electronics products, that of the video cassette recorder (VCR). Between 1978 and 1983, the West German market for VCRs expanded more than tenfold, so that, by the latter year, VCRs accounted for over a fifth of the overall consumer electronics market.[21] However, in this product segment, Grundig was the only West German firm which, in conjunction with Philips, managed to establish a foothold, while the other firms opted to assemble and/or sell VCRs manufactured according to one or the other of the two Japanese video technologies. By 1981, the West German VCR market was more tightly in the grip of Japanese firms than any other segment of the market. More than any other, this development accounted for the growing crisis of the West German consumer electronics industry in the early 1980s. The West German market stagnated, production declined as foreign firms conquered a growing share of the domestic market and this trend was not offset by an expansion of exports, production processes were rationalized to try to cut costs as prices fell, employment contracted,[22] and more and more plants were either shut down or—more frequently—taken over.

The relationship between the state and the consumer electronics industry in the long post-war economic 'boom' was of the 'arm's length' kind which corresponded to the West German philosophy of the 'social market economy'. The state's role was confined largely to 'holding the ring' for the firms and trying to ensure by means of competition policy that mergers and take-overs did not enable any single firm or group of firms to achieve a position of market domination and suspend the 'free play of market forces'.[23] The implementation of competition policy was the responsibility of the Federal Cartel Office (FCO), which must be informed of any planned mergers or take-overs if the two firms each have a turnover exceeding 1 DM billion or one of them has a turnover of more than 2 DM billion. The FCO *must* reject any proposed merger which, in its view, would lead to the emergence of a, or strengthen any existing, position of market domination.[24]

Decisions of the FCO may be contested in the Courts, and firms whose merger or take-over plans have been rejected by the Cartel Office may appeal for permission to proceed with their plans to the Federal Economics Minister. He is empowered by law to grant such permission when it is justified by an 'overriding public interest' or 'macroeconomic benefits', which may relate to competitiveness on export markets, employment, and defence or energy policy.[25] However, the state had no positive strategy for the consumer electronics industry and industry, for its part, appeared to have no demands on the state, other than that, through its macroeconomic policies, it should provide a favourable business environment. This situation changed only when, as from the late 1970s onwards, the Japanese export offensive in consumer electronics plunged the West German industry into an even deeper crisis.

The Politics of European Restructuring

The burgeoning crisis of not only the West German, but also the other national consumer electronics industries in the EEC in the early 1980s prompted pleas from the firms (and also organized labour) for protective intervention by the state—by the European Community as well as by its respective national Member States. The partial 'Europeanization' of consumer electronics politics reflected the strategies chosen and pursued by the major European firms to try to counter, or avoid, the Japanese challenge. These strategies contained two major elements: (*a*) measures of at least temporary protection against Japanese imports to give the firms breathing space to build up or modernize their production capacities and improve their competitiveness *vis-à-vis* the Japanese and partly also to put pressure on the Japanese to establish production facilities in Europe and produce under the same conditions as the European firms and (*b*), through mergers, take-overs, and co-operation agreements, to regroup forces with the aim of achieving similar economies of scale to those enjoyed by the most powerful Japanese firms. The first element of these strategies implicated the European Community in so far as it is responsible for the trade policies of its Member States. The second element did not necessarily involve the European Community, but had a European dimension to the extent that most of the take-overs and mergers envisaged in the restructuring of the industry involved firms from two or more of the EEC Member States, including the French state-owned Thomson (see above). As this 'regrouping of the forces' of the European consumer electronics industry was to unfold at first largely on the West German market, the firms could only implement their strategies once they had obtained the all-clear of the FCO or, failing that, of the Federal Economics Ministry.

The Politics of Video Recorder Trade between Japan and the EEC

The Dutch-based multinational conglomerate, Philips, was the first firm in the world to bring a VCR on to the market. Between 1972 and 1975, it had no competitors at all in VCR manufacture and, as late as 1977, it split up the European market with Grundig, with which Philips developed the V2000 VCR which came on to the market in 1980. By this time, the Japanese consumer electronics firms had already built up massive VCR production capacities and had cornered first their own market and then, unchallenged by the European firms, the American as well. With the advantage of much greater economies of scale, they were able to manufacture and offer VCRs more cheaply than Philips and Grundig when the VCR market did eventually 'take off' in Western Europe. German imports of VCRs, for example, increased almost eightfold between 1978 and 1981.[26]

The immediate background to the calls for protection against imported Japanese VCRs by European VCR manufacturing firms was formed by massive cuts in prices for Japanese VCRs, as a consequence of which, in 1982, the market share held by the V2000 VCR manufactured by Philips and Grundig declined sharply.[27] Losses incurred in VCR manufacture led to a dramatic worsening of Grundig's financial position. In November 1982 Philips and Grundig announced that they were considering taking a dumping case against the Japanese to the European Commission. The case, which was later withdrawn, can be seen as the first move in a political campaign designed to secure controls or restraints on Japanese VCR exports to the EEC states. This campaign was pursued at the national and European levels, both through the national and European trade associations for consumer electronics firms and particularly through direct intervention by the firms at the national governments and the European Commission. However, the European firms, many of whom had licensing agreements with the Japanese, were far from being united behind it.

Philips, seconded by its VCR partner, Grundig, was the 'real protagonist' of protectionist measures against Japanese VCRs. In pressing their case on EEC member states and the European Commission, they emphasized the unfair trading practices of the Japanese in building up production capacities which could meet the entire world demand for VCRs ('laser-beaming'), and the threats which the Japanese export offensive posed to jobs in Western Europe and to the maintenance of the firms' R. & D. capacity and technological know-how. Above all, however, was the threat which the crisis in VCR trade and the consumer electronics industry generally posed to the survival of a European microelectronic components industry, over half of whose output, according to Grundig, was absorbed in consumer electronics products.[28]

These arguments found by all accounts a very receptive audience at the European Commission, where, by common consent of German participants in the policy-formation process, Philips wields great political influence. By all accounts, Philips's pressure was also responsible for the conversion to the protectionist camp of the Dutch Government, which hitherto had been a bastion of free trade philosophy within the EEC. By imposing unilateral import controls through the channelling of imported VCRs through the customs depot at Poitiers (see above), the French Government had already staked out its position on VCR trade with Japan. It presumably required no convincing by Philips and Grundig on the issue, although it is interesting to speculate over the extent to which its stance also reflected the preferences of Thomson which in the past had been the 'chief of the protectionists' in the European industry.[29]

With the Dutch Government having been shifted into the protectionist camp by Philips, the greatest resistance to the imposition of some form of import controls on Japanese VCRs could have been expected to come from the West German Government. Along with the Danish and (hitherto) the Dutch Governments, the West German Government had generally been the stoutest defender of free trade among the EEC Member States. The Federal Economics Ministry's antipathy towards import controls may in fact have had some impact on the form of protection ultimately agreed by the EEC Council of Ministers, which was a 'voluntary self-restraint agreement' with Japan. However, even such self-restraint agreements had in the past been vetoed by West Germany in the Council. The West German Government's abstention in the vote on the agreement in the Council of Ministers signified if not a radical, then none the less a significant, modification of its past trade policy.

Within the Bonn Economics Ministry, the section for the electrical engineering industry—characteristically—had the most receptive attitude to the V2000 firms' case. Elsewhere in the Ministry, in the trade and European policy and policy principles divisions and at the summit, the Ministry's traditional policy in favour of free trade was given up much more reluctantly. The Ministry did not oppose the voluntary restraint agreement after it had been negotiated, but it may be questioned whether the Ministry's acquiescence in the agreement was motivated solely by its feeling of impotence *vis-à-vis* the united will of the other Member States. Abstaining on the vote in the Council of Ministers enabled the V2000 protectionist lobby to reap its benefits without the West German Government being held responsible for its implementation. The Government's abstention may equally have been the result of the pressure exerted on the Economics Ministry by the V2000 firms, particularly Philips and Grundig, both of which engaged in bilateral talks with the Ministry, and from the consumer electronics sub-association of the electrical engineering trade association of the ZVEI (Zentralverband der Elektrotechnischen Industrie), in which a majority of the member firms had sided with Philips and Grundig. The Ministry, by its own admission, did not listen as closely to the firms which were simply marketing Japanese VCRs as to those which actually manufactured VCRs in Europe: 'we were interested in increasing the local content (of VCRs) to preserve jobs.'

The success of the V2000 firms in obtaining any agreement at all from the Japanese to restrain their exports of VCRs to the EEC does not mean that they were happy with all aspects of the agreement, least of all with its contents concerning VCR prices and concrete quotas which were agreed with the Japanese. As the market subsequently expanded less rapidly than the European Commission had anticipated, the quota allocated to Japanese imports (including the 'kits' assembled by European licensees of Japanese firms) amounted to a larger share of the market than expected and the European VCR manufacturers did not sell as many VCRs as the agreement provided. Ironically, within a year of the adoption of the agreement, both Philips and Grundig announced that they were beginning to manufacture VCRs according to the Japanese VHS technology and by the time the agreement had expired (to be superceded by increased tariffs for VCRs) in 1985, the two firms had stopped manufacturing V2000 VCRs altogether.

The Politics of Transnational European Mergers and Take-overs

The wave of merger and take-over activity in the European consumer electronics industry which peaked around 1982 and 1983 had begun in West Gemany in the late 1970s, when Thomson swallowed up several of the smaller West German firms—Normende, Dual, and Saba—and Philips, apparently reacting to the threat it perceived Thomson as posing to its West German interests, bought a 24.5 per cent shareholding in Grundig.[30] The frenzied series of successful and unsuccessful merger and take-over bids which unfolded in 1982 and 1983 is inseparable from the growing crisis of the European industry and the major European firms' perceptions as to how they could restructure in order to survive in the face of Japanese competition.

The first candidate which emerged for take-over on the West German market was Telefunken, for which AEG, itself in desperate financial straits, had been seeking a buyer since the late 1970s. Telefunken's heavy indebtedness, which was largely a consequence of losses it had incurred in its foreign operations, posed a formidable obstacle to its disposal, however, and first Thomson, which had bought AEG's tube factory, and then Grundig, baulked at taking it on as long as AEG had not paid off its debts. While talks on Telefunken's possible sale to Grundig were still going on in 1982, Grundig's own financial position was quickly worsening as a result primarily of its mounting losses in VCR manufacture.

Grundig confessed publicly that if the firm carried on five more years as it was doing, it would 'go under like AEG', which, in summer 1982, had become insolvent. Grundig intensified his search for stronger partners, which he had apparently begun by talking with Siemens in 1981. In late 1982, at the same time as Grundig and Philips were pressing for curbs on Japanese VCR imports, Grundig floated the idea of creating, based around Grundig, a European consumer electronics 'superfirm' involving Philips, Thomson, Bosch, Siemens, SEL, and Telefunken. Most of the prospective participants in such a venture were unenthusiastic about Grundig's plans, however, and the outcome of Grundig's search for a partner or partners to secure its survival was that Thomson offered to buy a 75.5 per cent shareholding in the firm.

Political opinion in West Germany was overwhelmingly, if not indeed uniformly, hostile to Thomson's plan to take over Grundig. The political difficulties which Thomson and Grundig faced in securing special ministerial permission for their deal were exacerbated by the probability of job losses given a rapidly deteriorating labour market situation, and by the fact that, as late as 1982 and early 1983, an election campaign was in progress. Moreover, the Federal Economics Ministry was apparently concerned that, if Thomson took over Grundig, the West German Government would have been exposed to the danger of trade policy blackmail from the French Government, which could then have demanded increased protection for the European consumer electronics industry as the price for Thomson not running down employment at Grundig (and in other West German subsidiaries).

The decisive obstacle to Thomson's taking over Grundig, however, lay not with the position of the Federal Economics Ministry (or that of the Government or the FCO or the Deutsche Bank), but rather in that of Grundig's minority shareholder, Philips. Against expectations, the FCO announced that it would approve the take-over, but only provided that Philips gave up its shareholding in Grundig and that Grundig also abandoned its plans to assume control of Telefunken. As talks on Grundig's plan to take over Telefunken had already been suspended, the latter condition posed no problem to Thomson's taking over Grundig.

Once it had been put on the spot by the FCO's decision, Philips was forced to leave its cover and declare that it would not withdraw from Grundig. Apart from its general concern at being confronted by an equally strong competitor on the European consumer electronics market, Philips's motives in thwarting Thomson's take-over of Grundig were probably twofold. First, Thomson evidently did not want to commit itself to continue manufacturing VCRs according to the Philips–Grundig V2000 technology, but wanted rather to keep the Japanese (VHS) option open and, according to its public declarations, to work with Grundig on the development of a new generation of VCRs. Secondly, Philips was, ahead of Siemens, Grundig's biggest components supplier, with annual sales to Grundig worth several hundred million Deutschmarks. If Thomson had taken over Grundig, this trade would have been lost.

A sequel to the failure of Thomson's bid for Grundig was that in 1984, with bank assistance, Philips assumed managerial control of Grundig. Thus, at the end of this phase of the restructuring programme of the European consumer electronics industry, two main groups have emerged, one centred around Philips, the other around Thomson, and Blaupunkt is the only significant firm in West Germany left under West German control. But a common European response (i.e. one involving Philips *and* Thomson) to the Japanese challenge of the kind which Max Grundig had envisaged in 1982 had not come about, and may be less likely given Thomson's acquisitions in Britain and the US which make it a much more powerful competitor to Philips. But the acceleration in Japanese and also Korean inward investment in Europe in 1986–7, especially in VCR production where there are now a total of twenty Far Eastern-owned plants, suggests that the process of restructuring within Europe is far from complete.

Conclusions

The recent experience of the European consumer electronics industry points to the critical role of the framework and instruments of regulation in trying to account for the different responses of the various national industries and governments to the challenges posed by growing Japanese competitive strength and technological leadership. At one extreme is self-regulation by individual firms, where governments eschew any attempt to determine the responses which particular firms make to changing market conditions, whilst adopting policy regimes such as tax and tariff structures and openness to inward investment which critically affect the conditions under which self-regulation takes place.[31] At the other extreme is regulation by government intervention at the level of firm strategy, where governments seek specific policy outcomes by offering specific forms of inducement to selected firms and denying them to others.[32]

It would be mistaken, however, to interpret the differences in the role of governments in these contrasting regulatory regimes as evidence that they are determined by the actions and preferences of governments alone, or given the prevailing conception of the role of the state or nature of the legal system. Non-governmental actors, principally but by no means exclusively firms, can seek to induce regulation from often reluctant governments. Conversely, governments' regulatory objectives can meet resistance or non-collaboration from actors whose compliance is required for the objectives to be realized. What this points to is a conception of the process of regulation as a power struggle, where the resources of the various actors are constantly shifting with changes in market conditions and competitive pressures.

In Britain and West Germany the dominant form of regulation has been self-regulation, with government relatively indifferent to the pattern of ownership of firms in the sector or the fate of particular firms. In West Germany, for example, the outcome of the Thomson take-over bid for Grundig affair was determined not by the stance adopted by the Federal ministries but by the calculations of its own interests made by Philips as the minority shareholder in Grundig. By contrast the French Government sought not only to establish Thomson as a national and then increasingly as a European champion, but also sought to determine its investment decisions and its product strategy. In Britain the NEDO Sector Working Party attempted to open up space for a regulatory regime which would have given the state a much more direct role in restructuring the industry, but its initiative was forestalled by the election of a Government committed to a policy of abstentionism.

The capacity of individual national governments to determine the form of regulation in the consumer electronics industry has increasingly been limited, both by the characteristics of the state–firm relationship, and by the growing internationalization of the sector. As we have seen in the French case government–industry relations are dominated by a bilateral, direct relationship between the state and Thomson, without any significant intermediary role for trade associations, trade unions, or financial institutions. But as we have shown elsewhere,[33] the state is fragmented *vis-à-vis* Thomson: for various reasons, including the phenomenon of *pantouflage* (the career movement of civil servants out into industry) and Thomson's 'monopoly of legitimate expertise', the Ministry of Industry's capacity to influence Thomson has been weak, and the nationalization of Thomson did not fundamentally alter this. As a result this Ministry has been 'captured' by Thomson and has acted as its champion within government; by contrast the Ministry of Finance had clearer goals overriding those of the Ministry of Industry, namely the restoration of Thomson's financial health. Such an extreme case of capture can amount to the regulation of government by the firm. It points to the conclusion that regulation is crucially about the distribution of power between organizations, including different agencies of the state, and it can never be static as long as the organizations are subject to internal and external pressures for change.

The direct form of regulation of the firm by a national government becomes more and more problematic as international competition intensifies and the strategic response of firms involves transnational take-overs and mergers. This, as we have seen, has been a striking feature of the European consumer electronics industry in the last decade. In addition the regulation of the industry through tariff protection (rather than that of the firm through specific discriminatory measures) has shifted to the level of the European Commission, although national governments can bring pressure to bear at this level by tactics such as those the French Government used at Poitiers. But so too can firms, and we have pointed to the role played by Philips in persuading the Commission to initiate the voluntary export restraint agreement on VCRs with Japan. It raises the question of when firms will seek to turn self-regulation towards intervention in their competitive response to perceived external threats. In this case an examination of the organizational culture of Philips provides important clues in the analysis of the changing regulatory terrain. Traditionally a federal structure of national organizations, Philips has tended until recently to seek protection from competition rather than jeopardize by extensive rationalization and plant closures the local loyalties it has built up with national governments.

Growing internationalization has blunted the distinctive differences in the regulatory regimes in the three countries which were prominent in the mid-1970s, and has highlighted the opening up of regulatory space at the European level. We have noted the restriction on the scope for intervention by national governments that this represents, but we should also emphasize the implications for industry associations and trade unions. The growing Japanese presence in Britain has significantly diminished the capacity of the trade association to represent a coherent industry interest, and so far the European level industry association is conspicuous for its weakness. Likewise trade unions have found it difficult to organize at this level, although some efforts have been made, such as the convening of conferences which bring together representatives of Philips workers in different European countries. The organization which is in the most powerful position to dominate the regulatory space at the European level is the firm, and increasingly we must expect the political economy of industrial policy, in the consumer electronics as in other sectors, to be characterized by a process of bargaining between national governments, the European Community institutions, and multinational companies.

Notes

This chapter is based on research financed by the Economic and Social Research Council. This has included interviews with government departments, firms, trade unions, trade associations, and other bodies in the three countries.

1. This, according to industry estimates, is the position after Thomson acquired Thorn-EMI-Ferguson and General Electric-RCA in 1987. In respect of all consumer electronics products the positions for Philips and Thomson are 2 and 5.
2. *Mackintosh Yearbook of West European Electronics Data, 1987* (London: Benn Publications, 1986).
3. *Business Monitor*, 1975.
4. E. Arnold, *Competition and Technological Change in the Television Industry* (London: Macmillan, 1985).
5. Electronic Consumer Goods Sector Working Party, *Progress Report, 1978* (London: National Economic Development Office, 1978).
6. See A. Cawson, P. Holmes, and A. Stevens, 'The Interaction between Firms and the State in France: The Telecommunications and Consumer Electronics Sectors', in S. Wilks and M. Wright (eds.), *Comparative*

Government–Industry Relations: Western Europe, the United States, and Japan (Oxford: Clarendon Press, 1987).

7. R. Crane, *The Politics of International Standards: France and the Color TV War* (New Jersey: Ablex Publishing, 1979); R. Levacic, 'Do Mercantilist Industrial Policies Work? A Comparison of British and French TV Manufacturing', *National Westminster Bank Quarterly Review*, May 1984.
8. P. Messerlin, 'Managing industrial change' (unpublished paper, Sussex European Research Centre, 1983).
9. Cawson *et al.*, 'The Interaction between Firms and the State in France'.
10. *La Vie Française*, 3–9 Dec. 1984; *Financial Times*, 6 Feb. 1986, 23 June 1987.
11. *Libération*, 31 July 1981.
12. J.- M. Quatrepoint, 'Un échec exemplaire: l'affaire Grundig', *Revue d'économie industrielle*, 27 (1984), 31–41. See also Cawson *et al.*, 'The Interaction between Firms and the State in France'.
13. *Financial Times*, 14 June 1982.
14. *Libération*, 21 Nov. 1982.
15. See *Financial Times*, 6 Jan. 1983.
16. Quatrepoint, 'Un échec exemplaire'.
17. Trade Minister Edith Cresson claimed that Poitiers had served to influence the outcome of this agreement. See *Financial Times*. 29 Apr. 1983.
18. See *Financial Times*, 24 Mar. 1983.
19. From 25,000 in 1950, employment in the West German industry rose to a peak of some 117,000 in 1974. H. Neumann, 'Arbeitsplätze wie Schnee in der Sonne: Vorschläge der IG Metall zur Beschäftigungssicherung und zur Strukturpolitik in diesem Industriebereich' (manuscript, Frankfurt-on-Main, 1985).
20. Ibid. 24, 26.
21. Ibid. 86.
22. From 105,000 in 1978 to less than 64,000 in 1983. Ibid. 79–80.
23. Consumer electronics firms may of course have benefited from various measures of (non-sector-specific) state support. AEG-Telefunken, for example, received considerable subsidies for its research and development work in some sectors and received generous credits from the state under the Marshall Aid programme. See G. Hautsch, *Das Imperium AEG-Telefunken* (Frankfurt-on-Main, 1979), 47.
24. Bunderskartellamt, 'Das Bundeskartellamt' (press release, Berlin, n.d.), 8–9.
25. Bundesministerium für Wirtschaft, *Wettbewerbspolitik in der sozialen Marktwirtschaft* (Bonn, 1982), 36.
26. Neumann, 'Arbeitsplätze', p. 86.
27. *Handelsblatt*, 8 Dec. 1982.

28. *Frankfurter Allgemeine Zeitung*, 9 Nov. 1983.
29. Quatrepoint, 'Un échec exemplaire' pp. 34–5.
30. Ibid. 32–3.
31. This form of regulation is more likely to occur in sectors such as consumer electronics which are relatively open to international competition. For a contrasting case drawn from our work on telecommunications, see K. Morgan and D. Webber, 'Divergent Paths: Political Strategies for Telecommunications in Britain, France and West Germany', *West European Politics*, 9(4) (1986), 56–79.
32. This distinction closely parallels John Zysman's between the role of government as regulator and as player. See *Governments, Markets and Growth* (Berkeley and Los Angeles: University of California Press), 75.
33. Cawson *et al.*, 'The Interaction between Firms and the State in France'.

6

Regulation of Privatized Enterprises: Institutions and Procedures

Tony Prosser

Introduction

It is no exaggeration to claim that privatization has become the central theme in the domestic policy of the Thatcher Government in the United Kingdom. Although sale of council houses may have been the example which achieved the greatest impact under the Government of 1979–83, the sale of state enterprises is rapidly achieving pre-eminence. Other countries are also embarking on privatization programmes, notably France where around sixty-five state-owned concerns are to be sold in the next five years.

Governmental justifications of the British privatization programme have shifted from the economic to the political: sale will free nationalized concerns from governmental interference and leave their operation to the apolitical market.[1] However, regulatory arrangements will cover the most important industries sold. This chapter will assess how far these are in fact insulated from political intervention and examine their potential effectiveness and openness. Before looking at the institutions it will be necessary to describe the background of nationalization, for much of the appeal of the privatization programme is drawn from the failure of British governments to develop acceptable arrangements for nationalization.

Nationalization and the 'Public Interest'

According to a recent commentator

> in terms of the enterprises that really matter, privatization should be interpreted as the transition from one institutional mode of dealing with the failure of the market mechanism to allocate resources efficiently to another. Regulation by government Department, through direct control of capital allocations, investment plans, borrowing requirements and pricing

policy, is to be replaced with regulation by a quasi-governmental public agency, backed up by competition policy.[2]

Nationalization was mainly adopted after the Second World War as the solution to deal with those industries where, for example, economies of scale made monopoly inevitable. The central assumption lying behind this was that the change from private to public ownership would remove the profit motive and enable the boards of the industries to act in the 'public interest'. The boards themselves were to determine this at 'arm's length' from government, though inevitably certain powers of government over them were provided, notably power for the sponsoring minister to appoint board members and chairman, to issue general directions (which would be published) to the boards, and to approve investment programmes.[3]

The major defect in these arrangements was that the idea of a self-defining 'public interest' which could be discovered unproblematically by expert boards proved to be a will-o'-the-wisp. Instead, detailed governmental intervention on a range of matters (especially pricing) came to dominate industry decision-making. This was not implemented by means of published directions but through informal and usually secret processes. As a result, the ability of the industries to run their affairs suffered from an unpredictable environment of fluctuating short-term constraints, their image suffered as short-sighted government intervention caused financial problems, and, most seriously, accountability for decision-making was attenuated to vanishing point. Who could be accountable if it was not clear whether responsibility for decisions rested with the boards or with the government?[4]

Attempts to rationalize the arrangements through the adoption of financial targets, through economic pricing and investment rules, or improved corporate planning techniques were all unsuccessful, falling foul of the basic division of responsibility and the reluctance of governments to give up their ability to use the industries for general economic objectives. More recently some progress has been made in agreeing objectives for each industry, but the dominant control mechanism has become the external financing limit. This produces the same problems as earlier controls; control by external financing limits is extremely blunt, is essentially short term, and operates as an instrument of macroeconomic policy rather than providing a rational objective tailored to each industry. Thus manipulation of the external financing limits has served as a means of influencing the figures on public borrowing, raising surrogate taxation, and providing a boost to the economy in a pre-election period.[5] The problem of how the public ownership of industry can be incorporated into a broader political system whilst achieving some degree of accountability remains as far from a solution as ever.

At the time of the major examples of nationalization during the 1940s special arrangements were made to protect consumers in the form of consumer councils or consultative committees. Their powers were modest, due again to the assumption that the boards 'must regard themselves as the high custodians of the public interest'.[6] They have performed the role of handling complaints resistant to solution by the industries and of providing a limited degree of comment on policy proposals, in particular price increases. Some of the most active have recently attempted to undertake consumer audits.[7]

The record of the nationalized industry consumer councils has generally been dismal. Though their complaints-handling role has had some importance, it has been rare for them to use records of complaints to argue for general policy change. In some cases there is a statutory requirement that they be consulted before price increases, and on the boards' general plans. However, such consultation has been late and cursory, and underlying these problems has been the fundamental difficulty in obtaining information from the industries. Although one electricity consultative committee negotiated an important agreement on disclosure of information in 1980,[8] in general serious difficulties remain, highlighted, for example, by the decision by British Rail to refuse to give the Central Transport Consultative Committee statistics on quality of service after the Committee had used such figures as the basis for criticism of BR.[9] The Government has made it clear that any forthcoming reform of the consumer councils will not include the enactment of a statutory presumption in favour of disclosure.[10]

Other problems of the role and operation of the consumer councils include their inability to take any effective action in relation to price increases determined by the Treasury's external financing limits; yet such governmental decisions are the effective determinants of pricing policy. Indeed, the attitude of the Government to any attempt by a consumer council to get involved in such issues was vividly revealed by its refusal to renew the appointment of the Chairman of the London Electricity Consultative Council which was attempting to bring a challenge in the Courts against a potentially unlawful increase in electricity charges effectively caused by a change in the industry's external financing limit. The consumer councils generally also lack a properly structured procedure for handling consultation and face serious problems of follow-up.[11]

Thus nationalization in the UK has not resolved the problems of accountability to consumers or to a wider 'public interest'; indeed, the failure to develop workable and politically acceptable arrangements has been a source for much of the attraction of privatization. However, as suggested at the outset of this chapter, privatization does not remove the problems but instead provides the opportunity for the design of fresh institutions which may or may not be superior to those of public ownership. In particular, one must ask whether there will be continuing problems of the role of government. Together with a colleague I have described at length elsewhere the range of means available to governments for influencing privatized concerns; these include the use of residual shareholdings, special shares, and contractual devices.[12] What part does government play in the regulatory process? Another major problem was the lack of openness associated with nationalization, illustrated especially by relations with government and the consumer councils' difficulties in obtaining information. What arrangements exist to *ensure* openness in the new regulatory regime?

The Potential Regulatory Arrangements

Of course, government departments perform important regulatory functions, for example the role of the Department of Trade and Industry in the investigation of the affairs of companies. Given the stress in governmental rhetoric on the freeing of privatized industries from political control, institutions given a greater degree of separation from government are, however, more likely to provide suitable models. The most obvious example is the system of regulatory agencies and public service commissions in the United States. Thus at a Federal level there is a long history of agencies such as the Federal Communications Commission regulating telecommunications and broadcasting. The procedures of these bodies are governed by the Administrative Procedure Act,[13] which, as we shall see, imposes important protections in both rule-making and adjudication. At the state level, many states have public service commissions which regulate utilities; thus for example the New York Public Service Commission regulates power and gas utilities, telecommunications, and water companies.[14] The commissions are governed by state legislation such as the New York Public Service Law and some Federal legislation, notably the Public Utility Regulatory Policies Act.[15] Of course, de-regulation has become of considerable importance in the United States during the last few years. However, it has been most important in relation to airlines and other forms of transport together with long distance telecommunications; the energy sector, for example, has seen very little de-regulation apart from the de-control of oil prices and of some well-head natural gas prices.[16] There has also been a growing awareness post-deregulation that policy makers 'cannot just set rules designed to let competition flourish and then stand back. They also need to be ready to intervene to keep markets open.'[17]

Two aspects of United States regulation are of immediate relevance to the design of regulatory institutions in the UK. The first is the regulation of profits through a rate of return specified by the agency: this has been extensively discussed and heavily criticized in the British literature.[18] The second, and much less fully discussed, characteristic of regulation in the United States is the type of procedure used, and in view of the lack of coverage in official sources on this side of the Atlantic it is on this that I shall concentrate.

The procedures are far more open and participatory than anything considered in the UK (with the possible exception of some procedures of the Civil Aviation Authority). There is limited space here for any detailed analysis of the complex procedures in the different agencies at Federal and state levels,[19] but a few general principles can be established. To take rule-making first, the 'notice and comment' provisions of the Administrative Procedure Act provide for an informal system of participatory rule-making. Thus general notice of proposed rules and regulations must be provided in the Federal Register, and the agency must then afford interested persons the opportunity to participate through the submission of written data, views, or arguments. These must be considered by the agency, and reasons given for their acceptance or rejection when the rule is finally made. The Courts have required further action to make participation effective, for example by requiring informal conferences between agency staff and interested parties, oral hearings, two rounds of notice and comment so that participants can comment on the reasons for the rejection of their evidence, and so on. Some constraint was imposed on the judicial elaboration of procedures by the decision in the Vermont Yankee case,[20] but important hybrid techniques survive.[21] Further requirements for the subjection of proposed rules to cost benefit analysis have been imposed recently.[22]

For adjudicatory decisions a more formal procedure involving public hearings and a right to cross-examine is prescribed. At the state level, the most important examples of similar proceedings are the rate-making hearings at which tariffs are set and their burden allocated between different classes of customers.[23] Thus in New York the electricity utility will file a request for an increase in its rates and the commission will then publicly announce that it will hold a hearing. The utility prepares evidence to support its claim, and evidence is also prepared by the commission and by intervenors. These may include large companies, chambers of commerce, municipalities, Federal Government agencies, the state consumer office, organized consumer groups, environmentalists, and individual consumers. Crucially, the staff of the commission have extensive rights of access to the utility's information as do other participants in the proceedings. Thus, for example, the California Utilities Commission has ruled that any interested party should have access to the utility's own computer models.[24]

At the hearing the various parties present their evidence and cross-examine on it; the commission may also order a management audit of the utility to find whether it is using its resources efficiently. Finally, the commission will give its decision with detailed reasons (for example, 460 pages in relation to the increase in electricity tariffs in California of 9.7 per cent in 1983); in New York the decision must be made within eleven months of the application for the increase and in other states the time-limits are often much shorter.[25]

Regulatory procedures in the United States have been subjected to criticism, notably on grounds of legalism and capture by the regulated industries. This may be partly true, although convincing arguments can be made that the criticisms are exaggerated.[26] What has been lacking, however, has been any official attempt to consider the possible advantages of applying the relatively open and participatory procedures of the US in a British context. The reaction of the Department of Energy in relation to the regulation of the privatized gas industry is instructive. The Energy Select Committee of the House of Commons produced a pre-legislative report on the arrangements to be adopted for regulation. During the proceedings extensive evidence was presented to it outlining some advantages of the US system of regulation.[27] The Department claimed to have studied regulation in other countries in detail.[28] The Select Committee in its report recommended that 'the Government should study in depth the merits of the US system adapted to the UK system' and that 'at an early opportunity' the Government should make publicly available the information it had collected on foreign experience.[29] The Government replied that it had taken into account US practice but because of the diversity of sources in which it was contained the information on experience abroad could not be made available; instead it referred the Committee to earlier evidence.[30] When one examines this, however, it is so brief and vague as to be an insult to the Committee; the whole US experience is dealt with in five brief paragraphs, only one of which refers to agency procedures, and that without reference to any details.[31] It also became clear during oral evidence that the Secretary of State for Energy had misunderstood recent regulatory developments relating to gas in the United States.[32]

This sort of cavalier disregard for overseas experience does not augur well for the development of regulatory machinery after privatization in the United Kingdom nor have previous regulatory arrangements in the UK been beyond criticism. Thus the Independent Broadcasting Authority in allocating franchises to programme contractors has been fiercely attacked, both as regards its competence and its highly secretive procedures.[33] Indeed, if the primary intention of those designing the Authority had been to avoid openness and debate, it is difficult to see how this could have been achieved more effectively. By contrast, the Civil Aviation Authority, though plagued by difficulties in its relations with government, exercises regulatory functions through procedures which are far more open and which seem to have produced general satisfaction.[34]

An important model for the procedures to be adopted for regulatory institutions is thus the sort of model developed in the United States which highlights openness and provides important participatory rights. However, before one can decide whether this would be appropriate, one needs to know more about the purpose of regulation.

Why Regulate?

There has been remarkably little discussion of the rationale for regulation in relation to privatization in the UK. Thus in the case of the gas industry no White Paper or considered consultative document was published, and this in itself was a reason for the Select Committee investigation referred to earlier.[35] In the case of telecommunications a brief White Paper emerged, but this simply repeated a ministerial statement about the future of the industry with less than a paragraph on the proposed regulatory arrangements.[36] Somewhat fuller coverage was given in the White Papers on airports policy and on privatization of the water authorities, in the latter case no doubt because of the complexity of the regulatory arrangements involved.[37] Even in these cases, however, little was said about the rationale for regulation beyond stating that 'a system of economic regulation will be designed to ensure that the benefits of greater efficiency are systematically passed on to customers in the form of lower prices and better service than would otherwise have been provided.'[38]

Fuller consideration of the philosophy lying behind the regulatory framework is contained in the two reports prepared by Professor Littlechild on the regulation of British Telecom's profitability and on the economic regulation of privatized water authorities.[39] Thus the main purpose of regulation of telecommunications was seen as protecting domestic and small business subscribers against British Telecom's dominant market position; regulation would merely be a stopgap until the development of effective competition. Regulation was *not* to prevent the earning of excess profits, as the likely profits would be reflected in the price paid to the Treasury on flotation.[40] In the case of the water authorities, regulation would have to be permanent because of the element of natural monopoly present (though competition within the *capital* market would be feasible); but regulation would be necessary to ensure that the benefits of increased competition were passed on to consumers.[41] Thus the purpose of regulation is to create surrogates for market competition, either temporarily or permanently.

An important theme in the design of systems for economic regulation has been that the system should be as non-discretionary as possible, mainly to avoid the danger of capture by the regulated industry. Indeed this was a dominant reason for the adoption of the formula for price reduction for British Telecom tied to the Retail Price Index; similar formulae have been adopted for gas, and are to be adopted for the regulation of airport traffic charges and for water charges.[42] However, the general arrangements for regulation in practice involve extensive discretion on the part of the regulator; nor can decision-making take place through any quasi-scientific process of economic logic. This arises partly from the fact that many of the regulatory provisions actually adopted are not based on an economic rationale at all but rather on social or 'rights' arguments. Thus, for example, the pre-eminent duty imposed on the Secretary of State and the Director-General of Telecommunications is to exercise their powers in the manner best calculated to secure the provision of telecommunications services that satisfy all reasonable demands, including emergency services, public call boxes, directory information, maritime services, and services in rural areas.[43] This hardly sounds like an attempt to set a surrogate for market forces. Rather, it is suggesting that certain principles, such as the provision of a universal service, are so important as to prevail over the effects of market forces; rather than finding justification in utilitarian reasoning, the principles are justified by rights arguments.[44] Similar principles are also reflected in many of the conditions attached to the licence of British Telecom. In taking decisions which are based on provisions such as these the regulator cannot proceed by any system of economic calculation but rather must base decisions on wider social and philosophical arguments.[45]

Of course, other regulatory provisions are essentially economic and utilitarian in principle. Thus many of the privatized industries will be subject to little or no competition in their key markets, most notably the water authorities (if they are privatized) and the gas industry. In such areas regulation aims at creating surrogates for competition and 'to achieve the same "market place" goals of allocative and productive efficiency—in other words to keep costs and prices low and service and quality high.'[46] It might be thought that this can involve an essentially non-discretionary application of economic science to discover 'optimal' pricing policies. Indeed, this was the basis for the (notably successful) attempt to develop technical rules of pricing and investment as controls over the nationalized industries during the 1960s and early 1970s.[47] However, as Littlechild himself has noted, economists are now less convinced than in the past that a set of 'optimal' prices exists; indeed, the status of conventional neo-classical economics as a positivistic science has been effectively undermined.[48] Rather, writers at both ends of the political spectrum have come to stress the market-place as characterized by uncertainty and so taking the form of a process involving learning and the amassing of knowledge of preferences.[49] Thus any system acting as a form of surrogate for market forces will not be able to proceed through the application of formal and determinate rules but instead will have to learn from experience and amass expertise.

Any regulatory body will therefore be characterized by experiment and discretion; this is inevitable but is also desirable in permitting precisely that learning from experience which best substitutes for market processes.[50] This is by now something of a truism, but what has been overlooked is that this gives powerful a priori arguments for the adoption of an open and participatory set of procedures for regulation; as I have argued elsewhere, such a learning process *implies* that there be arrangements for participation and accountability through a free flow of information throughout the regulatory structures.[51] Such an argument can be made to rest on considerations of democratic principle.[52] However, it can also be convincingly argued that *effective* regulation depends on the availability of the fullest range of information possible to the regulator and also formal arrangements for the testing of information in an open forum. Thus to regulate effectively the regulator must be able to minimize unpredictable contingency in his environment and this depends on the free flow of information; some sort of open forum is necessary to provide for the testing of the information and to increase opportunities for learning from it.[53]

Much literature on regulation has stressed the importance of the availability of competing sources of information for the regulator. In the absence of this, the regulator is likely to become dependent on the regulated industry and so to be caught in the familiar US state of 'capture' in which the public interest comes to be equated with the interests of the industry.[54] One solution to this is to split up the industry into separate regional companies, so that each can generate information on, for example, costs of distribution, rates of return, and the effects of alternative pricing strategies.[55] Such splitting has not been adopted in the case of British Telecommunications or British Gas, although if the water authorities are sold separately they will provide competing sources of regulatory information. In the absence of splitting, it is even more important that procedures exist through which information can be tested and critical views be brought to bear on it.

Thus it would seem that there are powerful arguments of principle favouring the adoption of regulatory systems on the US model with extensive scope for openness, expression of views to the regulator, and the testing of evidence in an open forum. To what extent has this been implemented in the regulatory arrangements adopted after privatization in the UK?

Regulation and Government

As we have seen, there has been a lack of any detailed consideration of the US procedures in the design of regulatory institutions in the UK. Moreover, the pattern of large commissions regulating a range of utilities has not been adopted, despite strong arguments from, among others, the National Consumers Council in favour of this,[56] and instead a system of agencies linked to particular industries has been established. What the creation of new agencies has tended to overshadow, however, is that many of the most important regulatory powers are given directly to government rather than to bodies at 'arm's length'. Thus in some areas the relevant minister is the regulator; examples are the promulgation of traffic distribution rules at airports, the limitation of aircraft movements,[57] and regulation of the water environment.[58] In other industries where independent regulatory bodies have been established, notably telecommunications and gas, the Secretary of State retains important powers and the operation of the regulatory body is dependent on prior decisions of the minister laying down the principles to be applied. Thus the licensing of telecommunications systems is in the hands of the Secretary of State (after consultation with the

Director-General of Telecommunications).[59] This means that the development of competition is effectively in the hands of government, and indeed there has already been heavy criticism of 'the Government's illiberal policies on the licensing of public networks and resale'.[60] In relation to the gas industry similar provisions for authorization of public gas suppliers by the Secretary of State exist.[61]

The licence issued by the Secretary of State will also contain the key regulatory provisions in the form of licence conditions; the most important of these is that controlling price increases. The formula adopted is to relate certain prices to the retail price index; thus in the case of British Telecom a particular basket of charges cannot be increased by more than the retail price increase minus three points (the latter figure representing the expected efficiency gain) each year until 31 July 1989.[62] The negotiations on the actual figure to be set and on the range of prices to be covered were treated as a private matter between the Department and British Telecom; thus, for example, the Post Office Users' National Council which had previously represented consumer interests was not allowed to participate in the negotiations.[63] As we shall see when we examine the work of the telecommunications regulator, the scope and operation of the formula has proved highly controversial, and this is also likely to be so in the case of the British Gas Corporation.

Despite the fundamental importance of licences and authorizations in the regulatory schemes, there is limited public scrutiny over their terms. Thus in the case of telecommunications there are minimal procedural safeguards when the licence is drawn up, reflecting the fact that a large number of licences will be issued in most of which the complicated regulatory safeguards applying to British Telecom will be unnecessary. All that is required is that the Secretary of State must consult the Director-General of Telecommunications, and in the case of public telecommunications systems the Secretary of State must give notice that the licence is to be granted, state reasons, and consider representations and objections.[64] Originally, the Bill did not contain any provision for the laying of licences before Parliament, but eventually an amendment was accepted to the effect that the licence for a public telecommunications system should be so laid.[65] A licence does, however, have to be included in a public register except where the

Secretary of State directs.[66] In the case of gas there is no duty to lay any authorizations before Parliament.[67]

The general scheme is that, despite these major powers for the Secretary of State to set the initial conditions for regulation, the system shall operate at arm's length thereafter. However, in telecommunications the Secretary of State has other important powers, for example as regards approval of apparatus,[68] appointing the Director-General, and establishing and appointing advisory bodies,[69] and giving directions in the interests of national security or foreign relations.[70] In gas the Secretary of State for Energy prescribes quality standards,[71] has responsibilities as regards safety,[72] and appoints the Director-General and Consumers' Council.[73] The Secretary of State may also give general directions to the Director-General of Telecommunications indicating considerations to which the latter should have particular regard in determining his order of priorities in keeping under review activities connected with telecommunications, and indicating considerations to which the Director-General should have particular regard in exercising any of his functions.[74] It remains to be seen how these powers are to be exercised, but there are very limited procedural safeguards accompanying them and, for example, there is no obligation to publish the Secretary of State's general directions to the Director-General. This could be of particular concern were there to be a change of government, for the Labour Party is committed to take action in relation to privatized companies before passing legislation to bring a company into public ownership. This involves use of the minority shareholding retained in government hands and action to 'make . . . the existing regulatory agency, more effective.'[75] The danger is that existing powers of direction could be abused to exert behind-the-scenes pressure on the regulator in much the same way as pressure was put on the nationalized industries by government, precisely the situation which the privatization programme is supposed to render impossible. However, in the case of the gas industry the legislation was amended after concern had been expressed by the Select Committee to require the Director-General to publish any such directions in his annual reports.[76] Nevertheless, it should be noted that there is no prohibition on informal *ex parte* contacts between the Secretary of State and the regulator in either the telecommunications or gas legislation.[77]

We can now see that government is at the heart of the regulatory systems adopted after privatization. However, governmental decisions are generally subject to very limited scrutiny, as we have already seen in relation to the licences issued for telecommunications and gas operators. There are some limited exceptions to this where some attempt has been made to incorporate elements of outside participation in governmental decision-making,[78] but these are limited to civil aviation and land use where greater procedural protections have traditionally been afforded. In general, procedural safeguards are notable by their absence in relation to other aspects of regulatory decision-making by ministers.

As well as new regulatory functions being given to ministers, the Monopolies and Mergers Commission (MMC) has been given extended responsibilities with privatization. Of course, its normal functions under competition law are of very great importance, though there is not the space to discuss this here.[79] I shall deal later with the MMC's role in modifications of licences and authorizations.

The New Regulatory Institutions: Telecommunications

The first new regulatory institution is the Office of Telecommunications (OFTEL) headed by the Director-General of Telecommunications (DGT). In some respects his role is modelled on that of the Director-General of Fair Trading and, like the Office of Fair Trading, OFTEL is a non-ministerial government department. In some respects, the DGT acts as an adviser to the Secretary of State, as already noted in relation to licensing; he is also under a general duty to give information, advice, and assistance to the Secretary of State (and the Director-General of Fair Trading) either on request or on his own initiative.[80] For example, this provision enabled the DGT to give important advice to the Secretary of State in relation to his reference to the MMC of British Telecom's proposed take-over of the Canadian firm Mitel.[81]

In general, however, and subject to the points made above, there is a separation of responsibilities between the Secretary of State and the DGT. Thus once a licence has been issued the Secretary of State has no power to amend it;[82] this is to be undertaken by the Director-General with the agreement of the licencee or, where that is not forthcoming, through a reference to the MMC.[83] This cumbersome procedure has been justifiably critized by the National

Consumer Council as giving the regulator very little power to react to change in the telecommunications industry, and it is ironic that criticisms of the delay associated with the US procedures has been countered by a division of responsibilities which is bound itself to cause considerable delay.[84] The major danger is that the procedure will be bypassed by substituting informal agreements for licence modifications, and this has already arisen in relation to the merger of British Telecom and Mitel, where the majority of the MMC recommended that anti-competitive practices be restrained by undertakings rather than licence modifications because '[t]he provisions of the Telecommunications Act which govern amendments are such that in the short term it would be difficult to make the necessary changes to the licence without involving further delay and a risk to the future of Mitel'. This has raised problems of the enforceability of the undertakings.[85]

The DGT is also responsible for enforcing licences and their conditions.[86] This includes responsibility for the enforcement of the price limitation clause in the licence, and indeed pricing issues have been extremely important in his work. Other duties include keeping under review all activities connected with communications and publishing information and advice about this, and (of particular importance) investigating complaints about the supply of telecommunications services and apparatus.[87] However, perhaps the most important action of the DGT so far has been to agree the terms of connection between British Telecom and Mercury, its only competitor in the provision of the basic telephone business of the communication of messages.

The regulatory arrangements for telecommunications thus combine in one institution a wide range of functions requiring a variety of skills. It will be recalled that the report on which the price regulation scheme was based stressed the need for regulation to be non-discretionary. This is so to the extent that if the DGT wished unilaterally to change the pricing formula he would have to proceed by means of obtaining a favourable report from the MMC, but in other respects his task is highly discretionary. This is highlighted by the diversity of the general duties imposed on him. These are vague and the relation between them is often unclear; this can only be resolved through concrete decisions in practical situations. Indeed, as mentioned above, the implications of different duties may be contradictory; as the National Consumer Council has put it,

'OFTEL has been given conflicting objectives, especially in the field of competition. Trying to combine the provision of a universal service on standard prices and conditions is incompatible with competition in parts of the network; the former requires cross-subsidy, the latter requires the removal of cross-subsidy.'[88] This point is reinforced by the fact that the licence conditions designed to prevent anti-competitive behaviour by British Telecom also involve highly judgemental decisions by the Director-General.[89]

The major emphasis so far in the DGT's approach has been the promotion of effective competition: 'The duty to promote effective competition in my industry is absolutely fundamental to the whole regime.'[90] However, he has also stressed that this is not necessarily absolute, and demands careful planning in particular situations; 'although I believe that a presumption exists in favour of competition, and careful consideration must be given to the justification for any inhibitions of competition, nevertheless some planning of the path to competition and some limitations of the ultimate scope of competition is likely to be in the public interest.'[91] This provides many opportunities for difficult and controversial decisions.[92] Thus the issue of the procedures through which decision-making takes place is of considerable importance. There are few procedural protections in the Act itself. In the case of public telecommunications systems the Secretary of State must give notice that the licence is to be granted, state reasons for proposing to grant the licence, and consider representations and objections.[93] All licences must be included in a public register (except where the Secretary of State directs otherwise),[94] but there are no other procedural requirements when they are made. Where a licence is to be modified by agreement, the DGT must publish the proposed modifications and their effect, state reasons for them, and hear representations.[95] As has been noted, other amendments to licences take place through a reference by the DGT to the MMC. Oddly enough, although the wide powers of the MMC to require the attendance of witnesses and the provision of documents explicitly apply to such modification references, its procedural duties are not incorporated into the telecommunications legislation, though in the case of gas they *are* explicitly incorporated.[96] These provisions require the MMC to take into consideration representations from any persons or body appearing to have a substantial interest in the reference and to permit them an oral hearing unless it is not reasonably necessary or practicable to do so.[97] Otherwise, the MMC may determine its own procedure, in particular in relation to rights to be heard and to cross-examine, and as to attendance of the public. In earlier proceedings analogous to licence modification a number of oral hearings were arranged by the MMC; thus, in the Mitel reference, notices inviting evidence were placed in a number of newspapers and fourteen hearings were held.[98] Hearings do not permit competitive examination of evidence nor cross-examination,[99] but despite these limitations, the hearings do provide some opportunity for debate and challenge of evidence. Where a licence is to be modified by the DGT after a report from the MMC he must also give notice and reasons and consider representations.[100] Before making an enforcement order after breach of a licence condition the DGT must comply with similar requirements and notice and comment is also required before the designation of standards for approved equipment.[101]

There are thus some statutory procedural requirements to enable a degree of participation in regulatory decision-making, but they form a rather incoherent set of exceptions to a system of potentially closed decision-making rather than providing any general participatory schema such as is provided by the Federal Administrative Procedure Act in the United States. Moreover, they are mainly concerned with formal proceedings for modification and enforcement of licences which will form a tiny part of the DGT's work. However, he has, in his own words,

> made a commitment, in public statements, to be as open as possible in the discussion of issues arising out of my functions and duties. I intend to make public statements about major issues under review and to invite representations from any interested parties; I intend to establish contact with individuals, companies and representative bodies with interests in telecommunications so that I may become fully aware of their views on important issues; and I intend to give the fullest possible explanation of the basis for my conclusions, subject only to the need to respect commercial confidentiality . . .[102]

A variety of steps have already been taken to implement this commitment. The DGT has published a number of consultative documents on issues he is considering,[103] and invited representations on the basis of their contents. His consultative document on the future licensing of Value Added Network Services, for example, was followed by a forum attended by over 120 delegates, including representatives from licencees and users, equipment suppliers, and trade associations. On the issue of quality of service, he has also commissioned two studies of services in rural areas, and has issued a major Report on Quality of Service, using public opinion surveys, the monitoring of nearly 8,000 calls by volunteers, and some analysis of complaints.[104] At the level of general telecommunications policy, he has taken the initiative in establishing the Telecommunications Forum which he will chair. This is to provide a forum for debate on telecommunications issues and will include representatives from trade and technical associations and consumer and user organizations.[105] The DGT has also committed himself to making public his advice to the Secretary of State in so far as matters of commercial confidentiality do not arise, and a number of examples of this has been published.[106]

This degree of openness is most encouraging, though it is unfortunate that it is dependent on the initiative of this particular DGT rather than being required from all regulators. However, for it to have any real effect it requires the regulator to acquire and test a wide range of information; the lack of such powers dogged the nationalized industry consumer councils.

The DGT has the same powers to require information as does a civil court, though this is limited to his investigation of certain criminal offences and enforcement of licence conditions and investigation of complaints.[107] However, given the breadth of the issues which can be seen as a potential breach of condition these limitations are unlikely to prove restrictive in practice. Though there are problems surrounding the powers of courts in the area of public interest immunity the power to obtain information is thus wide and much greater than that of any of the old nationalized industry consumer councils. He is also empowered to publish information.[108] In addition, the British Telecom licence requires the publication of certain information by the company, for example on charges and other terms and conditions and separate statements of accounts for each business to avoid cross-subsidization. Most importantly, any information reasonably required by the DGT for the purpose of exercising any of his functions under the Act must be provided to him.[109]

Especially in view of the latter provision, the powers of the DGT to require information are thus extensive, and the MMC also has wide powers to require the attendance of witnesses and the provision of information.[110] In principle the DGT has expressed himself satisfied with his access to information, though he would prefer more information to be provided as a matter of course rather than on request and has criticized the lack of regular accounting information to enable him to deal effectively with pricing complaints.[111] The major problem to have arisen concerned the publication of performance indicators. The nationalized industries were encouraged to publish such indicators as a central means of accountability,[112] and, although the quality varied, they provided one of the most important tools through which consumer councils could assess performance. After privatization, British Telecom refused to provide such information. The DGT then made arrangements, as noted above, to use volunteers to monitor services and commissioned public opinion surveys. The first such exercise in examining the quality of British Telecom's service found that quality of service had remained broadly steady in recent years. Shortly before the publication of this report, BT agreed to the publication of key performance indicators.[113] This represents a considerable success for the DGT, and with the continuing monitoring from his Office should provide fuller information on service quality than was available under nationalization.

The DGT is also assisted by various advisory committees: the Secretary of State has established them for matters affecting England, Scotland, and Wales and Northern Ireland and the DGT has done so for matters affecting small businesses and persons who are disabled or of pensionable age.[114] The national bodies have some overlapping membership with the Post Office Users' National Council which previously had a consultative role and dealt with complaints when British Telecom was publicly owned. There are also over 160 local Telecommunication Advisory Committees recognized under the Act as representing consumers.[115] The committees will also play a major role in handling complaints. The existence of the various committees may go some way towards reducing the fears expressed by the Post Office Users' National Council that there would be no independent body continuing to represent consumers.[116] However, it should be remembered that the Council had important statutory rights, notably the right to be consulted before major changes in service including tariff increases: the advisory committees have no such right, and the lack of a single national body will surely lessen their effectiveness as a voice for the consumer interest. As we shall see, rather different arrangements will be made for the gas industry.

Nevertheless, the means by which the regulatory authority can obtain information from the regulated industry are in general far superior to the means for public scrutiny of decision-making whilst British Telecom was nationalized. It could be argued that under public ownership the exercise of pressure from government could be an effective means of making more information available; however, relations between government and nationalized industries were hardly characterized by openness and little information emerged. In this respect the arrangements after privatization represent an advance. What is lacking, however, especially in comparison to arrangements in the United States, is any structured forum in which information can be debated and tested. This is particularly needed where one company remains dominant in the industry (as is the case with British Telecom), so that a regulator is inevitably dependent on information from that source. As we have seen, the DGT has taken steps to develop various means for debating and testing information and has also made use of outside consultants. However, in view of the importance of the testing of claims one would have expected some more structured arrangements for this in the legislation.

A central theme in accounts of regulation in the United States is that of 'capture' of regulators by the dominant industry. The best indicator so far that this has not occurred in relation to the DGT is his decision setting out the terms for interconnection between British Telecom and Mercury. This was on terms which by no stretch of the imagination could be said to favour BT unduly, and which indeed were far more acceptable to Mercury than anything obtainable by agreement.[117] The DGT's proposed limitations on the ability of British Telecom to procure switching equipment from abroad also resulted in a hostile reaction from the company.[118] The matter on which there has been the greatest criticism of regulation has been that of British Telecom price increases where, although the total has remained within the price formula in the licence, prices have been 'rebalanced' at the expense of rentals and some local calls. However, this is not something which can be laid at the door of the DGT for it was clearly envisaged when the price formula was set, and, as we have seen, this took place through negotiations between British Telecom and the Government. Indeed, in an industry where prices do not directly reflect costs and where there has been a degree of cross-subsidization, such an outcome is an inevitable result of choosing this form of economic regulation. The decision of the DGT was by no means a rubber-stamping of the proposals, and he employed various forms of audit in examining the increases and threatened to initiate proceedings for license modification if the company was earning an excessive rate of return.[119] Thus any allegation of capture of the DGT by the regulated industry is most unconvincing; what is more worrying is the role of government in the regulatory process and the lack of any requirements of openness here.

New Regulatory Institutions: Gas

The arrangements for the regulation of the gas industry after privatization follow a broadly similar institutional pattern. A Director-General of Gas Supply (DGG) has been created; his Office has been christened OFGAS. There are many other similarities to the machinery adopted for telecommunications; thus the Secretary of State authorizes gas suppliers,[120] and authorizations may be amended by agreement between the public gas supplier and the DGG; other amendments require a report from the MMC.[121] The DGG is also responsible for enforcing conditions attached to authorizations. Procedural requirements are very similar to those in telecommunications.

However, in relation to gas, in the area of the tariff market (i.e. supply to those other than large commercial and industrial customers who negotiate individual contracts) there is not even the minimal competition which exists in some areas of telecommunications;[122] but arrangements for regulation go some way to recognizing this difference. Thus the DGG is under a duty to promote competition only in the contract market (i.e. for very large users); and this duty was only inserted into the Bill after much pressure from the Select Committee which had pressed hard for a general duty to promote competition.[123] The DGG also has power to direct public gas suppliers to use their pipelines for the carriage of gas produced by others;[124] this strengthens ineffectual provisions in earlier legislation to encourage suppliers of gas other than the British Gas Corporation.[125]

The most important recognition of the continuing monopoly nature of supply for the vast majority of consumers is, however, the creation of the Gas Consumers' Council supplementing the work of the DGG. The Council is appointed by the Secretary of State and will have members from each area corresponding to those of British Gas, and some regional staff.[126] It has been given the duty of investigating those complaints which relate to gas supply but not to enforcement of the authorization; it also has the power to investigate complaints about gas fittings and their installation, maintenance, and inspection or related matters.[127] It acts as adviser to the DGG on matters relating to tariff customers.[128] The Council thus resembles the previous consumer bodies existing before privatization. There is no statutory requirement that the Council be consulted, as there was with the old National Gas Consumer's Council, but the *Authorisation* issued to British Gas requires the company to give the Council details of its general policies and general arrangements for their implementation, and it must inform the Council of changes in the policies and general arrangements and proposed price increases. This, however, retains the deficiencies of the statutory provisions under nationalization; no time limit is laid down for consultation in advance and the detail in which information must be given remains indeterminate. The company must also give the Council information it reasonably requires in resolving complaints.[129]

The Gas Consumers' Council has begun life with only two-thirds of the staff of its predecessor under nationalization and no clear idea of its future budget; its money for promotion is less than one-hundredth of that to promote the flotation of British Gas and inadequate for publicity in national newspapers or television.[130] Nevertheless, the creation of a separate consumer body goes some way to meet the fears that it will not be possible for a regulator to combine a role of impartial arbitrator with that of a consumer advocate.[131] In the United States, a number of regulatory bodies have either established separate Public Advocates Offices to represent consumers at hearings, or have separated the public advocacy staff from the rest of the agency, and the Senate Committee on Governmental Affairs has recommended that such arrangements be substantially extended through the establishment of an independent consumer advocacy agency.[132]

The powers of the DGG are similar to those of his counterpart in telecommunications and, in particular, the *Authorisation of British Gas* requires the company to give him information he reasonably requires in exercising his functions.[133] The essentially non-competitive nature of most of British Gas's business creates two special problems regarding the acquisition of information for effective regulation. First, the pricing formula is far more complex than that for British Telecom.[134] In brief, as well as permitting British Gas to increase its prices by a figure 2 per cent below the rise in the retail price index, the company is permitted to take into account in full the increase in the average cost of gas acquired during the year. This assumes that British Gas is a passive-price taker in gas purchase, but in fact it will remain the dominant buyer; the formula removes the incentive for it to minimize the cost paid and so creates all the problems of US-style profit regulation without any of the means for scrutiny of efficiency available to US regulators. It would also be possible in principle for British Gas to purchase expensive gas to satisfy demand in more competitive areas of its markets which will be cross-subsidized from consumers within the regulated market.[135] In view of this the Select Committee recommended that the DGG should have the power to satisfy himself that contracts for the purchase of gas were prudently incurred to meet the needs of regulated tariff customers, and to have the power to disallow any costs not so allowed. This was firmly rejected by the Government.[136] The Committee also recommended that the company be obliged to publish the profits arising from the regulated tariff market separately and that this should be certified as a fair reflection of the market's revenues and costs by the DGG; however, this proposal was also firmly rejected by the Government.[137] The Government also resisted the Energy Committee's proposed duty for the DGG to require that British Gas develop a set of performance objectives against which to measure standards of service.[138]

It remains to be seen whether the regulator of the gas industry will be as imaginative in developing his procedures as that in telecommunications. Other new regulatory arrangements are to be adopted for airports involving the Secretary of State, the Civil Aviation Authority, and the Monopolies and Mergers Commission,[139] and if the water authorities are sold a system similar to that in telecommunications and gas will be set up.[140] But it is now time to draw the threads together and come to some conclusions about the regulatory arrangements which have accompanied privatization.

Conclusion

Major reasons for the failure of nationalization in the UK were the lack of any effective means for determining the 'public interest' which was supposed to guide the decisions of the industry boards, and the lack of any clear division of responsibilities between boards and government. Privatization, it is claimed, overcomes these difficulties by substituting the market-place as the decision-making guide and by freeing the industries from government. The very existence of regulatory machinery implies that the market-place is an inadequate guide; we can now see that government retains a major role in the regulatory process. One could argue that the intention is that government will be non-interventionist: but all past experience shows that governments of all political complexions will take full advantage of powers given them, whatever their rhetoric might claim. Indeed, I have argued elsewhere that in a modern economy it is *impossible* for any government to disclaim responsibility for economic performance with the result that decision-making in key industries *cannot* be divorced from the role of government.[141] Once this is recognized, the central question becomes the extent to which the means exist to ensure that this role is performed openly.

As we have seen, in relation to the regulatory bodies established on privatization there are improved arrangements for gaining information from the industries, and the Director-General of Telecommunications has taken a most imaginative approach to his task. However, especially in comparison to the United States, there is a marked absence of provisions *requiring* openness and debate before decisions are taken. Even more importantly, there is an almost total lack of openness in the decisions taken by government rather than by the new regulators. Even though I have suggested that important lessons could be learned from regulatory bodies in the United States, this suggests that the fundamental problem lies not so much with the regulatory bodies themselves but with the peculiar secrecy associated with British government. Whilst that remains, it is unlikely that privatization will resolve the problems which were so characteristic of British nationalization.

Notes

Inevitably events develop quickly in this area. The manuscript of this contribution was required by 15 January 1987 and so it has not been possible to incorporate events after 1 January 1987.

1. See e.g. J. Moore, *Privatisation in the United Kingdom* (London: Aims of Industry, 1986).
2. R. Rees, 'Is there an Economic Case for Privatisation?', *Public Money*, Mar. 1986, 19–25, at p. 19.
3. See T. Prosser, *Nationalised Industries and Public Control* (Oxford: Basil Blackwell, 1986), ch 2. For a detailed account of the implementation of nationalization see N. Chester, *The Nationalisation of British Industry 1945–51* (London: HMSO, 1970).
4. National Economic Development Office, *A Study of UK Nationalised Industries* (London: HMSO, 1976), and Prosser, *Nationalised Industries*, chs. 3–4.
5. Prosser, *Nationalised Industries*, ch. 4; see now the Chancellor's *Autumn Statement 1986*, Cmnd. 14.
6. H. Morrison, *Socialisation and Transport* (London; Constable, 1933), and see Chester, *Nationalisation of British Industry*, p. 641.
7. Prosser, *Nationalised Industries*, chs. 8–9.
8. London Electricity Consultative Council, *Making the London Electricity Board More Publicly Accountable* (London: London Electricity Consultative Council, 1983).
9. R. Ford 'Informed Sources', *Modern Railways*, 43 (1986), 351.
10. Department of Trade and Industry, *Nationalised Industries Legislation – Consumer Councils*, (London: HMSO 1985).
11. Prosser, *Nationalised Industries*, pp. 66–9; A. Henney, *Yes Minister—How the London Electricity Board Fixed Tariffs for 1984–5* (London: London Electricity Consultative Council, 1984). The criticisms made in National Consumer Council, *Consumers and the Nationalised Industries* (London: HMSO, 1976), generally remain valid.
12. C. Graham and T. Prosser, 'Privatising Nationalised Industries', *Modern Law Review*, Jan. 1987.
13. 5 USC ss. 551–9, 701–6, 1305, 3105, 3344, 5362, 7251.
14. A. Henney, *Regulating Public and Privatised Monopolies: A Radical Approach* (Newbury: Public Finance Foundation, 1986); Association for the Conservation of Energy, *The Regulation of Gas and Electricity Utilities in the USA* (London: Association for the Conservation of Energy, 1986).
15. 16 USC ss. 2601 ff. see generally A. Aman, *Energy and Natural*

Resources Law: The Regulatory Dialogue (New York: Matthew Bender, 1983), 3.03[I], and Henney, *Regulating Public and Privatised Monopolies*, p. 4.

16. See generally S. Breyer, *Regulation and Its Reform* (Cambridge: Harvard University Press, 1982) and N. Lewis and I. Harden, 'Privatisation, Deregulation and Constitutionality', *Northern Ireland Legal Quarterly*, 34 (1983), 207–21.
17. *Financial Times*, 31 Jan. 1986 (Leader).
18. S. Littlechild, *Regulation of British Telecommunications' Profitability* (London: HMSO, 1984), and *Economic Regulation of Privatised Water Authorities* (London: HMSO, 1986). The seminal criticism is J. Averch and L. Johnson, 'Behaviour of the Firm Under Regulatory Constraint', *American Economic Review*, 52 (Dec. 1962), 1052–69.
19. See J. Freedman, *Crisis and Legitimacy* (Cambridge: Cambridge University Press, 1978), Henney, *Regulating Public and Privatised Monopolies*, and Lewis and Harden, 'Privatisation'.
20. 98 S. Ct. 1197 (1978).
21. I. Harden and N. Lewis, *The Noble Lie* (London: Hutchinson, 1986), 216.
22. Executive Order 12,219, 46 Federal Register 13,193, and see Lewis and Harden, 'Privatisation', pp. 217–23.
23. See generally Aman, *Energy and Natural Resources Law*, s. 3.03.
24. For an account of the hearings see Henney, *Regulating Public and Privatised Monopolies* pp. 5–6, 30–3.
25. Ibid. 6; Association for the Conservation of Energy, *The Regulation of Gas and Electricity Utilities*, p. 14.
26. Henney, *Regulating Public and Privatised Monopolies*, pp. 11–13.
27. HC 15, 1985–6, Minutes of Evidence, evidence from e.g. National Consumer Council, Alex Henney.
28. Ibid., evidence from the Trades Union Congress, 196.
29. HC 15, 1985–6, para. 85.
30. Cmnd. 9759, *Regulation of the Gas Industry*, para. 73.
31. HC 15, 1985–6, Minutes of Evidence, 88–90.
32. HC 15, 1985–6, Minutes of Evidence, 205; cf. the Secretary of State for Energy's replies to Qs. 297–8.
33. N. Lewis, 'IBA Programme Contract Awards', *Public Law* (1975), 317–40, and A. Briggs and J. Spicer, *The Franchise Affair* (London: Century, 1986).
34. R. Baldwin, *Regulating the Airlines* (Oxford: Clarendon Press, 1985), esp. chs. 10, 12, and pp. 244–5. See also the Civil Aviation Authority Regulations, 1983, SI no. 550.
35. HC 15, 1985–6, para. 3.
36. Cmnd. 8610, *The Future of Telecommunications in Britain*.

37. Cmnd. 9542, *Airports Policy*, Cmnd. 9734, *Privatisation of the Water Authorities in England and Wales*; and Department of the Environment and Welsh Office, *The Water Environment: The Next Steps* (London: Department of the Environment, 1986).
38. Cmnd. 9734, para. 3.
39. Littlechild, *Regulation of British Telecommunications' Profitability and Economic Regulation of Privatised Water.*
40. Littlechild, *Regulation of British Telecommunications' Profitability*, ch. 4.
41. Ibid., ch. 2.
42. Ibid., para. 4.19.
43. Telecommunications Act, 1984, s. 3(1)(*a*).
44. A central theme of the work of Ronald Dworkin; see esp. *Taking Rights Seriously* (London: Duckworth, 1977), pp. 82–100.
45. Cf. Professor Carsberg's evidence to the Energy Select Committee, HC 15, 1985–6, Minutes of Evidence, Q. 239 and p. 69–70.
46. HC 15, 1985–6, para. 10.
47. Prosser, *Nationalised Industries*, pp. 36–41; National Economic Development Office, *UK Nationalised Industries*, esp. App. D.
48. M. Hollis and E. Nell, *Rational Economic Man* (Cambridge: Cambridge University Press, 1975); T. Balogh, *The Irrelevance of Conventional Economics* (London: Weidenfeld and Nicholson, 1982).
49. G. Hodgson, *The Democratic Economy* (London: Penguin, 1984), esp. pp. 72–7, 170–80; also see the writings of the Austrian School, and especially F. A. Hayek, 'The Use of Knowledge in Society', *American Economic Review*, 35 (1945), 519–30, and *The Political Order of A Free People* (London: Routledge & Kegan Paul, 1979), 65–70.
50. See G. Teubner, 'Substantive and Reflexive Elements in Modern Law', *Law and Society Review* (1983), 239–85.
51. T. Prosser, 'Democratisation, Accountability and Institutional Design: Reflections on Public Law', in P. McAuslan and J. McEldowney, *Law, Legitimacy and the Constitution* (London: Sweet and Maxwell, 1985), 170–90.
52. T. Prosser, 'Towards a Critical Public Law', *Journal of Law and Society*, 9 (1982), 1–19.
53. Prosser, *Nationalised Industries*, pp. 13, 111–12, 227–30, and Committee on Governmental Affairs, *Public Participation in Regulatory Agency Proceedings*, US Senate Document 95–71, chs. 1–2.
54. See e.g. P. Quirk, *Industry, Influence in Federal Regulatory Agencies*, (Princeton: Princeton University Press, 1981).
55. See e.g. M. Hammond, P. Helm, and D. Thompson, 'British Gas: Options for Privatisation', *Fiscal Studies*, 6(4) (Nov. 1985), 1–20,

and C. Price, 'Privatising British Gas: Is the Regulatory Framework Adequate?', *Public Money*, June 1986, 13–19, at pp. 14, 19.

56. National Consumer Council, *The Privatisation of Monopolies* (London: National Consumer Council, 1985).
57. Airports Act, 1986, ss. 31–2.
58. Cmnd. 9734, and Dept. of the Environment and Welsh Office, *The Water Environment.*
59. Telecommunications Act, 1984, s. 7; the power to delegate to the Director-General has not been exercised. Note also that only the Secretary of State can designate a public telecommunication system (s. 9).
60. J. Vickers and G. Yarrow, *Privatization and the Natural Monopolies* (London: Public Policy Centre, 1985), 45; see generally ch. 3 and pp. 81–3 therein.
61. Gas Act, 1986, s. 7, and Department of Energy, *Authorisation Granted and Directions given by the Secretary of State for Energy to the British Gas Corporation Under the Gas Act 1986* (London: HMSO, 1986).
62. Department of Trade and Industry, *Licence Granted by the Secretary of State for Trade and Industry to British Telecommunications Under Section 7 of the Telecommunications Act 1984* (London: HMSO, 1984), Condition 24.
63. Post Office Users' National Council, *Annual Report 1983–4* (London: Post Office Users' National Council, 1984), para. 101.
64. Telecommunications Act, 1984, s. 8(5).
65. Ibid., s. 9(2).
66. Ibid., s. 19.
67. Gas Act, 1976, ss. 7–8, 36.
68. Telecommunications Act, 1984, ss. 22–5.
69. Ibid., ss. 1, 54.
70. Ibid., s. 94.
71. Gas Act, 1986, s. 16.
72. Ibid., s. 18.
73. Ibid., ss. 1, 2.
74. Telecommunications Act, 1984, s. 47.
75. Labour Party, *Statements to Conference, Blackpool, 1986* (London: The Labour Party, 1986), 6.
76. Gas Act, 1986, ss. 34(3), 39(2).
77. For restrictions on *ex parte* contacts in the US, see Harden and Lewis, *The Noble Lie*, pp. 243, 246–9.
78. See Airports Act, 1986, ss. 32–4, and Dept. of Environment and Welsh Office, *The Water Environment*, para. 3.9.
79. In general see R. Merkin and K. Williams, *Competition Law* (London: Sweet and Maxwell, 1984), and N. Korah, *Competition*

Law of Britain and the Common Market, 3rd edn. (The Hague: Nijhoff, 1982).

80. Telecommunications Act, 1984, s. 47(4).
81. *Report of the Director General of Telecommunications for 1985*, HC 461, 1985–6, para. 3.21.
82. The Secretary of State has a very limited power of veto over licence modifications; see Telecommunications Act, 1984, ss. 12(5–6), 13(5–6), 15(5–6).
83. Telecommunications Act, 1984, ss. 12–15.
84. HC 15, 1985–6, Minutes of Evidence, p. 104.
85. Cmnd. 9715, *British Telecommunications PLC and Mitel Corporation: A Report on the Proposed Merger*, paras. 10.79, 10.82; P. Gist and S. Meadowcroft, 'Regulating for Competition: The Newly Liberalised Market for Private Branch Exchanges', *Fiscal Studies*, Aug. 1986, 41–65 at pp. 63, 65.
86. Telecommunications Act, 1984, ss. 16–19.
87. Ibid, ss. 47–9.
88. HC 15, 1985–6, Minutes of Evidence, p. 104; the duties referred to are in Telecommunications Act, 1984, ss. 3(1)(*a*) and 3(2)(*b*); see also Gist and Meadowcroft, 'Regulating for Competition', pp. 47, 63–4.
89. Ibid. 49–52.
90. HC 15, 1985–6, Minutes of Evidence, Q. 236.
91. *Report of the Director General of Telecommunications for 1984*, HC 457, 1984–5, paras. 1.4–1.5; see also his *Report for 1985*, paras. 1.2–1.4.
92. However, there are limits to the social arguments he is prepared to consider; see n. 45 above.
93. Telecommunications Act, 1984, s. 8(5).
94. Ibid., s. 19.
95. Ibid., s. 12(2–3).
96. Telecommunications Act, 1984, s. 13(9); Gas Act, 1986, s. 24(7).
97. Fair Trading Act, 1973, s. 81.
98. Cmnd. 9715, ch. 1.
99. For the procedures of the MMC see Korah, *Competition Law*, s. 2.2.4, and *R* v. *Monopolies and Mergers Commission ex parte Matthew Brown PLC* [1987], 1 All ER 463.
100. Telecommunications Act, 1984, s. 15(3–4).
101. Ibid., s. 17(1–5), 22(8).
102. *Report of the Director General of Telecommunications for 1984*, para. 1.27.
103. e.g. *Telecommunications—Quality of Service: A Consultative Document*, OFTEL, 1986.
104. *Quality of Telecommunications Services*, OFTEL 20/86.

105. *OFTEL News*, 2 (Mar. 1986), 2.
106. HC 15, 1985–6, Minutes of Evidence, Qs. 227, 235; and see e.g. *Advice on the Allocation of Frequencies for Private Mobile Radio Purposes*, OFTEL 5/85.
107. Telecommunications Act, 1984, s. 53.
108. Ibid., s. 48; note the limitations contained therein and in s. 101.
109. Department of Trade and Industry, *Licence*, Conditions 16, 20, 52.
110. Fair Trading Act, 1973, s. 85.
111. HC 15, 1985–6, Minutes of Evidence, Q. 254; *Report of the Director General for Telecommunications for 1985*, para. 1.15.
112. Cmnd. 7131, *The Nationalised Industries*, paras. 76–8.
113. *Quality of Telecommunications Services.*
114. Telecommunications Act, 1984, s. 54.
115. Ibid., s. 27.
116. *Annual Report 1983–4*, paras. 96–7, 103.
117. *Determination of Terms and Conditions for the Purposes of an Agreement on the Interconnection of the British Telecommunication Telephone System and the Mercury Telecommunications Ltd System*, OFTEL (1985).
118. *British Telecommunications' Procurement of Digital Exchanges*, OFTEL (1985), and *Financial Times*, 25 July 1985.
119. See *Report of the Director General of Telecommunications for 1984*, para. 1.19; his *Report for 1985*, para. 1.9; *British Telecom's Price Changes, November 1985*, OFTEL 1/86, and *Review of British Telecom's Tariff changes. November 1986*, OFTEL 18/86.
120. Gas Act, 1986, ss. 7–8; in the case of non-public gas suppliers the licensing power may be delegated to the Director-General of Gas Supply.
121. Gas Act, 1986, ss. 21–7.
122. Cf. Government claims as to the degree of competition even in the domestic market which notably failed to impress the Energy Select Committee; HC 15, 1985–6, paras. 15–22 and Cmnd. 9759, paras. 8–13.
123.. Gas Act, 1986, s. 4(2)(*d*); cf. HC 15, 1985–6, para. 69.
124. Gas Act, 1986, ss. 19–22.
125. Oil and Gas (Enterprise) Act, 1982; and see Price, 'Privatising British Gas', 14.
126. Gas Act, 1986, s. 2 and Sch. 2.
127. Ibid., ss. 32–3.
128. Ibid., s. 40.
129. Department of Energy, *Authorisation*, Condition 8; for problems of consultation under nationalization see Prosser, *Nationalised Industries and Public Control*, ch. 8.
130. *Guardian*, 20 Nov. 1986.

131. National Gas Consumers' Council, *British Gas—Safeguarding Consumer Interests After Privatisation* (London; National Consumer Council, 1985), para. 9; National Consumer Council, *Privatisation of Monopolies*, para. 15.3.
132. Association for the Conservation of Energy, *The Regulation of Gas and Electricity*, pp. 11, 27–8 Committee on Governmental Affairs, *Public Participation*, ch. 5.
133. Gas Act, 1986, s. 38; Department of Energy, *Authorisation*, Condition 7. Note that the statutory provision does not cover the Director-General's functions of keeping under review gas supply, advising the Secretary of State or the Director-General of Fair Trading, or publishing information and advice.
134. Department of Energy, *Authorisation*, Condition 3.
135. Price, *Privatising British Gas*, pp. 14–15.
136. HC 15, 1985–6, para. 37; Cmnd. 9759, paras. 46–9.
137. Cmnd. 9759, para. 53; see also HC 15, 1985–6, Minutes of Evidence, Qs. 310–17.
138. Cmnd. 9759, para. 64.
139. Airports Act, 1986, ss. 31–4, 36–56.
140. See above, n. 37.
141. Graham and Prosser, 'Privatising Nationalised Industries'.

7

Corporate Strategy and State Support in the European Motor Industry

Stephen Wilks

Introduction

The optimists are in the ascendant in current evaluations of the European motor industry. In the long run the threats posed by energy, pollution, and safety issues have dissipated and analysts are persuaded that the industry will continue substantially unchanged well into the twenty-first century.[1] In the medium term industrial restructuring is well under way, costs are being controlled, and motor companies are returning to substantially improved profit. In the short term, the industry is experiencing record car sales and the suicidal discounting which has marked recent years is being wound down. In 1974–5 the industry was in despair, with the product itself widely regarded as heading for extinction and every motor manufacturer making losses. As recently as 1983–4 pessimism was still the order of the day. The crisis was of over-capacity, structural maladjustment, continued heavy losses, and reliance on the state. The cycle of sentiment, even more volatile that the business cycle, is now on an upturn. The motor industry is back in business.

This chapter examines the basis for such optimism and concentrates particularly on the continued need for, and changing forms of, state support for the industry. It discusses the strategies of the major producers within an increasingly Europeanized industry, and outlines the way in which the motor industry distributes vital costs and benefits across Europe, significantly affecting levels of national prosperity. The British experience is examined in some depth in order to give substance to the general argument and to illustrate the importance of variations in the culture of state intervention. The British motor industry has become the weakest among the major producing countries. While Spain and Korea have leapt to prominence the British industry exhibits long-term contraction and its decline serves to underscore two concerns of this chapter. The first concern is to analyse the evolving strategies of the European producers. The crisis of the British industry has obliged indigenous producers (including now Nissan) to develop some of the most innovative and promising responses to competitive pressure. The second concern is to emphasize the importance of the state and the role played by considered 'industry friendly' regulative measures. In this area British government intervention has sometimes been favourable for the industry but on the whole neither friendly nor considered. Largely for the sake of manageability the discussion concentrates on the car industry and on the volume producers. It reflects conditions in the spring of 1987.

Among the factors making for greater optimism, regulatory issues loom large. For reasons which are expanded upon below, the regulatory environment has moved from one of hostility to become far more supportive of the industry. This applies at the national level and even more so at the European level. Strict regulative proposals on pollution, safety, and energy conservation have given way to proposals for expanding market opportunities and eliminating expensive contradictions between national regulatory regimes. The emphasis has moved from restrictiveness in the wider interests of society to facilitation in the narrower interests of the industry. This regulative relaxation has not emerged as unsolicited good fortune but as a result of government's concern at the weakness of the industry. Financial weakness has been reflected in companies plans for new investment, employment, and product development as expressed in their corporate strategies. The strategies of the companies are formal and elaborate, they are analogous to the policies of governments, and form the subject matter of bilateral discussion between the main manufacturers and government agencies. Companies can in this way indicate to government the harmful effects of restrictive regulatory regimes, and lobby for more favourable regulation.

Although the general picture within Europe is one of more industry friendly regulatory development, and constructive discussion between governments and the industry, it must be remembered that regulatory styles vary markedly between the various countries. British regulative practice appears particularly distinctive. The British tradition is to favour passive, framework regulation which is 'industry neutral' in that it aspires not to discriminate between sectors or between firms in any one sector. This tradition is congenial to Conservative ministers who have an ideological predilection for measures that do not distort the market. Norms of British regulation therefore stress a reactive, open-handed style of implementation with an emphasis on values of 'natural justice'. An outcome of this style is that there is a reluctance to bargain over the formulation and execution of regulations. It is foreign to British practice to use regulation as the Americans tend to use it, as a positive, goal-oriented instrument to achieve given industrial objectives. The style is one of 'problem avoidance' rather than 'goal seeking'. A further implication of treating regulation as part of an impersonal legal framework is that there is a reluctance to take regulative initiatives. British officials are anxious not to regulate unless it is absolutely necessary and to avoid impractical experimentation. Regulation is taken seriously and is conscientiously policed. This, at least for the apologists, is one reason why Britain appears often to be dragging its feet over European regulative initiatives in fields like pollution control.

Competition within the European Market

The motor industry has become fully internationalized over the past two decades. Decisions about corporate strategies and products are made on the basis of calculations about the European market and, for many manufacturers, the global market. All the same, the market remains strongly differentiated; we are still a long way from a 'common market' in cars. The main differentiating factors include national consumer preferences (the Italians buy small cars); personal tax regimes (over 60 per cent of new cars in Britain are bought by or through companies);[2] petrol and purchase tax variations; anti-pollution regulations and import restrictions (by France and Italy on the Japanese, by Spain on everybody). In the late 1970s, as international consumer preferences began to converge, there was much talk of the 'world car', produced on all continents, to similar specifications, and enjoying massive economies of scale. This seems to have been a chimera. The emphasis now is on tailoring products to market niches while flexible manufacturing has reduced the importance of single-model scale economies.

As national markets have opened up, competition on a European scale has grown steadily more intense. For the past decade six groups of volume producers have been vying for market leadership. As Table 2 indicates, each group has currently between 10 per cent and 13 per cent of the market and their profits are relatively modest. In contrast, the specialist producers, orientated towards the historically high dollar American market, have been very profitable. The Japanese use a concept of 'excessive competition' to describe an industry marked by duplication of effort, below optimum scale, low profitability, and dominance by short-term competitive tactics.[3] The European volume car industry could be seen as suffering from a similar syndrome. In 1984 the volume producers (including BL and SEAT) lost $1,313 million overall and Ford Europe is the only group not to have fallen into serious loss at some time since 1980. *The Economist* Intelligence Unit recently predicted that only two groups would survive as independent producers within Europe, probably Volkswagen and Fiat.[4] The Japanese solution to excessive competition is for the Ministry of International Trade and Industry (MITI) to engineer a consensus to manage competition, although the Japanese motor industry has not been one of its outstanding successes. The European Commission is not MITI and the future shape and distribution of the European industry will be decided partly by corporate strategies within the market, partly by competitive national governments.

Forecasting developments within the European market is difficult and very risky. Events have confounded prediction. Thus Bhaskar argued in 1980 that the take-over of Chrysler Europe by the Peugeot group was a shrewd strategic move—in fact it was a disaster;[5] General Motors' Bedford plants were said to 'appear to have a secure future'—they have just been closed.[6] The rapidity of change is quite startling. In the USA Ford made record losses in 1980–2, now it is making record profits. In the second quarter of 1986 alone Ford made profits of $1.1 billion and its 1986 profits exceeded those of GM for the first time since 1924. Chrysler's recovery has been even more incredible. It made the largest loss in American corporate history in 1980 and received a very controversial $1.5 billion in Federal loan guarantees.[7] These loans have now been repaid and Chrysler's profit of $1.6 billion in 1985 was a record. Its Chairman, Lee Iacocca, has become a cult figure,[8] a possible presidential candidate and the second highest paid corporate executive, 'earning' $11.4 million in 1985.[9] International

Table 1. European Car Producers

Company	Ranking by Production			Employees '000	Production '000	European Market share	Profit (loss)
	1985	1982	1978		1985	1985 %	1985 $ m.
Volkswagen Group	1	3	3	259	1735	12.95	1,164
Renault	2	1	4	144	1547	10.73	(1,600)
Peugeot Group (Citroen/Talbot)	3	2	1	177	1545	11.64	84
General Motors (Europe)	4	4	6	100	1333	11.31	(372)
Ford (Europe)	5	6	5	115	1307	11.94	326
Fiat Group	6	5	2	226	1207	12.30	1,099
Daimler Benz	7	7	8	199	538	3.75	2,708
Rover Group	8	8	7	102	465	3.98	(165)
BMW	9	9	9	54	431	2.74	471
Volvo (+ Dutch Volvo)	10	10	10	68	397	2.42	1,055
SEAT (now Volkswagen)	11	11	11	21	305	1.38	(258)
Alfa-Romeo (now Fiat)	12	12	12	28	158	1.50	(152)
Saab	13	13	13	45	112	0.56	385

Note: The table is compiled from various sources, mainly the financial press. Figures for profits and employees are the latest available but should not be taken as definitive. They are group figures and in some cases include non-motor activities. Profit/loss is before tax calculated at the $ exchange rate in December 1986.

developments of this nature are, of course, important for Europe. As discussed below, both General Motors (GM) and Ford have recently reappraised their European strategies and are devoting equal, if not more, attention to their relationships with Isuzu (34 per cent owned by GM) and Mazda (25 per cent Ford owned).

The 'third force' on the European scene, and the most significant threat, is the Japanese. In the first nine months of 1986 they took 12 per cent of the European market and are market leaders in several of the non-producing countries such as Ireland and Denmark. The Japanese influx emphasizes two issues which require a response from the community as a whole. The first is that of protectionism. Italy, France, and Britain have each raised barriers against Japanese imports. The Italians were fortunate in having a quota already in existence when they ratified the GATT and joined the Community. Japanese imports have thence been kept under 3,000 units. The British and French have established informal, voluntary quotas of dubious legality: in the French case 3 per cent in 1977, in the British case 10.8 per cent dating back to 1975. The West Germans still publicly endorse free trade, but in 1986 Japanese imports exceeded 15 per cent for the first time and Hans-Erdmann Schoenbeck, President of the VDA (Verband der Automobilindustrie) has protested, declaring ominously that 'I hope the Japanese will see sense'.[10] Indeed they have. MITI has introduced a voluntary export restraint analagous to the 1981 restraints on exports to the USA. The European manufacturers are collectively discussing the issue with the Commission. The Japanese may not, however, be so willing to exercise restraint in the future. They have real problems of their own with over-capacity and the rising yen. Nissan made an operating loss in the first half of 1986–7 for the first time since its incorporation in 1952.

The second Japanese-related issue is that of inward investment. The European manufacturers detest the idea of Japanese production in Europe and so do most Continental governments. On the other hand the British Government has been very welcoming to Nissan and to Honda. The European manufacturers are anxious that the European Commission should formulate the most stringent possible regulations over local content in order to deny the Japanese undue competitive advantage. The issue will come to a head when Toyota's plans for a European plant are eventually formulated and announced.

Corporate Strategy as a Focus for Bargaining

While industrial fortunes can change with disconcerting rapidity, the key to understanding developments within the industry is to gain an insight into the corporate strategies of the major producers. Large motor manufacturers cannot simply react to market signals. They must make strategic choices and to a limited extent they can control the market. In particular, a corporate strategy is essential because motor industry investment is lumpy and long term; and because companies 'internalize' transactions. Capital requirements for new model development are enormous and decisions taken now have ramifications lasting for decades. As Altshuler *et al.* point out,[11] an automobile designed now will take five years to bring to production, be produced for six to eight years, be driven for up to twelve years and will therefore be in use in large numbers in the year 2010. Within the company the detailed organization of design, development, production, and sales means marrying a myriad internal transactions into a coherent operation. Planning by a hierarchy within the company replaces the relative anarchy of the external market. Whether companies fail or succeed depends on their comparative advantage. This, in turn, may depend on the product, on production technology, on the work-force, on location, on managerial competence, on access to finance, and so on. Increasingly, however, it is recognized that the ability to devise and execute an effective corporate strategy is a comparative advantage in its own right. The strategy consists of a series of decisions and choices, many of which have a high discretionary content. All the big producers have elaborate corporate strategies—if they do not they are in danger of going under.

Curiously, the corporate strategies of the big car producers have a significant demonstration effect. To some extent they embody a 'corporate culture' and in turn affect the industrial culture of the society in which they operate. For instance, 'the development of work relations at Fiat sets the trend for the whole of Italy and the state of power relations at Fiat mirrors the situation in the country'.[12] Something more modest but similar might be said for Renault and Volkswagen which tend also to be pace-setters in areas such as internationalization, production automation, and quality control.

As I have argued elsewhere,[13] corporate strategies present challenges and opportunities for governments. A government interested in promoting or in controlling a major producer must understand the content of the company's corporate strategy and the process by which it is produced. The Ford example illustrates the relationship.

The Ford Motor Company was one of the first producers to develop a corporate strategy to plan and integrate its global operations. Ford Europe was established in 1967, an organization matched only in 1986 by General Motors when it established 'GM Europe: Passenger Cars', with a co-ordinating staff based at Zurich. Ford's strategy is global and is ultimately centred on the needs of the North American market. Currently Ford requires a small car for the USA with quality and cost factors which have led it to look to the Far East. It already owns 25 per cent of Mazda (Toyo Kogyo) and has just taken a 10 per cent holding in Kia Motors of Korea (a further 8 per cent is owned by Mazda). It appears that Kia will produce a Mazda-designed small car to be imported into the USA as the Ford Festiva. Korean cars are making a big impact in North America; Hyundai, for example, is now the largest importer into Canada. The Korean industry is taking off and is showing quite incredible signs of expansion. Respectable forecasters anticipate Korean car production will rise from 640,000 units in 1987 to 910,000 in 1990.[14] For Europe the concern is that Ford has moved its emphasis to the Far East in search of low-cost production, new technology, and joint ventures. Certainly, the company appears to be revising its attitude to its European operations. Ford's present policy appears to be to reduce the autonomy of its European operations, emphasize sound finance, and reverse the company's traditional insularity by pressing for joint ventures.

Britain is thus in the curious position for a major car producer of having a market leader with an equivocal commitment to British production—an equivocation denied by Ford.[15] Ford's strategy has in certain respects clearly operated against Britain's interests. One can cite three examples. First, the new Fiesta investment was located in Spain rather than Britain and Ford is currently negotiating with the Spanish Government for subsidies to fund the Fiesta replacement. Secondly, the emphasis on Mazda may remove technical innovation capability from Europe and opens up the possibility for Mazda captive imports; Ford is already importing a

Mazda van. Thirdly, the company has consolidated its lead in the British market on the basis of 'captive imports'. Only 57 per cent of the cars sold by Ford in Britain in 1984 were actually made there. One estimate, which includes component imports, argues that only 46 per cent by value of Ford cars is British.[16] Ford, therefore, has a large deficit on its British trade, £501 million in 1984.

It can, of course, be argued that Ford's international presence is a source of strength for Britain. Thus from mid-1986 the climate for investment in Britain improved with a weak pound and a strong D-Mark, better labour relations, industrial growth, and economic stability. Ford, as well as GM and Peugeot, responded by increasing British production and exports and by new programmes of investment in British facilities. But however the balance of advantage is assessed, the Department of Trade and Industry (DTI) has at least to accept that the British motor industry has a specific foreign-dominated structure which requires a distinctive policy approach and implies a significant reduction in the potential for control over that sector of the economy.

All this is by way of illustrating the impact of corporate strategy. Strategies must respond to a series of crucial challenges and opportunities. For instance, leading analysts argue that the future of the industry will be shaped by the four factors of flexible production technology, new product technology, new systems of social organization of production, and the failure of demand for a 'world car' to evolve.[17] From other perspectives many other factors could be added to the list, not least the policies and influences of national governments. Corporations are very aware of the interests of governments and of the rewards and penalties that governments can, deliberately or inadvertently, impose. It helps companies to have a 'home' or 'sponsor'. Maxcy's analysis of motor industry investment detected an overwhelming concern not to antagonize governments.[18] Indeed, one semi-Freudian interpretation of Ford's bid for Austin Rover, which would have presented Ford with grave problems of model and plant rationalization, was to suggest that Ford wanted an unambiguous European home and a national 'parent'.

The far from startling conclusion is that an intelligent government wanting to secure a greater share of benefits from its motor industry should do three things. First, it should analyse the strategies of the major manufacturers in order to anticipate developments and gain information about likely impact. Secondly, it should make its interests clear to the company involved, indicating, if not specific preferences, at least a general preference in favour of the national economy. Thirdly, a government should bargain with the company over key decisions which could reflect the national interest. These might concern new investments, sourcing policy, product strategy, or new finance. It might well be objected that this counsel is mercantalist, anti-European, and self-defeating (as with the 'subsidy auctions' which have already preceded several major investments).[19] It is possible that the European Commission would be a more appropriate agency. Although logical, this argument is also naïve. The motor industry is so important that an economic *realpolitik* comes into operation everywhere—except Britain. The pressures for government intervention are the subject of the following section.

Government Support: From Subsidy to Favourable Regulation

The motor industry is universally supported by governments through a variety of indirect or direct, and sometimes very generous, measures. The reasons for this are simple and obvious. The motor industry is central to a successful industrial economy. The total value of car output has been put at 8.8 per cent of all manufacturing output in the developed countries;[20] the industry represents over 15 per cent of world trade in manufactures;[21] estimates put European employment at two million direct, with another five million in the components industry.[22] The companies are also very visible. No European firm can rival General Motors with a turnover of $96 billion, profits of $4 billion, and 501,000 employees (world-wide in 1985) but, as was seen in Table 2, they are also massive employers. Volkswagen, Fiat, Daimler, and Peugeot are, respectively, 4th, 6th, 7th, and 10th in the league table of European employers.[23] Accordingly governments have been careful to see that their countries retain a motor industry. As Maxcy concluded, 'it is one of the contentions of this book that no industrial country is going to allow its domestic motor industry to disappear'.[24]

Economic Rationales for Support

There are three immediate areas of economic impact which provoke a response from government: employment, trade, and economic linkages. The quasi-automatic defence of employment levels has now largely disappeared. It is estimated that 410,000 people have left the industry in France, Italy, and Britain since 1979, compensated by small increases in West Germany.[25] The consequences of retaining labour were dramatically demonstrated by Renault who, with a tradition of no redundancies, made astronomical losses in 1984 and 1985 (of 12.55 billion frs. in 1984, around £1,300 million). After the appointment of the late Georges Besse in January 1985 the company entered into a radical restructuring and has shed 25 per cent of its work-force, largely by voluntary means. Nevertheless, motor companies are an important source of employment which governments must try to protect, not least because major contractions create intense political protest.

The second area is that of trade. Spain, France, and West Germany have a substantial trade surplus in cars; Italy and Britain a deficit. The British trade problem is returned to below. The third area is that of economic linkages. The motor industry is deeply integrated into the industrial economy which can make it a very suitable agent for growth but, equally, a serious retardant if it should contract. The British West Midlands has gone from boom to depression in twenty years, as the British motor industry has declined.[26] Clearly the component suppliers will be harmed by contraction, but the effect can be more subtle. The motor industry, it is widely argued, is 'de-maturing'.[27] It is pioneering a new social organization of work modelled, often, on Japanese practice; it is at the forefront of computer-aided design and manufacturing, of automation and robotization; and it is developing new technologies such as plastics, ceramics, and micro-computer control and information systems. If a country opts out of the motor industry it is jeopardizing its potential comparative advantage in all these areas.

Financial Assistance

It could be said of every motor company in Europe since 1965, with the exception of Daimler-Benz and the Americans, that without government aid it would have been in danger of going bankrupt at some point. The major recipients of aid have been Alfa-Romeo, which has made losses for the past thirteen years; SEAT, into which the Spanish Government has poured nearly $2 billion since 1980, as well as subsidizing every other producer in Spain; Dutch Volvo which has been receiving grants since 1977; Peugeot which, very reluctantly, accepted loans of around $300 million in 1983–4; the BL/Rover Group which received £2.4 billion from 1975–83, and now Renault which, on current projections, is likely to receive almost as much as BL has done. Fiat has undoubtedly received aid, although no one can find out how much, and it also benefits substantially from state lay-off pay through the *cassa integrazione* system. Ford and General Motors have also, of course, received very substantial promotional aid as they established new plants across Europe. Some companies have received aid almost as of right, in other cases the state has become involved very tardily as a result of political crisis. Mrs Thatcher's resentment at being manœuvred into granting £990 million to BL in 1981 is legendary and parallels the resentment of American new liberals. David Stockman, Ronald Reagan's 'supply-side' evangelist was similarly affected by the decision to give aid to Chrysler in 1981. He expressed outrage at the immorality of the proposition recalling that 'the notion that the Federal government should . . . refinance inefficient, bankrupt private enterprises was so loathsome to me that I resolved not only to vote against it, but to take the lead in trying to stop it. So I took the Floor of the House to speak out against this abomination that was about to pass.'[28] The biblical language is surely not accidental but, as Stockman concedes, such market purism was naïve; it is difficult indeed for the state to distance itself from companies as important as the major motor manufacturers.

Taking the industry on a European level, state aid of this magnitude is self-defeating and self-perpetuating. If market exit is perpetually impeded by government, crises of over-production and under-profitability are ensured. Ford has rather plaintively pointed out that 'Governments themselves have added to . . . problems. Massive state aid for ailing companies and lavish inducements to Japanese firms to create a European base are seriously distorting the European car and truck markets.'[29] This is a somewhat disingenuous point of view. Ford and General Motors have also used the massive financial resources of the parent companies to distort competition. From 1980 until very recently GM was the most aggressive competitor in the European market. Its declared aim was to 'catch up' with Ford overseas and it raised its market share by 40 per cent, from 8.3 per cent of the European market in 1981 to 11.1 per cent in 1985. It has been accused of blatantly 'buying' market share by aggressive discounting and promotions. Its British market share has risen spectacularly from 8.6 per cent in 1981 to 16.6 per cent in 1985.

Only in West Germany does government manage to refrain from extensive intervention. The competitive success of the West German industry is impressive although the Cassandras are prophesying that the strong D-Mark will bring serious problems. The West German case is interesting, as well as revealing of the West German model of organized capitalism. Volkswagen is still owned 20 per cent by the Federal Government (although privatization is being discussed), and 20 per cent by the Lower Saxony *Land* Government. Clearly it is not under the *tutelage* of government but equally it has a special relationship with the state. It is a creation of the state, and Brumlop and Juergens call it a 'state enterprise' arguing that 'the state representatives [on the Supervisory Board could] form a coalition with those from the employee and trade union side and . . . determine the composition and policies of the firm's management'.[30] It can therefore be argued that the state implicitly backs and underwrites Volkswagen. In addition the Supervisory Board provides for the state–management–labour–bank network of consensus formulation so characteristic of West German industry. The Deutsche Bank, for instance, which also holds 28 per cent of Daimler, is represented on the Board and by endorsing the company's strategy is doing so with the weight of the banking system.[31]

European Regulatory Responses

It is evident that there are considerable and harmful variations in European regulatory regimes where co-operation would be beneficial and the Commission might be expected to take an initiative. There are indications that the political institutions of Europe are beginning to catch up with economic realities. A weight of opinion is forming in favour of Europe-wide policy initiatives to defend the motor industry, to promote its restructuring, and to counter harmful societal side-effects. The Delors Commission has become activist and a triumvirate of Commissioners is pressing for a forceful Commission initiative.[32] In this they are supported by the collective lobby group of European manufacturers, the CCMC (Comité des Constructeurs d'Automobiles du Marché Commun), who in December 1986 submitted a confidential 'White Report' to the Commission calling for policy initiatives. The impetus for reform is the startling increase in Japanese import penetration outlined earlier in the chapter.

National corporate priorities are being effectively reproduced at the European level. The industry, through the CCMC, is pressing hard for Europe-wide controls on Japanese imports and Community regulatory harmonization. Equally provocatively, it is also looking for fiscal harmonization such as the removal of special car purchase taxes (over 200 per cent in Denmark and Greece, 10 per cent in Britain). As far as the Commission is concerned the manufacturers are pushing at an open door. The DG III policy is to pursue 'completion of the internal market' by 1992, and its motor industry officials see the car industry's salvation in creating an open, competitive, unrestricted home market of 320 million potential motorists.

The direction of policy development is indicated by the Beazley Report presented to the European Parliament in December 1986 and debated and approved at the end of January 1987.[33] The Report was prepared with the help and support of the Commission and it marks the beginning of a long, complex, and undoubtedly difficult period of policy development. The Commission will seek action on four main issues and there is an evangelical mood within DG III which portends unilateral action. The first issue is that of restraining Japanese imports through trade restraint, tariffs, or voluntary means. This will almost certainly imply lifting the existing barriers operated by the Spanish, the French, the Italians (and the British). Neither the French nor the Italians are likely to take such a step lightly or easily. Secondly is the issue of state aids. A system of enhanced transparency, scrupulous notification, and *post hoc* monitoring is already in place and is being policed with increased stringency by DG IV. The challenge, however, will be to construct a formula which allows some aid for restructuring, as in the Renault case, but which confines it within predictable, acceptable, market-related parameters. Such parameters are under discussion but are not yet formulated in any official, widely accepted fashion. The West German 'social market' principles offer one possible model.[34] The third issue is that of 'completing the internal market' by harmonizing vehicle-type specifications and other regulations, by equalizing tax regimes, and by unifying such other regulations as emission controls. In Eurospeak the aim is 'the creation of a single European Community market for motor cars by approximation of those national measures adopted by Member States in furtherance of protected national passenger car markets based on purely national interests'.[35] The fourth issue, and the poor relation, is to explore ways of ameliorating the social consequences of restructuring. The Beazley Report stresses consultation and training.

The Commission's main executive power lies in the responsibilities to assess and control 'state-aids' under Articles 92 and 93 of the Rome Treaty and to police competition under Articles 85 and 86. It is increasingly turning its attention to the transparency of all aid and to controlling subsidies. In this Peter Sutherland, the Commissioner responsible for competition, has argued publicly for measures to be taken against aid to the motor industry. This has met a less than sympathetic response from the Commission President, Jacques Delors, whose home government is a major culprit. All the same, Commission preferences are beginning to bite. It has been reported that Ford's decision to site its new 'lean burn' engine production at Dagenham was influenced by the British Government's threat to resort to European litigation if aid were given by the Westphalian Government to the proposed alternative location at Cologne.[36]

Environmental Regulation

The problems associated with Community-level regulation can be illustrated by the pollution control measures discussed during 1984–5 (which badly disrupted the West German car market). Action on engine emissions is long overdue. It is a false economy to employ dated technology which excludes European exports from the Japanese and American markets with their stringent anti-pollution regulations. As Altshuler *et al.* point out, the American market is so important that it becomes the world standard in regulatory provisions,[37] and, indeed, those companies such as

Daimler and BMW, whose vehicles already meet American standards, were content with the Commission proposals. The story is a complicated one and has been well told elsewhere.[38]

Under intense Green pressure the West German Environment Minister tried and failed to get agreement in the Council of Ministers to rigorous emission standards for nitrogen oxides, hydrocarbons, and carbon monoxide. The unsatisfactory compromise was a Council Decision to introduce limits differentiating between large, medium, and small cars. The deadline for large cars is 1988–9, the other regulations would not come into effect until after 1990. The Decision, yet to be given full effect in a Directive, has so far only been implemented in Denmark and West Germany. The final version of any Directive would be only permissive; other Member States are showing little inclination to introduce required restrictions and are still selling leaded petrol. The West German provisions are modest, granting tax concession to those buying cars with catalytic converters. About 20 per cent of new cars are being sold with converters. This situation is unsatisfactory for the industry, for consumers, for those interested in regulatory harmonization, and for the environment. It illustrates the tenacity of companies pursuing their particular interests both directly and through surprisingly sympathetic governments. Clearly there is a tension between Community regulation and national regulation with national governments pursuing more partisan interests in support of the corporate strategies of their national producers.

The pattern of state support for the motor industry in Western Europe has been to treat the industry as a 'manufacturing infrastructure'. The industry has been supported by governments, regardless of ideological predilection, in order to secure valuable economic benefits felt to be in the general interest. The history of state support has been of trade protection, favourable regulatory regimes and subsidy, and rescue when pressed. The term 'national champion' could have been coined with the motor industry in mind. But change is in the air.

While it is certain that state support will continue, the methods of support are beginning to change. Pressures for change include the sheer expense of continued subsidy and the increased effectiveness of EC subsidy limitations. The blanket subsidies seen at times for BL, SEAT, and Renault are likely to be resisted very strongly in favour of more specific support. A model has emerged of company reconstruction which might involve cutting capacity but which concentrates primarily on reducing the break-even level at which the company becomes profitable. This involves de-manning; increasing flexibility and productivity (targeted at Japanese levels); increasing plant utilization by, for instance, automation and multi-model assembly lines; improving quality; cutting stocks; entering joint ventures for new product development; and buying in a greater proportion of components. Support is therefore likely to be contingent on a plausible reconstruction plan devised by a trusted management team or managerial leader. In other words, to come full circle, support is given to a convincing corporate strategy. Clearly there are substantial national variations in this sort of pattern. The most atypical of the European countries is, paradoxically, Britain. Paradoxically because many of the reconstruction strategies were pioneered at BL yet, nevertheless, the British Government has insulated itself from the industrial economy,[39] and shown an eagerness to withdraw support from the national vehicle producer.

The Decline of the British Motor Industry

The decline of the British motor industry is a testament to industrial failure. It mirrors the decline of the British industrial economy and, indeed, such is its importance that it shares some responsibility for a wider industrial decline. Production has fallen from 11.1 per cent of world production in 1960 to 5.2 per cent in 1977 and 3.7 per cent in 1984.[40] Car import penetration has increased from 23 per cent in 1972 to 58 per cent in 1985, and commercial vehicles from 14 per cent in 1974 to 40 per cent in the first eight months of 1986.

The conventional, but mistaken, wisdom in the mid-1970s was that while Britain might have a comparative disadvantage in vehicle assembly, its components and commercial vehicle sectors were a source of great and lasting strength. In fact the component industry suffered very badly from the decline in British production and many firms, in effect, migrated abroad. Meanwhile the commercial vehicle industry disintegrated. The truck market collapsed in Europe and in key export markets. European production of trucks over 6 tonnes fell from 407,000 in 1980 to 247,000 in 1984; the British market very nearly halved between 1980 and 1982. In the face of this collapse the British truck industry proved to be the least resilient. Ford, as we have seen, sold its truck operations and their long-term future are now in serious doubt. General Motors simply closed its Bedford truck plants after fifty-five years of operation following opposition to its attempted take-over of Leyland Vehicles and Land Rover. The *coup de grâce* came at the beginning of 1987 when Leyland Trucks was merged into a minority joint venture with DAF.

The most effective way to illustrate the decline of the industry is to examine its trade balance. It has traditionally earned a considerable surplus and, indeed, an historical analysis of its present failings would point to the complacency and fragmentation generated in the immediate post-war years when it was treated merely as a dollar-earning money machine. The trade balance in cars went into deficit in 1975 and the balance for the industry as a whole went into serious deficit in 1982. Recent figures show a growing deficit in commercial vehicles and an emerging deficit in component trade to produce a deficit for 1986 of £3.9 billion. The motor industry thus provides not only the most striking sectoral example of manufacturing decline, but also its potential to produce a catastrophic balance of payments crisis. This perspective was highlighted by the House of Lords Select Committee on Overseas Trade which observed that motor vehicles displayed the largest single sectoral trade deterioration from 1978–84, and commented that 'motor vehicles, which makes the chief contribution to the growth of the deficit, provides the most striking example of this double decline (i.e. stagnant exports and rising imports)'.[41]

The causes of decline are multiple. Among the proximate causes are poor management, appalling labour relations, a slow growing home market, a complacent attitude to quality and delivery, and the destructive impact of macroeconomic policy. Government must take some share of blame, but up until about 1977 it could be said that the main feature of government policy was a curious lack of involvement with the industry, coexisting with a programme of massive support for the main British producer. Since 1977 relative indifference has at times bordered on hostility, as the recent acceptance, if not encouragement, of the dismemberment of BL/ Rover suggests. The main allegation against government is its reluctance to provide leadership and support. The liberal ideology of Mrs Thatcher's Conservative Government is, of course, totally antagonistic to industrial intervention, but it is startling to see principle overwhelm pragmatism. No other Government has allowed its motor industry to collapse, no other Cabinet has contemplated such a momentous gamble with manufacturing trade and employment.

Privatization and the Abdication of Responsibility

The stance of the British Government since 1979, as it concerns the motor industry, has exhibited two main features. First, a tolerance of the multinationals; secondly, a desire to remove BL from the public sector, both financially and legally. The former aspect of policy can be seen in the encouragement given to Nissan and the reluctance to act over the sourcing policies of Ford and GM.

In contrast to most European countries the British Government has been very welcoming to the Japanese. The Nissan plant in Tyne and Wear presents a threat to the established European industry. Apart from the simple addition to capacity, the plant raises three further fears. First, it embodies a new model of industrial relations. It is a single union plant with the Amalgamated Engineering Union (AEU) given sole rights in an agreement which embodies pendulum arbitration and virtually prohibits strikes. Moreover, the company has consciously copied West German labour practices and negotiates with a 'company council' which, like the West German works council, may contain non-union workers and is independent of the union. Membership of the union has also in practice been low. Secondly, it incorporates Japanese working practices such as quality circles and total labour flexibility. It promises very high productivity. Ford has estimated that cars produced in the Sunderland plant are likely to cost £330–£530 less to manufacture than those of its British competitors.[42] Thirdly, it is building up to 60 per cent local content, to meet Commission criteria as an indigenous producer. It is seeking in fact to attain 80 per cent local content, an informal target at which it is expected that opposition from European countries to British-built imports can be decisively dismissed. At this point it can avoid import restrictions and export freely throughout the Community. But even at 80 per cent it will still import substantially from Japan and may therefore undermine domestic component suppliers.

The British Government has supported Nissan with aid as well as enthusiasm. It will receive £112 million in direct regional aid and, exceptionally, has been guaranteed a continued regional development grant at 22 per cent even though the rate has been cut to 15 per cent. When Mrs Thatcher opened the plant in September 1986 the industry had confirmation that production would reach 100,000 at 80 per cent local content by 1991 and possibly 200,000 soon thereafter. Journalists were taken aback at the warmth of the Government reception. In the words of Gordon Kent, 'we were treated to a sickening sycophantic eulogy to Nissan quality from Margaret Thatcher . . . which some of us thought a bit thick considering the way she had bad-mouthed our own car company, Austin Rover, in Parliament'.[43] Ford and Renault have been exceptionally critical of the Nissan investment. They are pressing for mandatory local content to be defined at 80 per cent of ex-factory *cost*, instead of 80 per cent of ex-factory *price* (which includes overheads and profits). Ford allege that without this change the company could still manage to bring in power trains from Japan although Nissan have responded with plans to build an engine plant in Britain. In any event Britain, the stepping-stone for American multinational expansion in Europe, looks set to perform the same function for the Japanese. This will create discord, require a lead from the Commission, and, within Britain, create additional problems for Ford and the Rover Group.

The two American multinationals have been importing vehicles and components from their Continental plants since the mid-1970s. Ford has always argued that low productivity has necessitated this but the high sterling exchange rate has undoubtedly also played a part. Compared with GM practices, however, Ford is virtue incarnate. GM virtually gave up British production after 1978 in favour of assembling, or merely 'badging', vehicles from West Germany and Spain. It then proceeded, through aggressive discounting, especially in the fleet sector, to 'buy' British market share. By 1985 the position had become intolerable and Jones produced a telling critique of GM's strategy and its harmful effect on the British components industry and on Austin Rover. He pointed out that barely 22 per cent by value of GM car sales were of British origin and that 'severe doubt must arise as to whether General Motors . . . can still be regarded as a UK company'. Yet Vauxhall was still using its 'Britishness' to gain sales in the vital British fleet market which prefers, for rather obscure reasons, to 'buy British'. He went on to argue that 'the biggest threat to Austin Rover Group . . . is the aggressive discounting by General Motors . . . This is the main reason why Austin Rover Group's market share has not risen with the introduction of the Montego . . . Austin Rover Group has . . . been caught directly in the crossfire between Ford and General Motors'.[44] Following warnings from the Department of Trade and Industry in 1984 and 1985, GM promised to achieve 65 per cent local sourcing. Leon Brittan took up cudgels later in the year. He told the Commons that he regretted that 'after lengthy discussions, Vauxhall is not yet ready to go further in proving that it really is a British car producer'.[45] In partial response both Ford and Vauxhall significantly increased their British content in 1986–7, reflecting better British productivity and a rising D-Mark as well as government pressure.

A British government has few sanctions to apply against the sourcing policies of the multinationals. It was argued above that, despite the formal position, companies are careful not to antagonize governments and take their policies and preferences seriously. It is a weakness of the British position that governments have brought pressure to bear only belatedly and spasmodically.[46]

In contrast the Government cannot escape involvement with the state-owned Rover Group. The history of government relations with BL/Rover is long and complex, but a few straightforward, if controversial, points can be made. First, the decline of BL has been 'managed' by Government, but since 1977, with the appointment of Michael Edwardes, and especially since the Conservative rescue of the company in 1970, support has been fatalistic, a negative managing of decline rather than a positive strategy for recovery. To have liquidated BL in 1974–5 when it was nationalized on the basis of the Ryder plan would have been unbearable, politically and economically. To liquidate a shrunken Rover Group today would be damaging but manageable. Secondly, the appointment of Graham Day as Executive Chairman in May 1986 indicates some residual commitment to saving Rover. Day was given executive responsibilities, like Sir Michael Edwardes but unlike his immediate predecessor, Sir Austin Bide. Rover once again has a forceful leader and Day immediately made clear that although privatization was the eventual goal: 'I do not see it is my job—and neither has it been indicated to me that it should be my job—simply to move into BL and have as *the* . . . priority the fact of privatisation . . . I am putting as the priority the financial health of the business'.[47]

Thirdly, although Rover needs capital, its needs are not apparently anything like as great as in the past or on the scale of aid currently going to Renault in France. What the company undoubtedly does require, however, is consistent government support. Fourthly, unambiguous backing has not been forthcoming. Ministers have been willing to criticize the company while the encouragement of Nissan is clearly contrary to the interests of Rover and the proposed sale to Ford was little short of a gesture of contempt. Fifthly, the Government has become obsessed with the desire to privatize the company almost regardless of the commercial or national logic of doing so. As Peter Morrison, the DTI Minister of State, recently told the Trade and Industry Committee, 'of course as a matter of fact we are basically in the business of privatisation'.[48]

In February 1987 this eagerness to disengage was again evident when Paul Channon, Secretary of State for Trade and Industry, announced that Britain was, in effect, withdrawing from truck manufacture. Leyland Trucks and Freight Rover were to undergo a minority merger with DAF of Holland. Engine and heavy truck manufacture was gradually to be transferred to Holland with Britain concentrating on light commercial vehicles. As late as the end of the 1960s Britain had been the premier truck manufacturing nation of Europe but now, with only modest public concern, the industry was quietly disappearing. The Rover Group was to keep a 40 per cent holding, £750 million in aid was announced, although it later appeared that the true figure was £680 million representing the writing-off of accumulated debt incurred by the truck and bus operations, making them saleable. Further details were not entirely clear but the suggestion was that, while the Government was subscribing new equity, no 'fresh' money would be going into the cars division. The Rover Group would gain in that it would be free from truck losses and the related debt burden and the Government also announced the approval of its five-year corporate plan.[49]

Channon announced to the House of Commons that Rover was being 'given every single thing they asked for', but it seemed that their requests had been restrained. The Government reiterated the emphasis on eventual privatization and on product and manufacturing collaboration with Honda. The tenor of the statements was more positive than in the past but the impression given remained one of fatalistic acceptance of decline with the problem of Rover cars postponed until after the next election. Above all, the

Rover Group was dealt with as an individual corporate problem. There was no clear suggestion that its future was being assessed in the context of prospects for, let alone policy towards, the motor industry sector of the economy. This was perhaps to be expected from a Conservative Government committed to disengagement from industry. Labour, in contrast, would favour a far more interventionist approach. Their pre-election industrial policy statements gave great prominence to manufacturing regeneration and to the central importance of the motor industry. For Kinnock the Conservative's 'attempt to flog off BL in 1986 was not simply economically unwise, it was a downright betrayal of responsibility'.[50] As might be expected, there was no indication that a Conservative Government would intervene on behalf of the Rover Group in the event of re-election, which is strange.

The stance of the Government was strange partly because of the sheer magnitude of state investment. Successive governments had invested about £2.5 billion in BL/Rover since 1974. From 1975 to 1984 this amounted to *just over £1 million per working day for nine years*. This was a lot to abandon, especially when a return on investment was in prospect, which introduces the more important point. BL/Rover had done almost everything that was expected of it. BL confronted its own work-force between 1977 and 1980 in a fashion that was followed by Fiat in Turin in 1980, by Peugeot/Talbot at Poissy in 1982, and by Renault in 1984–5. Productivity at Rover had increased, it had cut costs, raised quality, renewed its model range, increased exports to Europe, begun exporting to the USA, and, most important, entered into a very productive series of joint ventures with Honda.

Observers were divided on these developments. On the pessimistic side Williams *et al.* predicted that Rover would lose all independence: 'the present management has accepted the inevitable and adopted a strategy of assembling Hondas.'[51] On the optmistic side Jones saw a potential for Rover to succeed,[52] and Rhys concluded that 'for once the UK is ahead of the game', adding that 'the UK industry now has the cost structures to survive' and that (Vauxhall and) Rover 'are pointing the way for the European industry at large'.[53] As regards Rover's future the post-General Election stance of government will obviously be decisive but perhaps the strangest feature of Rover's decline is the self-fulfilling character of overt government policy. Motor car companies, like many other concerns, thrive on confidence and expectations of success. When government, as the main shareholder, and as the regulator and guardian of the national interest, demonstrates scepticism and promotes fragmentation then customers, suppliers, and the management and work-force themselves are working in an atmosphere conducive to decline.

Conclusions

The purpose of this chapter is not only to analyse developments within the European motor industry but also to draw out of the discussion some insights into the development of European capitalism and into regulatory responses. The discussion has identified three particular developments which are of a wide and lasting significance. First, the importance of corporate strategy; secondly, the tendency for the imperatives of industrial profitability to emphasize economic and de-emphasize social regulatory objectives; thirdly, the continuing growth of corporate power. The following discussion takes each in turn.

Within the economic literature the analysis of corporate strategy has become increasingly sophisticated. It is widely accepted that large oligopolistic corporations must have an elaborate administrative hierarchy and associated strategy in order to organize their internal transactions profitably.[54] Similarly, the constraints and determinants of such strategies are eagerly analysed.[55] The current content of corporate strategies is the very stuff of business analysis. The strategies of leading corporations are analogous to the policies of governments. They operate under different constraints and certainly have more specific and limited objectives, but they are evolved through an internal organizational process which can be studied, just as public policy-making can be studied. While the study of public policy tends to emphasize external influences on policy-making, the study of corporate strategy often appears to assume that it emerges fully developed from an internal decision-making process. That may be true in some cases but even a superficial analysis of the strategies of the motor manufacturers shows that it is not always the case. It is important then to ask which outside agencies become involved in the formulation of corporate strategy and with what implications for the content of strategy and for its implementation.

An important participant is the state. Government agencies are closely involved in the formulation of corporate strategies in both Renault and Rover, both of which are state owned. The position in Volkswagen is ambiguous. It is likely that the Federal and *Land* Ministries would be consulted but Streeck's work on Volkswagen gives little indication that they participate actively.[56] It might be supposed that government involvement in strategic planning in Rover and Renault would give a decisive opportunity to pursue governmental policy objectives. In fact the relationship is far less simple. What is clear is that government is divided in dealing with these companies. In France the Finance and Industry Ministries, have each made separate and at times conflicting assessments of Renault's financial plans. In Britain the annual approval of Rover's corporate plan has become a set-piece inter-departmental battle which involves the Cabinet Office as well as the Treasury and the DTI. Mrs Thatcher's personal advisers in the Cabinet Office have been intensely critical of the company, the DTI is more inclined to favour support. In this area the regulatory and promotional capabilities of European governments vary considerably. It has been argued that the institutions, organization, and resources of British central government, particularly the DTI, are simply not competent to handle detailed assessment of, and intervention into, industrial affairs.[57]

In contrast, the unions are closely involved in debates over corporate strategy in Volkswagen, have some involvement in Renault and SEAT, appear to be excluded in Fiat and Peugeot, and are undeniably excluded in the Rover Group. Indeed, Rover excludes its own divisional management. Renault has two worker representatives on the Board. In the past both were CGT (Confédération Générale du Travail) members and clashed with Georges Besse over the Renault rationalization strategy, after which they were marginalized. In Volkswagen, however, IG Metall is active on the supervisory board while worker representatives have the forum of the works council in which to debate the company's policies. The work-force has been extensively involved in aspects of strategic development and it is perhaps significant that there have been no compulsory redundancies. Similarly the banks are more involved in Volkswagen's strategic decision-making than is typical of the other European manufacturers.

The development of a corporate strategy requires a sequence of strategic choices in key areas. Clearly those choices will be affected by the range of external and internal parties who participate in them and are a function of inter-organizational relationships, even though they are often symbolically identified with a 'leader' (Graham Day for Rover; the late Georges Beese for Renault; Vittorio Ghidella for Fiat). It would be difficult to suggest that the openness of the decision-making process affects the suitability of the strategy. Volkswagen's more open processes have brought success but so have Fiat's far more insular methods. What can be more firmly maintained is first, and obviously, that more open processes are conducive to societal accountability and, secondly, that plan implementation should be more uncomplicated and effective if it is initially based on wide agreement. Practices vary widely across Europe. Attempts to open up strategy formulation systematically, as with the Vredeling Directive, have proved controversial and have been strongly resisted. The increasingly acknowledged importance of corporate strategies does, however, mean that they will be the subject of intense study. Moreover, to bargain with a company over or through its corporate strategy provides an attractive alternative to the much blunter manipulation of the regulatory environment which is the conventional Anglo-Saxon approach to influencing industrial activity. The Labour Party's continued commitment to 'planning agreements' reflects a desire to negotiate improvements in corporate strategy. Hence strategy formulation is likely to become a centrally important forum for debates over the proper development of the industrial economy.

A second striking trend to emerge from analysis of the motor industry is the way in which pressure for economic success, defined in terms of company profitability, has led governments to downgrade social regulatory objectives. The twin pressures of a need to reduce subsidies from the public purse on the one hand, and the industrial advantages to be gained from large national car producers on the other, have led governments to define their responsibilities in the same terms as those of industrial management. This convergence of governmental and managerial objectives has implications for the power of management and has led governments to downgrade traditional social and welfare priorities. The British Government was the first to abandon priorities of regional employment protection, followed by a more general support of labour-shedding across the industry; this was followed by restrictive union legislation. The British were also particularly opposed to strict environmental controls which, as British experience shows, impose additional costs on producers. But pollution imposes substantial costs on society. That it was West German ministers and companies which pressed for European emission regulations illustrates West German environmental sensitivity as well as the financial health of the West German industry and its strength in American markets.

The policy agenda on the future of, and regulation for, the European motor industry has thus become dominated by economic arguments. Problems include the loss of export markets, Japanese imports and European production, fragmentation of the R. & D. effort, 'catching up' with Japanese work organization and productivity levels, and so on. The criteria are industry growth and profitability with the imperatives of international capitalist competition driving out questions about the societal distribution of costs and benefits. Radical writers have long argued that 'Europe's division into separate states . . . enables European capital to present a united front against "national" political forces, and thus the European Left has suffered successive defeats throughout the 1970s. Under such conditions Europe can only be the Europe of European capital.'[58] The experience of the car industry would appear to lend credibility to this argument.

Central to corporate strategy and the ascendancy of managerial priorities is the issue of corporate power. In current debates on political economy the emphasis is now on the independence and influence of major corporations. The attacks on the allegedly unfettered power of multinational corporations have, however, been superceded by more sober analysis. Lindblom's study of *Politics and Markets*[59] has been influential in stressing the structural privilege of business; the mechanisms, biases, and outcomes of business privilege are being subject to closer academic scrutiny.

The large motor companies could be expected to feature prominently among the bastions of corporate power unless, that is, they are clients of the state. Conventional wisdom would hold that a company in need of state support would be dependent on the government and therefore relatively weak. In fact, in some cases, state dependence can perversely strengthen industrial management.

Most obviously, in their confrontation with their work-forces managerial ultimatums have been given credibility by the strictures of conditional state support. This appears true of BL, Fiat, and Renault. More subtly, work by Cawson and his colleagues has persuaded them that the 'national champion' relationship in France has led companies to colonize agencies of the state, rather than vice versa.[60] The Industry Department, they argue, is inclined to act as the advocate of firms such as Thomson, pressing its interests in government and in international negotiations. Indications are that a similar relationship of company dominance exists in respect of Renault. It is less plausible that such an argument could be applied in Britain to the influence of the Rover Group. As argued earlier, the British Government's relationship with its national motor manufacturer is internationally atypical. While financial support has been forthcoming there has been a constant pressure to privatize the enterprise and no sense of conviction that the Government is committed to the long-term survival of the company.

In general, however, in the current stage of industrial restructuring, with the emphasis on profitability within the European market, industrial management is being strengthened in its relations with the work-force and with government itself. The deployment of corporate power may be purely industrial and specific, such as the ability to attract research support or influence changes in the fiscal regime; or it may be wider and more social in impact such as influence on union legislation or on foreign policy—towards South Africa or Japan. As Cawson argues, 'the privileged position of business has two dimensions: i) governments constrain their policy-making options by anticipating possible adverse reactions by business and; ii) business groups are privileged participants in policy deliberation processes'.[61] The latter possibility leads to business being so closely involved in policy-making as to become, in Middlemas's phrase, 'governing institutions',[62] a possibility much explored in corporatist analysis. It can be maintained that Volkswagen, Renault, Peugeot, and Fiat are 'governing institutions' as, to a lesser extent, are Ford and General Morors. The Rover Group is not. Once again this illustrates the distinctive, non-corporatist, insular pattern of the British Government's relations with industry. There is a dilemma here. Economic success may involve sacrificing economic sovereignty to large corporations. This is obnoxious to economic liberals and to socialists alike and is culturally repugnant to the British polity. Yet to resist corporate dominance may carry the penalty of economic failure, with even more damaging results for economic sovereignty and individual well-being.

This chapter opened by noting an atmosphere of optimism in the European motor industry early in 1987. There are transitory grounds for such optimism but within the industry itself optimism perhaps reflects also the feeling that the tide of political approval has moved in favour of industrial priorities. Certainly in Britain the themes of wealth creation, managerial prerogative, and entrepreneurial flair are ideas 'in good currency'. In this atmosphere suspicion of corporate power is reduced if not dissipated. Within the large motor companies this is indeed cause for optimism, whether such optimism should be widely shared across society is less certain.

Notes

The author would like to thank officials in DG III and DG IV of the European Commission who generously supplied information on the development of European policy; also colleagues who kindly commented on an earlier draft, especially Dan Jones of the SPRU, University of Sussex, and delegates to the 1987 Annual Conference of the Universities Association for Contemporary European Studies. None of these individuals should be held in any way responsible for the arguments developed above.

1. For an authoritative review see A. Altshuler, D. Jones, D. Roos, and J. Womack, *The Future of the Automobile* (London: George Allen & Unwin, 1984).
2. K. Williams, J. Williams, and C. Haslam, *The Breakdown of Austin Rover: A Case Study in the Failure of Business Strategy and Industrial Policy* (Leamington Spa: Berg, 1987), 114.
3. But see C. Johnson, *MITI and the Japanese Miracle: The Growth of Industry Policy, 1925–1975* (Stanford: Stanford University Press, 1982), 76, for a more critical discussion of the idea.
4. See the *Financial Times*, 23 June 1986.
5. See K. Bhaskar, *The Future of the World Motor Industry* (London: Kogan Page, 1980), p. 144 and again p. 192 where the 'basic industrial logic' of the take-over is described as 'faultless'.
6. *Mea culpa* at this point, the source is S. Wilks, *Industrial Policy and*

the *Motor Industry* (Manchester: Manchester University Press, 1984), 248.

7. M. Edmonds, 'Market Ideology and Corporate Power: The United States', in K. Dyson and S. Wilks (eds.), *Industrial Crisis: A Comparative Study of the State and Industry* (Oxford: Basil Blackwell, 1985) (first published 1983), 93–4.
8. See his best-selling autobiography, L. Iacocca with W. Novak, *Iacocca: An Autobiography* (New York: Bantam, 1984).
9. *Business Week*, 3 Nov. 1986, 50.
10. *Financial Times*, 9 Oct. 1986.
11. Altshuler, *et al.*, *The Future of the Automobile*, p. 9.
12. M. Rollier, 'Changes of Industrial Relations at Fiat', in O. Jacobi *et al.* (eds.), *Technological Change, Rationalisation and Industrial Relations* (London: Croom Helm, 1986), 116.
13. Wilks, *Industrial Policy and the Motor Industry*, ch. 9.
14. See DTI, *World Automotive Forecast Report*, Nov. 1986, 5.
15. Ford Motor Company Ltd., Written Evidence, in *Report from the Select Committee on Overseas Trade*, HL, 1984–5, HLP 238–II, pp. 217–22.
16. D. Jones, *The Import Threat to the U.K. Car Industry* (Brighton: SPRU, 1985), 7.
17. Altshuler *et al.*, *The Future of the Automobile*, ch. 8.
18. G. Maxcy, *The Multinational Motor Industry* (London: Croom Helm, 1981), 272.
19. For further detail see S. Wilks, 'Multinational Strategies and National Subsidies', paper given at the ECPR joint sessions of workshops, Barcelona, Mar. 1985.
20. S. Sinclair, *The World Car* (London: Euromonitor, 1983), 1.
21. D. Jones, 'Structural Adjustment in the Automobile Industry in the 1980s', SPRU paper on work in progress, Oct. 1986, 4.
22. Bhaskar, *The Future of the World Motor Industry*, p. 4.
23. Publicly quoted companies, 1985 figures from *FT 500*, 1986.
24. Maxcy, *The Multinational Motor Industry*, p. 220.
25. Jones, *Structural Adjustment in the Automobile Industry*, p. 4.
26. See F. Gaffkin and A. Nickson, *Jobs Crisis and the Multinationals: De-Industrialisation in the West Midlands* (Birmingham: Birmingham Trade Union Group, 1984).
27. For an early statement of this position see D. Jones, 'Technology and the UK Automobile Industry', *Lloyds Bank Review*, 148 (Apr. 1983).
28. D. Stockman, *The Triumph of Politics* (London: The Bodley Head, 1986), 44.
29. Ford Motor Company, Writen Evidence, p. 220.
30. E. Brumlop and U. Juergens, 'Rationalisation and Industrial Relations: A Case Study of Volkswagen', in Jacobi *et al.*, *Technological Change*,

Rationalisation and Industrial Adjustment, p. 74.
31. See W. Streeck, *Industrial Relations in West Germany: A Case Study of the Car Industry* (London: Heinemann, 1984), for an outstanding study of decision-making in Volkswagen.
32. The triumvirate is composed of Lord Cockfield, Karl-Heinz Narjes (DG III), and Peter Sutherland (DG IV).
33. European Parliament Document A 2-171/86, *Report of the Committee on Economic and Monetary Affairs and Industrial Policy on the European Community Automobile Industry*, Rapporteur, Peter Beazley, 8 Dec. 1986. Debated and approved by the European Parliament, see *Official Journal*, 23 Jan. 1987.
34. For a discussion of subsidy control see S. Wilks, 'The Practice of the Theory of Industrial Adaptation in Britain and West Germany', *Government and Opposition*, 19 (1984).
35. Ibid. 7.
36. *Financial Times*, 4 July 1986.
37. Altshuler, *et al.*, *The Future of the Automobile*, p. 64.
38. I. Turner, 'Interest Group Activity and EC Policy-Making: A Case Study of the 1985 Car Exhaust Emmision Control Decision', unpublished paper, Henley Management College, 1986.
39. See S. Wilks, 'Has the State Abandoned British Industry?', *Parliamentary Affairs*, Jan. 1986, for development of this theme.
40. The figures are for cars and commercial vehicles produced in the 8 leading producing countries.
41. Select Committee on Overseas Trade, *Report*, 1984–5, HLP 238–I, p. 16.
42. See comments by Paul Roots reported in the *Financial Times*, 12 June 1986.
43. *Car Magazine*, Nov. 1986, 121.
44. Jones, *The Import Threat to the U.K. Car Industry*, pp. 7, 20, 26.
45. *Financial Times*, 24 Oct. 1985.
46. For development of this theme see Wilks, *Industrial Policy and the Motor Industry*, ch. 9.
47. Select Committee on Trade and Industry, *Minutes of Evidence*, 'BL plc', 1985–6, HCP 291, May 1986, para. 5.
48. Ibid., 'Department of Trade and Industry', June 1986, para. 15*b*.
49. See e.g. the *Financial Times* and *Guardian*, 20 Feb. 1987.
50. N. Kinnock, *Making Our Way: Investing in Britain's Future* (Oxford: Basil Blackwell, 1986), 77.
51. K. Williams *et al.*, *The Breakdown of Austin Rover*, p. 111.
52. See Jones, 'Structural Adjustment in the Motor Industry', p. 21.
53. D. G. Rhys, 'The European Motor Industry—A Future of Change', paper read to the Manchester Statistical Society, 18 Mar. 1986, 29, 30.

54. See, for instance, O. E. Williamson, 'The Modern Corporation: Origins, Evolution, Attributes', *Journal of Economic Literature*, 19 (1981): and A. Francis *et al.* (eds.), *Power Efficiency and Institutions: A Critical Appraisal of the Markets and Hierarchies Paradigm* (London: Heinemann, 1983).
55. As in H. Ergas, 'Corporate Strategies in Transition', in A. Jacquemin (ed.), *European Industry: Public Policy and Corporate Strategy* (Oxford: Clarendon Press, 1984), p. 330, where he stresses technological choice.
56. Streeck, *Industrial Relations in West Germany*.
57. Wilks, *Industrial Policy and the Motor Industry*, pp. 64–6.
58. S. Amin, 'Preface', in F. Clairmonte and J. Cavanagh, *The Worlds in Their Web: Dynamics of Textiles Multinationals* (London: Zed, 1981), p. xvii.
59. C. Lindblom, *Politics and Markets* (New York: Basic Books, 1977).
60. See A. Cawson, P. Holmes, and A. Stevens, 'The Interaction Between Firms and the State in France: The Telecommunications and Electronics Sectors', in S. Wilks and M. Wright (eds.), *Comparative Government–Industry Relations: Europe, the United States, and Japan* (Oxford: Clarendon Press, 1987), 10–34.
61. A. Cawson, 'Hostile Brothers: The Role of Firms in the Politics of Industrial Sectors', paper presented to the XI World Congress of Sociology, New Delhi, Aug. 1986, 9.
62. R. K. Middlemas, *Power, Competition and the State*, (London: Macmillan, 1986).

8

Regulating the Company

Cosmo Graham

The original inspiration for this chapter was dissatisfaction with the narrow view of company law in Britain. Academic company lawyers have been concerned with the minutiae of statute and case-law to the exclusion of insights that might have been obtained from such disciplines as economics and political science. This is a characteristically English denial of law 'as the great interpreter of the pattern of politics'.[1] Company law has been seen as an apolitical, technical subject concerned solely with the rules of private law.[2] The major concern of English company lawyers has been to elucidate the formal legal rules governing the relationship between the shareholders in the company and the directors; workers and other interests have only rarely intruded. This is, I shall argue, a nineteenth-century view of the company and one which fails to recognize that internal organization of companies is a matter of public concern.

This chapter is concerned with the 'modern' corporation. I argue that the internal forms of corporate governance of such companies is a matter of public interest. Historically this was the case, as corporations were the recipients of delegated public power, created to carry out public purposes. In the United States, Horwitz has argued that the conception of the corporation as a private entity was only fully developed in the nineteenth century.[3] But corporations now exist in the modern welfare state. The growth of the welfare state was due, in part, to the pragmatic necessity to respond to market failure, but two major reasons obstruct successful resolution of the problem. First, there are contradictory steering imperatives: the state wants to solve the problems thrown up by the markets without unduly disturbing the system of private property. Secondly, the complexities of modern society are such that effective purposive intervention is, if not impossible, extremely difficult. For example, there are gaps in the state's information about the external environment.[4]

At its extreme such an argument suggests that reasoned state intervention is impossible. A more limited position argues that these technical limitations to state action engender severe problems regarding the nationality of state action. The answer, it is argued, is to look for new legal and organizational forms which can cope with the complexities of modern society. Such forms will concentrate on the internal decision processes of groups and the co-ordination of the actions of groups. What this implies for companies is that reform of their internal decision-making procedures may be necessary if the state is to respond effectively to market failure.[5]

So the focus of this chapter is to interpret all theories of company law as answers to the question: why should a group of persons receive special privileges from the state, notably limited liability? The answer, which has varied in different historical periods, has been to impose some conditions on a company's organization. In addition, I shall maintain that all models of the company assume particular models of the state, law, and the economy, which support their view of the company. Choosing between these competing views of the world is not merely an empirical matter.[6] The differences are conceptual, with normative implications. Nor is economic analysis conclusive, because it ignores the very pre-suppositions of economic analysis which are at issue.[7]

I sketch three models of the company: the 'classical' model, the 'pluralist' model, and the 'neo-classical' model. I argue that the first model is no longer viable, and therefore a choice must be made between the pluralist and the neo-classical models. Outlining the dispute between pluralists and neo-classicists clarifies the point that behind questions about internal corporate governance lies differing normative views of the roles of law and the state. Finally, after a brief look at West German law as a point of comparison, current developments in the UK will be surveyed, in order to illustrate the problems facing company law.[8]

This chapter has a limited and modest compass.[9] It will not discuss the regulation of companies in the sense of regulation by administrative agencies, self-regulation, or the equivalents. Nor will questions which are traditionally defined as labour law be examined.

The Classical Model

This is the nineteenth-century response to the question why companies were allowed the privilege of incorporation. In the UK at least it remains the dominant paradigm. In describing the model I have leant heavily on the previous work of Stokes.[10] The classical model of the internal organization of the company is underpinned by assumptions about the role of the economy, law, and the state. The elements of this model are familiar and developed from the mid-nineteenth century in Britain when incorporation, with the associated privilege of limited liability, became freely available.

The first strand was the conception of the economy as composed of numerous private firms, of more or less equal power who competed amongst each other for customers. Those who were efficient prospered and those who were inefficient went bankrupt. The legitimating element was that no one firm could dominate the market: success depended on doing better than competitors, which judgement was made by the free choice of consumers.

It was not only the product market which provided a restraint on corporate power. An equally crucial restraint was provided by the internal organization of companies. The dominant theory was what Stokes has called the contractual model.[11] The shareholders decided on the business of the company, a decision incorporated in the contract contained in the memorandum and articles of association. The memorandum was originally unalterable, which seemed to assume that there was always an identifiable business the company could be held to, hence the foundation of the *ultra vires* rule. Directors were appointed to manage the company on the basis of this contract. It seems to have been assumed that shareholders would scrutinize the activities of directors closely and intervene when they felt directors were not being efficient, either directly in the management of the company or through the power of removal.

The role of the law was limited. The Courts would ensure that the terms of the contract were obeyed, through enforcing the *ultra vires* and the capital maintenance rules. Law also imposed fiduciary duties on directors, that is, a duty to act bona fide in the best interests of the company and not to put themselves into a position where duty and self-interest conflicted. The clearest illustration of the limited scope of court intervention can be seen in the conditions allowing a dissenting minority shareholder to sue in the name of the company. This was limited to cases where the majority controlled the company and had acted fraudulently, that is, if they had appropriated 'money, property or opportunities' belonging to the company. The Courts did not intervene to see whether the contract was executed well or badly, but only to deal with fraud, which constituted a breach of contract.[12] The other area in which the law intervened concerned disclosure obligations, this being seen as the price of limited liability. Here law was used to ensure that the shareholders could monitor the contract they had entered into effectively.

In ideal-typical terms, this is the law of a *laissez-faire* state, which enacts only general, formal–rational law, pursues fraud, and sets the ground rules for competition in the market. Within the view of the world, corporations are perceived as *private* entities. This was historically novel. Most previous corporations, for instance the East India Company, are perhaps best seen as carrying out public tasks even though they would make a profit for their private members. The *laissez-faire* view also contained unresolved tensions, for if companies were true private entities, how could the privilege of limited liability be justified?[13]

This nineteenth-century model became increasingly unreal in the twentieth century. In the economic sphere, the growth of large firms meant that there was no longer always a competitive product market. A company's power was less constrained by the existence of competitors.[14] The growth of the large corporation and widely dispersed shareholdings saw the effective breakdown of shareholder monitoring, a point made famous by Berle and Means,[15] as the 'divorce of ownership and control'. Some recognition of this can be seen in the English case-law which tentatively accepted the notion of managers running the company free from interference by the shareholders.[16] These two developments combined to ensure that corporate managers had more power with less constraints than in the classical era. As for law and the state, there developed a more interventionist and activist state which in turn impinged on company law. The consequent blurring of the public–private divide meant that the formal legal status of an entity was no longer a clear guide to its function. All these developments raised questions about corporate power and the viability of the classical model for its legitimation.

The Pluralist Model

In the United States the Great Crash of 1929 dramatized the 'problem' of the large corporation. The repercussions of the Crash can be seen in the classical debate over the power of corporate managers between Berle and Dodd, the starting-point for the American debate over the future of corporation law.[17]

This dialogue was prompted by the separation of ownership from control in the modern corporation. For Berle and others this raised problems of legitimacy, because managers were invested with power through an archaic, ritualistic process and lacked any effective oversight.[18] The modern corporations' increasing economic importance, so Berle felt, obliged them to take on wider functions than merely profit-making.[19] As Mason remarked, once the management of a corporation claims equity as a goal, as well as profits, then the divide between public and private disappears.[20] The problem is then to find a structure which will ensure that managers take into account all the various interests affected by the company's action.

From this beginning the American debate has generated a pluralist model of the corporation. It is pluralist in two senses. First, it is a theory of the state and the role groups play within it. Secondly, it is a set of ideas about corporate governance. The theory of the state sees, to follow Connolly,[21] the social system as a balance of power among overlapping groups, each of whom are constrained through the process of mutual group adjustment and all of whom share a broad value consensus. The role of the state in this process depends on the view of the theorist and Connolly identifies two main accounts: arena theories and umpire theories. In the former, the state is the territory for group struggle. In the latter, which is specifically identified with Berle, the state is an umpire between competing groups.

Berle saw the economy as marked by imperfect competition. Large corporations could create demand as much as be its subject. The internal organization of these corporations was characterized by the separation of ownership and control. Constraints in this type of institution are not provided by shareholder accountability but by the professionalization of top corporate management. The corporate management develops a soul.[22] The 'soulful' corporation was not a personal peculiarity of Berle's, other commentators, such as Bell and Kerr *et al.* claimed to discern its development.[23] Also, he does indicate that there is a need to develop the internal governance structures of the corporation to cope with this new situation.[24]

Even on its own terms a key part of Berle's response to the breakdown of the classical model seems unconvincing. As Hurst has pointed out,[25] the notion of benevolent managerialism was unstable because, after twenty years or more of talk of corporate statesmanship, the idea lacked specific substance, in fact and in law. So it is best to see Berle as beginning the debate about the separation of ownership and control and imperfect competition. But there is an additional point: if the modern corporation is a quasi-public entity, a range of interests wider than those of shareholders can legitimately be taken into account. Berle never fully addressed the ensuing problem of institutional design. For such developments we need to look to the work of Nader and Stone, even though there were earlier theorists who recognized the need to reform the internal governance structures of the corporation rather more clearly than did Berle.[26]

Stone begins by arguing that markets cannot restrain corporations because of blockages and information costs. The 'classical' legal strategies of aiming measures at the corporation's profits and at key individuals suffer from similar problems. Regulating corporate activities directly encounters the problems of information deficits and agency capture. So the way forward is to reform the corporate decision-making process to make it more 'responsible'. This means not only that the corporation reflects upon what it is doing but also does this by reference to a moral vocabulary.[27]

Part of the scheme for reforming corporate decision-making would involve the appointment of public directors to corporations.[28] General public directors would be appointed in large corporations, would ensure that the law was complied with, serve as a liaison in the legislative process, act as a check on the effectiveness of fundamental internal systems, serve a 'hot-line' function for whistle-blowers, oversee the preparation of impact studies, and act as an information interface between the corporation and its environment. Special public directors would only be appointed for a narrower range of tasks, when it was clear that a particular firm or industry was delinquent. These proposals are part of a wider scheme. He also suggests that the company should be required to gather certain information and before making certain decisions it should prepare an impact statement and ensure that all relevant interests are consulted, on an analogy with the Federal regulatory agencies.

The proposals produced by Nader *et al.* are similar. Their proposals differ in detail from Stone's but both are schemes for implementing a pluralist idea. The foundation of Nader *et al.*'s argument is the equation of the modern corporation with a public entity: thus in discussing the role of representative directors they draw an analogy with the American constitution. Likewise, their argument for ending corporate secrecy is that knowledge is essential to democracy.[29]

If the ideas of Stone and Nader are added to arguments begun by Berle and Dodd we can discern a potentially coherent model of corporate regulation. The strength of the argument comes from its grounding in classical theories of democracy,[30] the acknowledgement of the com-penetration of public and private spheres in the modern world, and the difficulties of using law to deal with the problems of a complex society. Nor is it without empirical referents. There have been developments in American case-law on corporate gifts which can be seen to be consistent with the pluralist view, there are examples of both general and special public directors in the US and UK, while the notion of the 'social audit' shows a similar inspiration.[31]

But this model has also been heavily criticized. Before examining these criticisms I want to deal with the second major strand in company regulation, the European debate on industrial democracy, because most of the criticisms directed at the pluralist vision can also be applied to industrial democracy.

Industrial Democracy

This has been largely a European debate, with the West German experience foremost. Although the notion of workers' control began as an explicitly socialist demand in West Germany and the UK, by the time concrete proposals surfaced this radical tinge had been lost.[32]

In West Germany and the UK two major official reports were produced, arguing the case for industrial democracy: the Biedenkopf Report and the Bullock Report.[33] Their starting-points were the problems faced by the pluralist model—the changing economic nature of the corporation and the breakdown in the traditional model of the company. The difference from the American debate resides in a more activist conception of the state and the greater power of the trade unions.

A variety of different schemes have been proposed; some have been implemented.[34] The key points in Bullock and Biedenkopf were the proposals to give the workers a place on the Board of Directors. But both recognized that effective worker representation required more than mere board representation.[35] Although the details differ they have one point in common; *only* the workers are incorporated into the decision-making process. Biedenkopf justifies employee involvement on the grounds that the necessity for organization and direction is inherent in the company where there is a division of labour. Therefore it cannot be said that the employee decides to be subordinate to the employer's authority. This right of authority exists independently of the parties' agreement. So there are certain characteristics of a public law nature, which mean that public law principles are transferable. The missing contractual agreement needs to be replaced with other forms of co-operation.[36] As for wider interests, the majority thought it was primarily the task of the markets and the state to promote the public interest.[37] Bullock rejected the need for consumer representatives very briefly, on the grounds that their interests in the company were different, that there were serious practical difficulties, and there were other means for protecting their interests.[38]

But the distinction between the position of workers and consumers is dubious, for in some markets consumers may have no choice of firms. In addition, the industrial democracy debate was prompted by the inability of other mechanisms to protect workers' interests. The argument about rationality crises implies that the problem is not confined to workers. Finally, it is by no means clear that the practical difficulties are insuperable. Stone and Nader *et al.* have produced detailed schemes for the representation of other interests. So the industrial democracy argument does not seem coherent on its own terms.[39]

A similar point can be made against the pluralist theorists, who often ignore or under-emphasize the role of employees. For example, Nader *et al.* seem to see industrial democracy as a difficult practical problem and suggest instead an employees' Bill of

Rights.[40] If the idea is to give all affected groups a voice in any decisions which affect them, then the work-force is an obvious candidate. The Biedenkopf analysis discussed above cannot be faulted. The explanation lies perhaps in the American origins of the debate and the weak power position of the unions. However, if the position is to be made theoretically coherent it must take on board the workers' interests just as the industrial democracy argument must acknowledge other interests.

I am suggesting it is indeed possible to develop a credible definition of corporate pluralism,[41] but that both the versions of corporate governance examined so far are imperfect versions, due to particular historical contingencies. The starting-point for developing such a real definition is the argument, rehearsed above, that the large, modern corporation is a quasi-public entity which should take into account a wider group of interests than simply its shareholders. This raises difficult problems, not only of deciding which interests should be taken into account, but also of designing institutions which will allow their views to be so taken into account.

The Neo-classical School

My argument so far has assumed that the conditions of the classical model have broken down and therefore the justifications for giving companies special privileges has become problematic. This is, however, disputed in the neo-classical model—so called because of its appeal to neo-classical economic analysis and its invocation of a night-watchman state.[42]

The neo-classical school have a positive and negative case. The positive case is that corporate power is restrained by market mechanisms; the negative that trying to replace market constraints is impossible. Corporations, it is suggested, must maximize profits, otherwise they will be overtaken by more efficient competitors and will go bankrupt. This applies regardless of whether a competitive market or an oligopoly exists. It has been argued against the profit maximizers that the theory cannot deal with information costs and a changing environment. Therefore, they may be free to pursue non-profit-maximizing strategies.[43]

A more common suggestion, therefore, is that profit maximization offers the only legitimate guide to corporate action, a point made by Friedman when arguing against corporate social responsibility.[44] He argues that social responsibility simply allows a corporate manager to spend other person's money in a way they would not have wished. This means he is performing a governmental function and thus should be subject to a political process. Even granted the legitimacy of corporate social responsibility there exists an insuperable problem in identifying appropriate action. Hayek puts the point in a different context:

> If we possess all the relevant information, if we can start out from a given system of preferences and if we command complete knowledge of the available means, the problem which remains is purely one of logic . . . This, however, is emphatically not the economic problem which society faces.[45]

Because of these fundamental limits on political–administrative processes we should, say the neo-classicists, place our faith in market mechanisms. Although the product market is still seen as a constraint, more emphasis has recently been placed on two other markets: the market for corporate control and the market for managerial services.

The first of these is associated with Manne.[46] Control of a corporation is an asset existing independently of any economies of scale or monopoly profits, and there is an active market for corporate control. This is premised on a high positive correlation between corporate managerial efficiency and the price of shares. Managers will strive to be efficient in order to keep up share prices, and to prevent take-overs.

The argument about the market for managerial services was originally developed by Fama,[47] who suggested that firms should be seen in a 'set of contracts' perspective. He separated management and risk-bearing, saying each is faced with a market for services providing alternative opportunities and, in the case of management, a motivation towards profit. The managerial motivation is the market for new managers, internal monitoring of managers, and the monitoring of the company board. He then sets out the conditions in which such a market would impose a wage revision process with full *ex post* settling up and says that the extent to which a wage revision process imposes full *ex post* settling up is an empirical matter, but is at least one of the ingredients in the survival of the modern corporation. It should be added that these markets are seen as connected. This approach also has implications for other parts of company law. For example, its proponents are by no means convinced of the importance of disclosure, it often being asserted that this question must be decided on the basis of a cost-benefit analysis.[48]

It is clear that this is a modified classical model, with one major difference. The monitoring role played by shareholders is now superseded by almost entire, albeit modified, reliance on market mechanisms. The internal organization of firms need only be reformed in so far as it obstructs market mechanisms. For example, there is a strong argument that defensive tactics by managers in take-over bids should be prohibited.[49] The explanation may be the American location of the argument which allows neo-classical theorists to argue that chartering gives shareholders a chance to choose what sort of governance structure they desire.[50] By and large the major effort is expended on attempting to show that external market constraints will ensure the modern corporation's legitimacy.

Resumé

The dispute between the pluralists and the neo-classicists cannot be settled in the space of this chapter, but some indication needs to be given of the relative strength of the competing arguments.

First, a body of economic literature takes issue with the assumptions of the neo-classical economics.[51] It attempts to incorporate insights abut managerial discretion and 'satisficing' into economic theory. Perhaps the best way of viewing this material is as an attack on the foundations of neo-classical economics. The argument is 'that neo-Classicism is not so impossible but nonetheless impracticable; that, given our world, a social order must, in reproducing itself materially, endow the institutions with certain properties in conflict with the neo-Classical assumptions.'[52]

Secondly, once the goal of a corporation becomes *long-term* profit maximization, it has been argued that it then becomes very unclear whether certain corporate actions are profit-maximizing or socially responsible.[53] If this is indeed the case, then the problem of political authority reappears. Thirdly, an efficient corporation will presumably be a corporation that plans for uncertainty. Any planning process demands proper information and alternative ideas and strategies. If this is the case, then why not institutionalize the voice of those actors who are affected by the corporation's actions? Hodgson, in a very different context makes the same point:

> . . . any politico-economic strategy for the transition to socialism, and any economic plan within socialism itself, is based on inadequate information, suffers partial distortions, and embodies faults of a more or less serious nature. This ever-present potential for failure means that alternative plans and strategies must be given scope for political expression. The most suitable way of achieving this is through some form of political pluralism.[54]

Fourthly, there is a tendency to assume markets are free, spontaneous growths. However, even in the classical *laissez-faire* model, the ground rules for the market are set by the minimal state. The selection of one particular rule against another will create a different type of market. As Frug puts it: 'There is . . . not "a" market mechanism, but as many markets as there are possible rules to define them.'[55] This leads to the final point, which is the paradox at the heart of the neo-classical view. It is a mistake to see the minimal state as a weak state. In order to guarantee the conditions that will allow markets to flourish the state must be strong and active.[56]

Now that the models have been outlined, I want to use them to examine current trends surrounding companies in the UK. Before doing this, a brief look at the West German experience is necessary, partly because it indicates that the problems faced by British company law are not unique, and partly because it gives some indication of the types of answer that might arise when the question of institutional design is posed.

The German Experience

The dominant paradigm for British company law was the classical model, but it is worth emphasizing certain key characteristics, in order more sharply to draw the contrast with the West German model. First, English law takes the interests of the company as being 'Present and future members of the company . . . on the footing that it would be continued as a going concern, (balancing) a long-term view against short term interests of present members'.[57] Secondly, when questions are put to decision in a general meeting members can, in the absence of fraud, vote in their own selfish interest, owing no duty to consider the company's interests or to minority shareholders.[58] Thirdly, the business of the company is managed by the Board of Directors, who are, in a loose sense, the agents of the shareholders.

West German law offers contrasts in all three areas, though I deal only with a limited range of West German business organizations—the private limited company (GmbH) and the public limited company (AG).[59] These are legal forms that most large business organizations take in West Germany.

The most striking distinction from the British viewpoint is that AGs (and those GmbHs who adopt this structure) have a two-tier board structure composed of a board of management and a supervisory board. The management board is appointed by the supervisory board and is responsible for the conduct of the business of the company. In undertaking this the management is under a general duty of care and confidence, as well as specific obligations to disclose information to the supervisory board. The supervisory board's role is to undertake a general oversight of the business. It cannot take any steps in the actual management of the company. Members of the supervisory board are chosen by the shareholders and, if the company is subject to the co-determination laws, by the employees. Members are also under a duty of care and confidence. The object of the structure was to give the shareholders a representative institution which would look after their interests, after the state loosened its hold on the regulation of companies in the late nineteenth century. Hadden concludes that this system, with its disclosure obligations, provides a more effective means of making management accountable to the shareholders than does the British unitary board.[60]

As for the shareholders of an AG, certain matters are reserved for them by law and the company's constitution. But a shareholder, in exercising these rights, must take into account the interests of the company. There is a parallel in American law where a majority shareholder may owe, in certain circumstances, a fiduciary duty to a minority shareholder.[61] The analytical significance of such a provision lies in the way it opens up the question of the interests of the company. Under the classic British system a court, faced with a challenge to a decision by shareholders, need only decide whether there is fraud. If there is no fraud, then the majority view of the shareholders takes precedence, and there is no need to examine motivations or reasons. Under the West German and American systems the Courts cannot avoid this inquiry—they are forced to develop some concept of the interests of the company and must inquire further into shareholders' reasons.

The third point which is striking to British eyes is co-determination. There exist two systems: the works council system and the supervisory board system. A works council is obliged to be formed in all plants with more than five employees. The council has rights of co-determination, in the absence of statute and collective bargaining, on matters such as health and safety and the conduct of workers in the plant. It also has rights to be consulted over important structural changes in plants and terms of employment. Finally, where the plant has over one hundred employees, it must establish an economic committee which has the task of consulting the employer on economic matters and reporting back to the works council.[62]

The supervisory board system provides for employee representation on the boards of all enterprises employing more than 2,000 people. Although there is parity of shareholder and employee representation, the chair, who is elected by the shareholders, has been given a casting vote in the event of deadlock. This scheme exists alongside normal trade-union channels and the works council scheme.

The supervisory board system was brought into operation in 1976 amid much controversy. It apparently applies to fewer than 500 companies,[63] and information on its workings, in English, is limited. It is by no means a panacea for sweeping away management–worker conflict nor has it greatly extended the work-force's practical opportunities to participate in company decision-making. (However, it does appear to have made more information available to the work-force.) As for the effects on the aims of company policy, such as profitability or social responsibility, the conclusion of the Beidenkopf Report was that co-determination did not have a detrimental effect on company policies.[64]

Any major conclusion from this brief survey is plainly impossible. Nevertheless, in the West German case we are dealing with a model of the company very different from that in the UK. But recent British experience shows that similar developments are possible.

Current British Trends

The core notion of the classical model is majority rule, with the majority taking their own interests into account, subject only to the *ultra vires* rule and a narrow definition of fraud. Courts have no need to adjudicate on questions of commercial judgement. But these ideas now seem to be being undermined in what are, ostensibly, technical areas of 'black-letter' law.

The best starting-point is the Cork Report on insolvency law reform,[65] which, despite the title, has had implications for company law. Cork started from two assumptions: that insolvency is not a purely private matter between debtor and creditor, and that limited liability is a privilege granted by the state which may be forfeited in certain circumstances. Two of the proposed areas of reform are of special interest: wrongful trading and disqualification of directors.

On the former, the position when Cork sat was that there was solely a prohibition against fraudulent trading which encompassed both civil and criminal remedies. Cork proposed a wider prohibition on wrongful trading, which is now embodied, albeit in a modified form, in the Insolvency Act, 1986. The point of such a reform was to aim, not at fraud, but at irresponsibility. In other words, it is not sufficient for the state to police fraud; a minimum level of responsible behaviour must be ensured. The task of identifying criteria of irresponsibility is largely left to the Courts' discretion.

Disqualification of delinquent directors raises similar issues. The Government began with a scheme whereby all directors of companies undergoing compulsory liquidation would suffer automatic disqualification unless they could exculpate themselves before a court. This was bitterly opposed in all the parliamentary stages and was eventually replaced with a procedure which confines the power to apply to court for a disqualification order to the Secretary of State.[66] One of the matters which the court should take into account when the company has become insolvent is the directors' responsibility for the causes of the company becoming insolvent. Again, the state is moving beyond fraud to examine, in limited circumstances, questions of competence as part of the qualification for the privilege of limited liability.

If the reforms prompted by the Cork Report represent only a limited undermining of the classical model, the same cannot be said of the proposed abolition of the *ultra vires* rule, one of the pillars of the classical model. The Prentice Report,[67] which makes the case, argues, correctly, that the *ultra vires* rule no longer provides protection for the shareholder and creditor. Therefore it should be abolished and these interests should rely on other safeguarding devices, such as minority shareholder actions.

Even within the most technical areas of company law an echo of wider debates can be heard. In recent years, for instance, there is grudging and highly qualified recognition in the case-law and statutes that interests of creditors and employees should be taken into account as well as those of shareholders.[68] In addition, there is a tendency, when faced with disputes about whether or not certain company decisions constitute 'fraud', to seek a new approach to resolving the question by, for instance, looking for an independent body of shareholders to make a decision. This raises practical and theoretical problems, for if the shareholders' subjective view of the best interests of the company is not decisive, then other criteria are demanded. There is an argument for the view that only procedural criteria can be found. The heart of this procedural argument is that all interests must be taken into account and only the force of better argument should prevail. Again we can see a connection with the pluralist school.[69]

These developments merely undermine the classical model, they do not provide a coherent alternative to it. One might assume from rhetoric that the Thatcher Government's preferred alternative is neo-classical. But this rhetoric has accompanied another strand, which emphasizes the increase in accountability obtained by substituting private shareholders for state ownership. This latter argument is empirically dubious; we shall see that no easy identification can be made between privatized industries and 'normal' private sector companies. Intellectually the neo-classical approach probably underpins the criticisms which Sealy has recently made of English company law.[70] He complains of too much unnecessary formality and red tape and too little concentration on bringing the law into tune with commercial reality.

Certainly the concerns of Sealy seemed to be recognized in *Burdens on Business*,[71] which assumed that businesses were clogged by too much red tape which included, *inter alia*, the formalities of company law. However, by the time of the follow-up paper, *Lifting the Burden*,[72] the only progress as regards company law was the removal of the prohibition on a company purchasing its own shares introduced in 1981. Ironically, Sealy criticizes just this provision as being too complex and unintelligible to serve its purpose.[73] At the moment the emphasis is on helping small businesses and some thought is going into the question of annual accounts and returns to the Register of Companies.

But does not the privatization programme represent a revival of the neo-classical model? It is important in this case to distinguish the rhetoric from the reality of the programme. I have written about this elsewhere,[74] so will be brief. The key point is that even after privatization the Government retains links through such company law techniques as government shareholding or government directors. Now, although the present Government has maintained that it will not use these devices, such self-denying ordinances are not legally enforceable. More important for the present argument is the use that the Government has made of the 'golden share' in companies such as British Telecom and British Airways. The effect is to prevent any shareholdings of above 10 per cent to 15 per cent being built up by parties considered undesirable by directors or by the golden shareholder. When the particular limit is breached the person concerned can be divested of the shares. The effect of such a provision in the articles of the company is to replace the market for corporate control by negotiation with government, thus abolishing a key element of the neo-classical model.

Nor must we forget the other powers government will have over the privatized industries. These include the power of the contractor, and the retention of strategic powers in such areas as oil and gas imports. It is thus unrealistic to see privatized companies as pure private sector companies dependent on the market. For many of these companies the government *is* the market and no important decisions can be made without negotiation with the authorities. This was illustrated in the Westland affair where, throughout, the affairs of a purportedly private sector company were dictated by government reaction to developments.[75] Even in the last instance it is not clear that market forces in any simple sense were operating.[76]

Thus, behind the rhetoric of market forces we can see the same com-penetration of public and private sectors that is such a marked feature of the modern state. Beyond the rhetoric and reality of privatization, however, two developments are worth noting. The first is the growing interest in Employee Share Ownership Plans (ESOPs). There is no space here to look at the various arguments surrounding this innovation.[77] But there are profound implications for company law. If employees base all or most of their investment in one firm, they may well become more risk averse than capitalist entrepreneurs, and thus more likely to demand a share in the firm's decision-making process.[78] A move towards greater employee share ownership thus may significantly affect the structure of company law.

Of course mere ownership of shares or a place on the Board of Directors does not guarantee a meaningful voice without any further protections. One of the prerequisites for meaningful participation is information about decisions. The pressure here comes from Europe via the Vredeling Directive on informing and consulting workers.[79] There are said to be two core obligations:

> The employer must supply specified information to employee representatives at least once a year and must inform and consult the relevant employee representatives before taking a proposed decision which has serious consequences for the workforce.[80]

These proposals have implications well beyond labour law. The idea behind 'information and consultation' is to inject the workers' views into the management's decision-making process. It lies 'on a continuum between negotiation and co-determination',[81] and implies a broader view of what interests a company ought to take into account than is offered in the prevailing English model.

Once we look outside the traditional areas of company law in the UK ideas like this no longer seem particularly foreign. There is, for example, the obligation to consult employees contained in Section 1 of the Employment Act, 1982, as well as various instances where information has to be provided by the company to trade unions.[82]

Recent developments have therefore undermined the explanatory and descriptive power of the classical model. These same developments cannot, it seems, be encompassed by the neo-classical model. This raises the possibility of a pluralist response, as illustrated by the Labour Party's policy document *Social Ownership*. It plans, first, to extend social ownership in the industrial and financial sectors; secondly, to set up British Enterprise, a new holding company, which will establish new socially owned companies and enter into joint ventures with the private sector; thirdly, to encourage socially owned industries to enter joint ventures with the private sector; fourthly, to develop industrial democracy in socially owned industries; and, finally, to make socially owned industries more responsive to consumers.[83] It is argued that greater social ownership must be matched by extending social planning throughout the economy. As a result, when public financial assistance is given, a Labour Government would be rigorous in scrutinizing its effects, while firms supported by British Enterprise would be required to draw up business plans between management and unions.

Labour also plans changes in the structure of the fully socially owned industries, including a proposal to give employee representatives *and* consumer representatives a right to a 'significant share' of the seats on boards. This will be backed up by giving workers greater rights to information, consultation, and representation throughout the enterprise. Consumers will also be given greater rights of information, mainly through consumer committees and a new national consumer agency. Finally, it is planned to carry out social audits of the socially owned industries to provide an independent appraisal of their performance.

There is no guarantee that the Labour Party will be in any position to implement this programme. I have nevertheless spent time on it because it is, ostensibly, a comprehensive policy statement bearing directly on the concerns of this chapter. Nor is the Labour Party alone. For example, the Limehouse group within the SDP has also argued that one of the steps in transforming capitalism will be to dissolve the public–private divide. They argue for systematic promotion of industrial co-ownership, in the shape of employee share schemes, until the point has been reached where employees are represented on the Board of Directors.[84]

Recent developments in English company law suggest that the classical model is being abandoned. But if it is indeed abandoned, what is to be the replacement? One legislative response has been to require more decisions to be taken through the company in general meetings. This seems misplaced nostalgia for the classical model and would be transformed if the Courts adopted a different notion of fraud. I have argued that there are only two modern strategies for company law and lawyers to adopt. A choice between them must be made on rational grounds.

Notes

I am grateful to my colleague, Norman Lewis, for his very helpful comments on a draft of this chapter, and the editors, for their helpful suggestions.

1. K. Dyson, *The State Tradition in Western Europe* (Oxford: Martin Robertson, 1980), 32.
2. Recent notable exceptions are K. W. Wedderburn, 'The Legal Development of Corporate Responsibility: For Whom Will Corporate Managers Be Trustees?', in K. Hopt and G. Teubner (eds.), *Corporate Governance and Directors' Liabilities* (New York: Walter de Gruyter, 1985), 3–54; K. W. Wedderburn, 'Trust, Corporation and the Worker', *Osgoode Hall Law Journal*, 23 (1985); 203–52; and M. Stokes, 'Company Law and Legal Theory', in W. Twining (ed.), *Legal Theory and Common Law* (Oxford: Basil Blackwell, 1986), 155–83.
3. M. Horwitz, *The Transformation of American Law* (Cambridge, Mass.: Harvard University Press, 1977), ch. 4.
4. For these arguments see J. Habermas, *Legitimation Crisis* (London: Heinemann, 1976); J. Habermas, *Communication and the Evolution of Society* (London: Heinemann, 1979), ch. 5.
5. See G. Teubner, 'Corporate Fiduciary Duties and Their Beneficiaries', in Hopt and Teubner, *Corporate Governance and Directors' Liabilities*, pp. 149–77, and J. W. Hurst, *The Legitimacy of the Business Corporation* (Charlottesville: University Press of Virginia, 1970).
6. For the arguments see M. Hollis, *Models of Man* (Cambridge: Cambridge University Press, 1977): D. Beyleveld and R. Brownsword, *Law as a Moral Judgement* (London: Sweet and Maxwell, 1986): M. Hollis and E. Nell, *Rational Economic Man* Cambridge: Cambridge University Press, 1975).
7. e.g. R. Romano, 'Metapolitics and Corporate Law Reform', *Stanford Law Review*, 36 (1984), 923–1016, pp. 1015–16. The classic criticism is D. Kennedy, 'Cost-benefit Analysis of Entitlement Problems: A Critique', *Stanford Law Review*, 33 (1981), 387–445.
8. A note about the concepts is required. The meaning I attach to terms such as 'pluralism' will be clarified in the course of the chapter. They are not the same meanings attached by other recent writers such as Romano, 'Metapolitics and Corporate Law Reform', and Stokes, 'Company Law and Legal Theory', who use them within a different conceptual framework.
9. From certain Marxist/socialist perspectives most of this chapter would be irrelevant 'reformism'. For the arguments and a contrary view see J.

Tomlinson, *The Unequal Struggle? British Socialism and the Capitalist Enterprise* (London: Methuen, 1982). A recent example is P. Ireland *et al.* 'The Conceptual Fundations of Modern Company Law', *Journal of Law and Society*, 14 (1987), 149–65.

10. Stokes, 'Company Law and Legal Theory'.
11. Ibid. 162.
12. For the relevant cases see *Ashbury Railway Carriage* v. *Riche* (1875), LR 7 HL 653; *Trevor* v. *Whitworth* (1887), 12 AC 409; *Burland* v. *Earle* (1902), AC 83.
13. To some extent these problems can be seen surfacing in the corporate entity theory. See Stokes, 'Company Law and Legal Theory', pp. 162–5.
14. See Hurst, *The Legitimacy of the Business Corporation*, ch. 2.
15. A. Berle and G. Means, *The Modern Corporation and Private Property* (New York: Macmillan, 1932).
16. *Automatic Self-Cleansing* v. *Cuninghame* [1906], 2 Ch 34.
17. A. Berle, 'Corporate Powers as Powers in Trust', *Harvard Law Review*, 44 (1931), 1049–74; E. Dodd, 'For Whom are Corporate Managers Trustees?', *Harvard Law Review*, 45 (1932), 1145–63; A. Berle, 'For Whom Corporate Managers *Are* Trustees: A Note', *Harvard Law Review*, 45 (1932), 1365–72. For a review of the debate see J. Weiner, 'The Berle–Dodd Dialogue on the Concept of the Corporation', *Columbia Law Review*, 64 (1964), 1458–67.
18. A. Berle, *Power Without Property* (New York: Harcourt Brace, 1959), 104–10.
19. A. Berle, *The Twentieth Century Capitalist Revolution* (New York: Harcourt Brace, 1954), ch. 5; Berle, *Power Without Property*, pp. 100–3.
20. E. Mason, 'Introduction', in E. Mason (ed.), *The Corporation in Modern Society*, (Cambridge, Mass.: Harvard University Press, 1959), 1–24, p.11.
21. W. Connolly, 'The Challenge to Pluralist Theory', in W. Connolly (ed.), *The Bias of Pluralism* (New York: Atherton Press, 1969), 3–34.
22. Berle, *The Twentieth Century Capitalist Revolution*, chs. 3, 5.
23. D. Bell, *The End of Ideology* (New York: Free Press, 1960), 81; C. Kerr *et al.*, *Industrialism and Industrial Man* (London: Penguin, 1962), 283.
24. Berle, *The Twentieth Century Capitalist Revolution*, ch. 3.
25. Hurst, *The Legitimacy of the Business Corporation*, p. 107.
26. R. Nader *et al.*, *Taming the Giant Corporation* (New York: Harper and Row, 1975). For an earlier example see A. Chayes, 'The Modern Corporation and the Rule of Law', in Mason (ed.), *The Corporation in Modern Society*, 25–45, p. 41.
27. Stone, *Where the Law Ends*, chs. 6–7, 10–12.

28. Ibid., chs. 15–16.
29. Nader *et al.*, *Taming the Giant Corporation*, pp. 124–5, 136.
30. For the 'classical theories' of democracy see C. Pateman, *Participation and Democratic Theory* (Cambridge: Cambridge University Press, 1970), ch. 2.
31. See Teubner, 'Corporate Fiduciary Duties and Their Beneficiaries', pp. 151–4; H. Schwartz, 'Governmentally Appointed Directors in a Private Corporation—the Communications Satellite Act of 1962', *Harvard Law Review*, 79 (1965), 350–64; L. Solomon, 'Restructuring the Corporate Board of Directors: Fond Hope—Faint Promise?', *Michigan Law Review*, 76 (1978), 581–610; Public Accounts Committee, *Roles and Responsibilities of Nominee Directors* (London: HMSO, 1985–6; HC 33); R. Bauer and D. Fenn, *The Corporate Social Audit* (New York: Russell Sage, 1972); M. Dierkes, 'Corporate Social Reporting and Auditing: Theory and Practice', in Hopt and Teubner, *Corporate Governance and Directors' Liabilities*, pp. 354–79.
32. For background see J. Clark *et al.*, *Trade Unions, National Politics and Economic Management* (London: Anglo-German Foundation, 1980); J. Elliott, *Conflict or Co-operation?: The Growth of Industrial Democracy* (London: Kogan Page, 1977).
33. *The Biedenkopf Report Co-Determination in the Company* (Belfast: Queens University, 1976), trans. by D. O'Neill; *Report of the Committee of Inquiry on Industrial Democracy* (London: HMSO, 1977; Cmnd. 6706).
34. See D. Vagts, 'Reforming the Modern Corporation: Perspectives from the German', *Harvard Law Review*, 80 (1966), 23–89; E. Batstone and P. L. Davies, *Industrial Democracy: European Experience* (London: HMSO, 1976).
35. See P. Brannen *et al.*, *The Worker Directors* (London: Hutchinson, 1976); E. Batstone *et al.*, *Unions on the Board* (Oxford: Basil Blackwell, 1983); R. E. Pahl and J. Winkler, 'The Economic Elite', in P. Stanworth and A. Giddens (eds.), *Elites and Power in British Society* (Cambridge: Cambridge University Press, 1974), 102–22; C. Brookes, *Boards of Directors in British Industry* (London: Department of Employment, 1979).
36. *The Biedenkopf Report*, p. 72.
37. Ibid. 133.
38. *Report of the Committee of Inquiry on Industrial Democracy*, pp. 54–6.
39. A point also made by O. Kahn-Freund, 'Industrial Democracy', *Industrial Law Journal*, 6 (1977), 65–84, pp. 76–9; Teubner, 'Corporate Fiduciary Duties and Their Beneficiaries', p. 157.
40. Nader *et al.*, *Taming the Giant Corporation*, p. 183.

41. For some discussion of real definitions see Hollis, *Models of Man*, ch. 7–8; D. Beyleveld and R. Brownsword, 'Law as a Moral Judgement vs. Law as the Rules of the Powerful', *American Journal of Jurisprudence*, 28 (1983), 79–117.
42. For an overview of the arguments see R. K. Winter, *Government and the Corporation* (Washington, DC: American Enterprise Institute, 1978).
43. See Winter, *Government and the Corporation*, pp. 18, 20–1. Against are S. Winter, 'Economic "Natural Selection" and the Theory of the Firm', *Yale Economic Essays*, 4 (1964), 225–72; Hollis and Nell, *Rational Economic Man*, pp. 218–23.
44. M. Friedman, 'The Social Responsibility of Business is to Make Profits', in G. Steiner (ed.), *Issues in Business and Society* (New York: Random House, 1972), 141–7; similarly F. Hayek, *Studies in Philosophy, Politics and Economics* (London: Routledge & Kegan Paul, 1967), 304–5.
45. F. Hayek, 'The Use of Knowledge in Society', *American Economic Review*, 35 (1945), 519–30, p. 519. See also D. Engel, 'An Approach to Corporate Social Responsibility', *Stanford Law Review*, 32 (1979), 1–98, and H. G. Manne, 'The "Higher Criticism" of the Modern Corporation', *Columbia Law Review*, 62 (1962), 399–432, pp. 414–16.
46. H. G. Manne, 'Mergers and the Market for Corporate Control', *Journal of Political Economy*, 73 (1965), 110–20.
47. E. Fama, 'Agency Problems and the Theory of the Firm', *Journal of Political Economy*, 88 (1980), 288–317.
48. See Winter, *Government and the Corporation*, pp. 54–5; L. S. Sealy, 'The "Disclosure Philosophy" and Company Law Reform', *Company Lawyer*, 2 (1981), 51–6.
49. R. Gilson, 'A Structural Approach to Corporations: The Case against Defensive Tactics in Tender Offers', *Stanford Law Review*, 33 (1981), 819–41; F. Easterbrook and D. Fischel, 'The Proper Role of a Target's Management in Responding to a Tender Offer', *Harvard Law Review*, 94 (1981), 1161–204. See also J. N. Gordon and L. A. Kornhauser, 'Takeover Defense Tactics: A Comment on Two Models', *Yale Law Journal*, 96 (1986), 295–321 and the replies in the same issue.
50. See e.g. B. Baysinger and H. Butler, 'The Role of Corporate Law in the Theory of the Firm', *Journal of Law and Economics*, 28 (1985), 179–91.
51. For a review see R. Marris and D. Mueller, 'The Corporation, Competition and the Invisible Hand', *Journal of Economic Literature*, 18 (1980), 32–63.
52. Hollis and Nell, *Rational Economic Man*, p. 233.

53. G. Frug, 'The Ideology of Bureaucracy in American Law', *Harvard Law Review*, 97 (1984), 1276–388, p. 1362; Vagts, 'Reforming the Modern Corporation', p. 46.
54. G. Hodgson, *The Democratic Economy* (London: Penguin, 1984), 162.
55. Frug, 'The Ideology of Bureaucracy', p. 1365.
56. A. Gamble, 'The Free Economy and the Strong State', in R. Miliband and J. Saville (eds.), *The Socialist Register* (London: Merlin Press, 1979), 1–25. See also A. Gamble, *The Free Economy and the Strong State* (London: Macmillan, 1986).
57. L. C. B. Gower, *Modern Company Law* (London: Stevens, 1979; 4th edn.), 578.
58. *Northwest Transport* v. *Beatty* (1887), 12 AC 589.
59. For an introduction to German law in this area see N. Horn *et al.*, *German Private and Commercial Law* (Oxford: Clarendon Press, 1982), ch. 14.
60. T. Hadden, 'Employee Pariticipation—What Future for the German Model?', *Company Lawyer*, 3 (1982), 250–7, p. 256.
61. *Jones* v. *Ahmanson*, 81 Cal. Rptr. 592 (1969), *Pearlman* v. *Feldman*, 219 F 2nd 173 (1955).
62. F. Wooldridge, 'The System of Co-Determination in Western Germany and its Proposed Reform', *Anglo-American Law Review*, 5 (1976), 19–40, pp. 23–4.
63. Hadden, 'Employee Participation', p. 251.
64. *The Biedenkopf Report*, pp. 45–54.
65. Report of the Review Committee, *Insolvency Law and Practice* (London: HMSO, 1982; Cmnd. 8558), chs. 43–5.
66. Company Directors Disqualification Act, 1986, s. 7.
67. Department of Trade and Industry, *Reform of the Ultra Vires Rule* (London: Department of Trade and Industry, 1986).
68. See *Lonrho* v. *Shell* [1980] 1 WLR 627 per Lord Diplock at 634; Companies Act, 1985, s. 309, 659, 719.
69. For the case-law see *Prudential* v. *Newman* [1981], ch. 257; *Estmanco* v. *Kilner* [1982] 1 WLR 2; *Smith* v. *Croft*, *Financial Times*, 11 Feb. 1987. An interesting statutory parallel is Companies Act, 1985, s. 164(5). For the argument about procedure see Habermas, *Communication and the Evolution of Society*, ch. 5; Teubner, 'Corporate Fiduciary Duties and Their Beneficiaries'.
70. L. S. Sealy, *Company Law and Commercial Reality* (London: Sweet and Maxwell, 1984).
71. Department of Trade and Industry (London: HMSO, 1985).
72. (London: HMSO, 1985; Cmnd. 9571), 38.
73. Sealy, *Company Law and Commercial Reality*, pp. 8–10.
74. C. Graham and T. Prosser, 'Privatising Nationalised Industries: Some

Constitutional Problems and Some New Legal Techniques', *Modern Law Review*, 50 (1987), 16–51.

75. See M. Linklater and D. Leigh, *Not With Honour* (London: Sphere, 1986).
76. Ibid. ch. 13 and p. 207.
77. For a useful review of the issues see K. Bradley and A. Gelb, *Share Ownership for Employees* (London: Public Policy Centre, 1986).
78. J. Meade, *Different Forms of Share Economy* (London: Public Policy Centre, 1986), 11; see also Bradley and Gelb, *Share Ownership for Employees*, p. 82.
79. OJ No. C297 and 15/11/1980, p. 3, Bull. Supp. 3/80. See C. Docksey, 'Information and Consultation of Employees: The United Kingdom and the Vredeling Directive', *Modern Law Review*, 49 (1986), 281–313.
80. Ibid. 284–5.
81. Ibid. 289.
82. Ibid. 287.
83. Labour Party, *Social Ownership* (1986).
84. R. Gravil, 'Three Steps We Could Take Towards Utopia', *New Statesman*, 2 Jan. 1987, See also R. Gravil (ed.), *Equality and the Ownership Question* (London: Tawney Society, 1986).

PART 3

Labour Markets

9

Whither Regulation? 'Disorganized Capitalism' and the West European Labour Market

Martin Rhodes

Introduction

The pace of change in West European industrial relations has recently been described as 'Promethean'.[1] Under the combined pressures of recession, intensified international competition, rapid process and product innovation, and changes in the structure of employment, both the nature of trade unions and traditional forms of collective bargaining have been thrown into question. Since the late 1970s, trade unions in Western Europe have been undermined by a crisis of support, representation, and strategy. Membership has declined in most European countries, although it remains higher by and large than in the early 1970s; the growing complexity and segmentation of the labour market makes representation increasingly problematic; and the scope and character of collective bargaining have been altered considerably by the unwillingness of employers and governments to engage in political exchange.[2] But perhaps the most serious threat to traditional forms of union support, representation, and strategy comes from the basic shift in the balance of power between capital and labour. This shift stems from the impact of new technology which allows firms to diversify and decentralize their operations and reduce both the scope of collective bargaining and the efficacy of protective legislation. This trend has been reinforced by a climate of neo-liberalism and popular supply-side economics in which traditional forms of unionism and collective bargaining are synonymous with societal 'rigidity' and sclerosis, and where demands from employers for 'flexibility' and 'de-regulation' are justified as the only alternative to competitive decline and increasing unemployment.[3]

While Britain has witnessed probably the most virulent ideological and legislative attack on trade-union powers—as well as some of the most interesting innovations in plant-level politics—the industrial relations systems of all West European countries are now undergoing radical change. Due to the crisis of traditional unionism and the decline everywhere of worker militancy, this is for the most part a silent revolution, the steel strikes of the early 1980s, the British coal miners' strike, and the 35-hour week strikes in West Germany notwithstanding.[4] But while the trade-union movement is now on the defensive, this does not mean that it has been totally disarmed nor that the current process of de-regulation and 'flexibilization' of labour markets is a smooth or painless one. Indeed it has now become the primary terrain of political and industrial struggle.

This chapter considers the nature of this struggle in four European countries—Britain, France, West Germany, and Italy. Specifically, it aims to assess the capacity of their unions and industrial relations systems for reconciling traditional forms of labour market regulation—based on universal norms and collective agreements—with the new demands and pressures for change. The key questions are these: can flexibility be linked to what unions consider an adequate degree of social protection and collective regulation; and, most importantly for the labour movement, is 'disorganized capitalism' of the type which seems to be emerging compatible with cohesive, encompassing, industrial trade unions? If it is not, are alternative organizational forms available which would allow trade unions to resist attempts by employers to exclude them and find new ways of defending the (sometimes competing) interests of a highly segmented work-force? The answer to this question depends on the adaptability both of the unions themselves and of existing modes of regulation.

Regulatory Tradition: Relations of Power and Legal Frameworks

Jean-Daniel Reynaud has drawn a clear distinction between two sets of rules in this domain:

> on the one hand, the rules set by collective bargaining to limit the employers' and individual employees' freedom of contract and to govern work relations; and, on the other hand, the rules derived from the law,

custom or mutual acceptance which determine the rights and obligations, or rather the powers, of each party (association, recognition, means of pressure, negotiating procedures) i.e. the rules making up the system, the rules of the game.[5]

Together these rules constitute the 'regulatory frameworks' which govern industrial relations systems. But, as Reynaud also reminds us, social actors—employers, workers, and their representative organizations—are not content to maximize their gains within a given setting, but are simultaneously always trying to modify the rules of the game in their favour. Thus, regulation—or, as Reynaud refers to it, social control—and the rules and distribution of power through which it operates, are always 'stakes' of industrial and political struggle.[6]

Of course, the rules of the game, and thus the nature of social control or regulation, differ, often fundamentally, from one country to the next. These differences reflect divergent state and legal traditions, the national character of trade unions and employers' associations, and historically determined differences in the balance of industrial power. The variables involved, and the interplay between them, are therefore extremely complex. The most important differences derive from the way in which the two sets of rules—rules established by collective bargaining and rules established by law or custom—interact to create a regulatory system. As this section illustrates, key variations derive from differing degrees of 'juridification'. In the context of labour law this concept embraces all forms of state intervention which 'reduce the freedom of action of employees and employers in shaping relations at work', and lead to a 'reduction in the regulatory jurisdiction of the collective bargaining parties'.[7] It also refers to the respective importance of substantive rules and procedural rules. The former primarily concern individual labour law and protective statutes, while the latter concern collective labour law and procedural arrangements established for regulating the forms, scope, and levels of bargaining and consultation.[8] The degree of juridification will also depend on statutory protection, positive rights to organize and strike (guaranteed by legislation or by the constitution), and common law regulation (liability or non-liability in tort for trade-union action).[9] Finally, of course, regulatory systems depend on trade unions to ensure that the rules are applied. To quote Otto Kahn-Freund:

> The law has important functions in labour relations, but they are secondary if compared with the impact of the labour market . . . the law does of course provide its own sanctions, administrative, penal and civil, and their impact should not be underestimated, but in labour relations legal norms cannot often be effective unless they are backed up by social sanctions as well, that is by the countervailing power of trade unions and negotiations with the employers and ultimately, if this fails, through withholding their labour.[10]

Finally, the institutional regulation of particular labour markets, whether in determining job- and skill-related issues such as training, upgrading, labour-utilization, and other employment conditions or in setting the boundaries between different types of labour market, will depend once again on a combination of the two sets of rules mentioned above as well as on the organizational strength of both employers and employees. The rules which structure *internal* company labour markets, and which govern exit to and entry from *external* labour markets, often exert a determining influence on employers' labour market strategies. They help explain to some extent diverse reactions in different countries to recession and intensified competition.[11] This point will be discussed in greater detail below.

West Germany

Of the four countries examined in this study, West Germany has the most extensively regulated system of industrial relations. Reflecting the origins of the German 'strong state' tradition in the paternalism and authoritarianism of the Bismarckian period, West German unions have traditionally relied on the state for reform and benefits. Their conduct has been closely regulated by 'law, legalisms and a "primacy of legislation" '.[12] Organized according to legal–rational principles, this highly regulated system of industrial relations has produced a 'tense but fruitful compromise' between capital and labour,[13] creating in the post-war period a 'virtuous circle' of industrial relations peace, high productivity, and bargained rewards for work-force moderation. The state as such has rarely played a directive role, but has a pervasive presence through formal law in three major areas: legal protection of the individual employee ('substantive labour law'), the regulation of bargaining through collective, procedural, labour law, and the regulation of work issues through the Works Constitution Act, 1972, and the

Company Co-determination Act, 1976. Within this system, strikes and legal powers of lock-out have generally been used as last resorts with both parties accepting a commitment to the so-called 'peace obligation' (*Friedenspflicht*) and respecting mediation by the West German Labour Courts.[14]

Regarding union conduct and organization, national industrial unions have a legal monopoly on strike action and wage bargaining, while the officially autonomous works councils (*Betriebsräte*) are restricted to shop-floor and job-security issues, in many of which they share decision-making. Under the co-determination laws (applied in 1952 in iron and steel, but extended, in slightly modified form, to all companies of more than 2,000 employees in 1976), employee representatives (albeit with limited powers) sit in equal numbers to employers on company supervisory boards.[15] In firms of more than twenty employees, companies are required to negotiate a *sozial plan* with works councils in order to minimize job losses. In the absence of agreement, the works council can call on a commission of conciliation to *impose* a social plan. While the delays associated with such procedural regulation have placed constraints on employers' powers of dismissal, works councils have collaborated closely with employers in 'co-managing' internal labour markets, a form of collaboration favoured by the 'regulative' rather than 'counter-power' tradition of the German Labour movement and reinforced by a consensus on the need for modernization, as long as the core work-force (skilled, young, male, and German) is protected. The uneven impact of restructuring and job losses have, however, threatened the equilibrium of this system in recent years.[16]

France

Industrial relations in France differ quite radically from those of West Germany. The seventeen West German industrial unions grouped within the German Trade Union Confederation (Deutscher Gewerkschaftsbund) have been described in Weberian terms as 'professional–bureaucratic': they are unitary, centralized, highly professional organizations with a strong financial base and a high rate of membership (around 40 per cent of the work-force). By contrast, their counterparts in France can be described as 'charismatic'.[17] Highly politicized and chronically divided, French trade unions have traditionally been excluded from decision-making by hostile employers (and governments) and, with the exception of the socialist CFDT (Confédération Française Démocratique du Travail), have typically eschewed co-management as 'class collaboration'. Lacking the financial and organizational resources of the West German unions—as well as the legitimacy accorded to the latter by the majority of West German employers—French union powers of regulation have traditionally been weak.

Unlike West Germany where proposals for a codified system of labour law have recently been rejected, the voluminous French Code du Travail would suggest a high degree of substantive and procedural regulation by law. In reality, the poorly organized professional basis for industrial relations in France—exacerbated by low union membership (around the 20 per cent mark) and the corresponding lack of legitimacy for trade-union activities—has been perpetuated by a legal framework for bargaining and representation in which the application of rules has been highly dependent on the relative strength of employers and unions. In many areas, union weakness and division have encouraged unilateral decision-making on issues vital to the work-force by managements—an example *par excellence* to illustrate Kahn-Freund's dictum that 'Everywhere the effectiveness of the law depends on the unions far more than the unions depend on the effectiveness of the law.'[18] In France, the effectiveness of the unions has been undermined by the absence of strong, well-institutionalized structures of representation within the firm. Although a trade-union presence was permitted for the first time within firms following the strikes of May 1968 (through *sections syndicales*), statutory rights to representation have for the most part been restricted to larger firms: until the Socialist Government's Lois Auroux of 1982, workers representatives were legally entitled to carry out their duties in firms of ten or more workers, but union delegates, health and safety committees, and works committees (*comités d'entreprise*) were required by law only in firms of fifty workers or more.[19]

As far as bargaining is concerned, company-level bargaining along West German lines has traditionally been opposed by unions as well as by employers. Since the late 1960s, agreements have proliferated at all levels—departmental, regional, and national—covering such issues as vocational training, conditions of work, and minimum wages. However, securing the application of such agreements has often proven extremely difficult, given both the weakness of the unions and their failure to secure the valuable rights to information (on company employment plans, for example) long enjoyed by West German works councils and more recently by Italian unions as well. One area where both procedural and substantive regulation may have been more effectively applied in limiting managerial autonomy is that of dismissals. The new legislation introduced after May 1968 increased union presence in firms of more than fifty workers and extended the powers of the French Labour Inspectorate. In 1975, new procedures were required for dismissals for economic reasons involving consultation of the *comité d'entreprise* and the approval of the Inspectorate. Employers have subsequently complained that such procedural rules have been costly and time consuming and have limited the adjustment capacities of firms.[20] Reducing such constraints has since become one of the main objectives of their campaign for de-regulation.

Italy

If the West German regulatory system has been strongly supported by the twin pillars of collective bargaining and legal statute, regulation in France has been weak in both respects. Italy, by contrast, has seen a weak and fragmented labour movement transformed into a powerful force, and in the late 1960s and early 1970s, Italian unions were able to secure 'a set of labour laws among the most extensive in Western Europe and collective agreements among the most "normative" '.[21] Until that time, collective bargaining was focused largely on issues such as general wage rates at the national level. Workers representation at the level of the firm remained weak. Following the 'Hot Autumn' of strikes in 1969, the system of regulation was revolutionized. Between 1968 and 1972 union membership leapt from 27 to 52 per cent of the work-force and unity among the three major federations—the CGIL, CISL, and UIL—made organized labour a powerful new force to be reckoned with. A major achievement was the passage in 1970 of Act 300, better known as the Statuto dei lavoratori (the Workers Charter) which became applicable in firms of fifteen workers or more. Subsequently, industrial relations became highly regulated by law at the level of individual protection and rights, and well regulated also in favour of the unions by collective agreements. Trade-union influence also extended to government policy, most notably through the Italian system of wage indexation (the *scala mobile*). A system for protecting surplus workers from outright redundancy—the Cassa integrazione—and public sector investment plans were adapted to meet union demands.[22]

Some of the most impressive—and constraining—advances were made in the area of substantive rights. Henceforth, the frontier between internal and external labour markets, as well as the deployment of labour on the shop-floor were rigidly governed in the workers' favour. Management control of the pace and organization of work was heavily constrained, as was the process of recruitment and dismissal: fixed term contracts were generally prevented, limiting part-time and seasonal work to certain sectors and workers; irregular dismissals incurred heavy fines and required compulsory reinstatement; and through the system of *collocamento numerico* (numerical hiring), employers have been obliged to respect the recruitment priority lists established by local employment agencies. In certain large industrial plants, workers were able to narrow wage differentials, abolish the distinction between salaried and blue-collar staff, and, in some cases, subcontractors on industrial sites were given protection and status equal to that of employees in the hiring firm.[23]

Britain

The regulatory tradition in British industrial relations differs in many ways from those on the Continent. In contrast to the varying degrees of juridification present in the West German, French, and Italian systems, the British system has rested largely on the *abstention* of the law. In place of positive, constitutional rights to organize and strike (as exist in the other three countries) British unions enjoyed until the 1980s a set of 'immunities' from liability in common law.[24] Legal protection has traditionally concerned only those workers not covered by arrangements freely agreed to by employers and unions. Wage councils, for example, have intervened to protect particular categories of workers since, unlike in France, there is no general minimum salary fixed for all workers by the state.

An attempt to formalize this system was made in the early 1970s by the Conservative Government of Edward Heath. The Industrial Relations Act, 1971, aimed to impose in certain respects a degree of Germanic 'social control' on what was seen as a fragmented and indisciplined system of bargaining, responsible for excessive shop steward power, unofficial strikes, and uncontrollable wage drift.[25] According to the terms of the Act, a new National Industrial Relations Court would oversee a new regulatory system requiring trade-union registration, establishing a list of unfair practices, making unofficial strikes illegal, restricting the legality of the closed shop, and, as in West Germany (but unlike Italy and France), making agreements legally binding. In its attempt to strengthen central union authority over shop stewards by allowing national officials alone legitimately to call official strikes, the Act was quasi-corporatist in intent. It aimed to *incorporate* rather than *exclude* the union movement from economic life, and in this respect, at least, it was quite different from the labour legislation enacted by the Thatcher Government after 1979.[26] The 1971 Act was, however, a failure: resisted by the labour movement, and largely ignored by employers, it provided yet further evidence that law is secondary to social forces in human affairs. With the Trade Union and Labour Relations Act of 1974, and the Employment Protection Act of 1975, the Wilson Labour Government restored trade-union immunities from legal liability and further extended employment rights. But this did not mean a full return to legal abstentionism. Indeed, regardless of the new Labour Government's intention to 'de-juridify', the importance accorded to substantive labour law meant that British industrial relations were now significantly less voluntarist and independent from the state than hitherto.

Finally, it is worth noting briefly the important 'regulatory' powers of British shop stewards in shop, plant, and company bargaining and in maintaining traditional demarcations and job territories. Apart from constraining, often severely, the 'functional flexibility' of British managers (i.e. the ability to redeploy labour in line with fluctuations in demand and changing technologies) this power has tended to fragment the labour movement between national officials and work-force representatives. The strength of plant unionism has arguably weakened the national unions and this weakness has been compounded in recent years by splits between public and private sector unions and between skilled and semiskilled workers, allowing a hostile Conservative Government after 1979 to divide and rule an increasingly impotent and demoralized labour movement.[27]

The 1980s: De-Regulation, Decentralization, and the Quest for Flexibility

Already by the late 1970s, even the most powerful of Western Europe's industrial unions were in retreat, battered into submission by six years of economic crisis, and unable—even in the case of the stronger and more cohesive Italian and West German unions—to resist the assault upon the interests of their members. The plight even of the once mighty metal unions in the face of the steel crisis reveals all the strategic problems involved in counteracting job losses and new managerial initiatives. This is true not only of Britain and France where fragmentation has progressively weakened the countervailing powers enjoyed by the unions in more prosperous times, but also of West Germany and Italy where the strength and internal cohesion of the metal unions has been steadily undermined by the extent and duration of the crisis. Their plight illustrates the problems faced more generally by industrial unions and notably their incapacity in most West European countries for anything other than defensive bargaining.

Thus, even in those areas where in the past they have been able to 'co-regulate' industrial relations through collective agreements or by exploiting the provisions of the law in the interests of their members, industrial unions are being forced—if, indeed, they are even consulted—to make an increasing number of concessions to employers demands. As is to be expected from their achievements in the 1960s and 1970s, the West German and Italian labour movements have best been able to withstand the employers' offensive. This is in part because of the advantages conferred upon them by statutory regulations; but it is also because they retain greater countervailing powers than unions in Britain and France.[28]

In all West European countries, the neo-corporatist tendencies identified in the 1970s—involving a centralized and institutionalized form of bargaining and decision-making between mutually supportive social partners—either failed to bear fruit or gave way to centrifugal pressures. These stemmed from union disaffection and fears of co-optation; from the diminishing resources available for political exchange in a time of recession; and from the lack of incentives for capitalists to engage in industrial level bargaining and conflict resolution. Even the strong regulatory framework of the West German system, and the commitment of both capital and labour to the 'modernization pact' of Modell Deutschland, did not prevent the demise of sectoral neo-corporatism (as in steel) or increasing attacks on the principles of 'socially controlled welfare capitalism'.[29]

In the past the industrial union has provided one of the key pillars of support in the labour market. It is from the sectoral or meso-level of industrial relations that workers can best be mobilized for solidaristic ends, and from which vital support can be gained by national confederations. Yet the developments of the past decade suggest that it is precisely the industrial union which is most threatened by contemporary trends. Its current crisis derives primarily from declining membership (although financially, unions often remain, as in Britain, quite strong) and from an inability to provide the collective goods (purchasing power and job security) required for gaining and maintaining their membership's allegiance.[30] Increasingly, when negotiating the form of industrial adjustment, it is forced to trade one collective good for another—purchasing power in return for greater job security for example. While this may spread the burden of the crisis, it may well also alienate the highly skilled 'core' work-forces. The differential impact of the recession—which undermines solidarity and encourages competition among workers for a diminishing number of jobs—may also provoke a fragmentation of the union base.[31] Finally, organizational cohesion and solidaristic policies are threatened by new management strategies in companies and plants. These aim either to bypass traditional forms of representation altogether or to modify and complement them with alternatives such as quality circles and work-life improvement schemes.[32]

These trends have far-reaching consequences for regulation. New managerial strategies—linked to more traditional forms of work-force segmentation such as subcontracting—threaten to undermine not only the collective bargaining side of the regulatory equation—with its norms and standards applied across the board to employees—but the statutory and legal side as well. Indeed, attacks in recent years on constraints on employers' freedoms, and the spread of 'atypical' forms of employment such as short-term, part-time, and unregulated clandestine work have led some to proclaim 'a legitimation crisis in labour law'.[33] To quote E. Córdova:

> atypical employment practices point to an undermining of the foundations of labour law and of the socio-economic system within which employment regulations are drawn up . . . the expansion of atypical work which is accompanied by a lack of or curtailment in protective regulation will, in the short term, bring about unstable and precarious working conditions. In the long term, it will cause a real crisis in the development of labour legislation and social security.[34]

And if the flexibility and freedom from constraint demanded by employers are incompatible with protective legislation covering all employees, the *raison d'être* of the industrial union—which is to maintain a system of uniform agreements—is also undermined: the 'legitimation crisis of labour law' is clearly then also a crisis of traditional trade unionism.

Analysts of the industrial relations scene concur that behind these developments lie deeper, long-term trends. Depending on one's point of view, these derive from a basic contradiction between a high degree of regulation and successful economic growth and/or a fundamental shift in the structure of production and the nature of employment. Both interpretations suggest that a return to growth would do little in itself to recreate the conditions in which industrial unionism has traditionally thrived. Claus Offe suggests that the crisis of labour law and collectivism is linked to a more general crisis of the capitalist welfare state; that the norms and decisions which derive from 'juridification' in industrial relations—from state 'labour policy' and the 'industrial citizen rights it confers'—may contradict fundamentally the interests of capitalists whose investment policies ultimately ensure that there are employees to protect: 'the greater the consequent burdens of state policies—which are *no longer modifiable by contract since they are established by legal regulation*—the more will investors react hesitantly to investment opportunities in the market.'[35] As Offe goes on to suggest, an over-regulated labour market may be incompatible with the long-term protection and growth of employment: 'The safer and more institutionally protected employment is made for employees, the less attractive it will become for investors to employ still more workers. The advantages for the employed thus form risks for employment because of the rational market strategies of investors and employers.'[36]

As Spiros Simitis argues, this legitimation crisis for labour law—and by implication for industrial unions—is illustrated by the unintended results of protection against dismissal. While protecting those already in employment, such measures restrict entry by others to the internal labour market and thus inadvertently discriminate against those seeking work.[37] This involves a process of social closure which, for Offe, reveals the dual tendency for unions to practise 'external exclusion' in order to build up 'internal solidarity'.[38] Extreme examples of this are the closed shop in Britain and the exclusion with union consent of older, unskilled, and foreign workers from secure employment in West Germany. More generally, the existence of substantive individual rights and rigid procedures are put forward to explain at least in part the emergence of a dual labour market between a core of protected and a periphery of unprotected employees.

Others argue that the crisis of labour-market regulation stems from a clash between institutional forms appropriate to the age of Fordism (with its standardized mass production and consumption) and the emergence of a 'new technological paradigm'. The definining characteristics of this new era are claimed to be 'flexibility, de-regulation, dualisation and polarisation and segmention' leading in the sphere of production to 'flexible specialisation'.[39] New flexibility in a world of decentralized, high technology work, will bring with it a necessary 'deregulation of government legislation and labour stipulations . . . rendering the trade unions peripheral in many capitalist countries'.[40] For many analysts, the impact of microelectronics, robotics, and new flexible manufacturing systems signals the demise of Taylorism. If they are correct, this will have far-reaching consequences for unions. Indeed, the portents of this new era are already with us. Technological change has focused managerial concern increasingly on to the workplace where traditional shop-floor bargaining is rapidly being replaced by 'human resource management'; intermediate and low-skilled workers—the traditional union's clientele—are being shifted from 'core' to 'peripheral' status in the workforce.[41] Once again, traditional forms of labour-market regulation—with their emphasis in many countries on the protection of skills and status—would appear to be less readily applicable in a context of rapid technological change and fast-evolving skill requirements.

In their quest for flexibility, firms are responding to three major pressures for change: the need to consolidate productivity gains, market fluctuations, and uncertainty, and the increasing pace of technological development.[42] According to the model of the 'flexible' firm, developed by the British Institute for Manpower Studies, employers are seeking broadly four types of flexibility. First, firms seek *numerical flexibility*, to enhance their ability to adjust their use of manpower in line with fluctuations in output (involving greater use of part-time, temporary, short-term contract and casual workers, as well as changes in the working time patterns of existing employees). Secondly, they seek *functional flexibility*, to allow them to adjust and deploy the skills of their workers in line with changing workloads, production methods, and technology (involving the erosion of traditional skill boundaries and clashing, in the case of British industry, with traditional demarcation lines and job territories). Thirdly, *distancing strategies* may be adopted and 'involve the displacement of employment relationships by commercial ones, as employers opt, for example, to sub-contract rather than reorganise their internal manning practices'. Fourthly, *pay flexibility*, may allow 'the company's pay and reward structure to support and reinforce the various types of numerical and/or functional flexibility which are being sought'.[43] The model of the 'flexible' firm is thus characterized by 'a "core" group of employees surrounded by peripheral groups of workers who may or may not be employees. The peripheral groups, with appropriate contracts and conditions of service, provide numerical flexibility. Functional flexibility is achieved in the core, supported by appropriate incentives and rewards, possibly including enhanced employment security.'[44]

Despite the pure formality of this model, it increases our understanding of both the motives behind employers' demands for de-regulation and the response to these demands from trade unions. As the pressures for flexibility would suggest, the areas of dispute in the 'flexibility debate' are the following:

1. laws and collective agreements governing 'numerical flexibility'; determining, that is, the freedom of the firm to dismiss and recruit workers as required;
2. laws and agreements covering part-time work, which also set limits on the firm's pursuit of 'numerical flexibility' and recourse to the external labour market;

3. laws and agreements covering the length and organization of working hours, which constrain the achievement of 'functional flexibility' in the firm's core work-force;
4. and customs and agreements determining salaries and the degree of flexibility in real wage costs (an area currently under dispute in Britain where the Conservative Government wishes to abolish national pay bargaining and tie wage rates closer to local labour markets and the ability of the individual firm to pay).

The 'regulatory frameworks' discussed in the first section of this chapter have determined the general character of company employment policies since the early 1970s. Thus, in Italy, the importance of substantive rights and shop-floor control have severely restricted both numerical and functional flexibility in larger firms, leading manufacturing industry to adjust through 'distancing strategies', decentralizing production to factories of between ten and forty-nine workers which are less well unionized, and impose fewer labour costs in the form of wages, benefits, pension payments, and social insurance. The Statuto dei lavoratori is not applicable in firms with fewer than fifteen workers. Consequently, permanent employment in manufacturing has fallen by 270,000 since 1976 (despite the sector's 3.9 per cent growth in output in real terms) while the number of people in various forms of 'atypical' employment has increased by one million, the large majority of whom are women. The informal sector of the economy is estimated at around one-third of GNP.[45] France has also seen its informal sector expand as firms, after the Grenelle accords of 1968, attempted to increase their flexibility through subcontracting, temporary help services, decentralizing production, and a similar recourse to female labour. French firms have also enjoyed greater numerical flexibility through the use of part-time, short-term, and seasonal workers, and greater managerial autonomy on the shop-floor where workers' control of production has always been weak.[46] In the West German system, works councils have considerable say both with regard to recruitment and dismissals and in influencing the acquisition of, and boundaries between, skills; but managers have enjoyed much greater functional flexibility in job design and manpower deployment than have their British or Italian counterparts. Works councils have assisted in encouraging workers to believe that their interests are coterminous with those of the firm—reflecting their 'regulative' rather than 'counter-power' function.[47] However, recruitment and dismissals have often been heavily constrained both by substantive and procedural rules and by works council influence. Finally, in Britain, employers have typically been more constrained with respect to their 'functional flexibility'—shop-floor control and rigid demarcation rules have maintained the traditional craft character of the work-place—but less so by statutory constraints on dismissals, despite procedures requiring advance notification of the union concerned.

The flexibility debate in each country reflects the extent to which some employers—typically those most exposed to external competition—feel constrained by regulation. Likewise, the formulation and implementation of policies designed to enhance flexibility have been shaped by existing relations of power between capital and labour, by the cohesion and strength of national and confederal unions, by the established system of labour law, and by the political complexion of governments. Thus, in West Germany, employers have a considerable stake in the efficient functioning of the existing system and, although there clearly exists an anti-union ethos amongst certain small employers, the larger companies are unlikely to push for decentralization and labour exclusion to the same extent as their counterparts in France. The purpose of the following discussion, then, is twofold: to examine recent changes in labour market policies and to assess the capacity of trade unions for adjusting to—and influencing the shape of—the newly emerging systems of labour market regulation.

In all countries, employers have sought to increase external flexibility through relaxed regulations on dismissals and irregular forms of work contract and internal flexibility by reducing obstacles to manpower deployment in the firm. The latter may involve the erosion of traditional demarcation lines, the introduction of various types of flexi-time and new incentive and reward schemes, and the removal of restrictions on weekend and night work. In each of these areas, employers have often obtained the overt support of governments—irrespective of their political complexions. In response, certain trade unions (the communist-oriented CGT in France, the British TUC, most British sectoral unions, and the European Trade Union Congress) remain unreservedly hostile to most of the new demands, and argue that flexibility is simply a euphemism for cutting real wages and social security protection while increasing inequalities, job insecurity, and the pace of work.[48] But a growing number of unions now feel that it is far better to negotiate flexibility and accept some de-regulation than have changes imposed by intransigent employers or governments.

In this respect, while strategies for increasing flexibility can in principle be imposed or negotiated, in practice most countries have seen a combination of both whether at the micro-level of the firm, the meso-level of the industrial sector, or the macro-level of national bargaining and legislation.[49] As far as the law is concerned, flexibility can mean either outright de-regulation—suspending all existing norms and rules governing the work relationship—or less radical adjustment in the form of bargained *re*-regulation. While the former can in principle be negotiated as well as imposed, the best hopes for continued union involvement clearly lie in their securing a *bargained* process of adjustment.[50]

Britain: Re-regulation and Labour Exclusion

In Britain, the Conservative Government of Margaret Thatcher has created a political and legislative climate hostile to bargaining. At the national level, unions have been wholly excluded from influence over labour legislation. This exclusion, coupled with leadership disarray, has prevented a coherent response to a strong reassertion of employer prerogatives. Indeed, as a result of trade-union weakness (in the last ten years they have lost more than three million members) and the disciplining effects of recession, employers have never been better placed to demand greater flexibility.[51] And while functional flexibility remains constrained in many cases by a determined defence of demarcation lines (with the exception of a number of notable flexibility agreements in British firms such as Austin Rover, and more notoriously in Japanese firms like Nissan and Hitachi) greater flexibility is indicated by a massive recourse to the external labour market and by the expansion of 'atypical' work (accounting for an estimated 34 per cent of all employment in 1985).[52]

Since the late 1970s, certain pace-setting firms have centralized strategic decision-making, while decentralizing the management of industrial relations to plant and shop levels. In a growing number of cases, 'Japanization' is producing new forms of work-force participation—and acquiescence.[53] New technology deals involving *union* influence rather than quasi-independent shop stewards have been achieved by only a small number of white-collar unions,[54] and flexibility agreements—designed to remove traditional demarcations between crafts, trades, jobs, and tasks—'aim to produce a workforce able and willing to operate, maintain and service plant and equipment with optimum efficiency and productivity without the constraints of traditional work or trade-union practices'.[55] Where industrial unions have attempted to negotiate nationally on such issues—as in shipbuilding—the arrangements have been overturned at the local level. And from their origins in high-tech companies such as the Japanese Hitachi and Toshiba or the Brtish Inmos and Lucas Electrical, single-union, no-strike deals (which suspend the right to strike during negotiations and may include single-status conditions, and pendulum arbitration for dispute settlements) have recently spread into areas of mainstream manufacturing such as steel.[56] A recent and worrying trend for the unions are the new tactics of de-unionization and de-recognition. In the publishing industry, and in other industries at senior management levels, employees are now being actively seduced away from unions by individual contracts and unions sometimes excluded from influence within firms.

Nationally, the trade-union movement is bitterly divided in its response to changes which have undermined the traditional *rapport de force* between capital and labour and which have sometimes seen hard-won concessions bargained away. The TUC is equivocal in its position and sceptical of employers' claims that a less rigid labour market could allow the creation of around 600,000 jobs. Even among its most innovative sections, the labour movement is divided between those unions like the electricians (EETPU) and engineers (AEU) who accept the inevitability of 'Japanization' (including no-strike deals and pendulum arbitration as a strike-substitute mechanism); those who accept it in part (single-union, single-status) such as the General Municipal and Boiler Makers (GMBU); and those like TASS (the left-wing engineers) who accuse the former unions of complicity in the development of a dual labour market. Others, such as the TGWU (Transport and General) are attempting to counter their own membership crises by coming directly to terms with labour market trends.[57] Such strategies include recruitment drives among the once 'atypical' but now expanding part-time labour force—a potentially large pool of members traditionally ignored by the large unions. In September 1987 a debate on the issue of single-union, no-strike deals was deferred by the TUC until its 1988 conference in order to avert a serious split in the labour movement. But a violent dispute subsequently erupted between the TGWU and the AEU over the latter's single-union deal with Ford in Dundee, Scotland. This has had serious repercussions for bargaining within the motor industry as a whole and may indicate that a serious split within the TUC is unavoidable.

The employers' offensive and union disarray have been promoted by government legislation. This is the *de jure* counterpart to *de facto* de-regulation through the greater use of casual contract labour which bypasses union agreements and accepted levels of pay, benefits, and security of employment.[58] In 1979, the Government doubled the qualifying period in work for protection against dismissal—excluding more than one million workers from protection; in the Employment Act of 1980 it made protection against dismissal dependent on even longer service in firms of fewer than twenty workers; and in 1982 the Government denounced ILO Convention No. 94 in order to rescind various 'fair wages' resolutions. Also in 1982, legal immunities were repealed, trade unions were exposed to liability in tort (opening them to claims for heavy damages), the closed shop was restricted, and political funds made subject to ballot; and in 1984 the Government intervened in trade-union internal affairs to regulate leadership election procedures.[59] In 1986, the Government's White Paper on the de-regulation of employment law ('Building Business not Barriers') proposed increasing hours thresholds for entitlement to employment protection rights from 16 to 20 hours per week and to restrict further the possibilities for claiming unfair dismissal. At the same time, the British Wages Act of 1986 removed all employees between the ages of eighteen and twenty-one from cover by Wages Councils, adding a further half-million people to the growing number of unprotected workers. Part-time workers in Britain are now reported to suffer the worst pay and employment rights in the EEC.[60]

But perhaps the most important aspect of these reforms lies in the juridification and 're-regulation' of industrial relations through the new union liabilities in tort: as Clark and Wedderburn point out, 'every economic common law right "restored" is an industrial trade union right destroyed . . . [and] the only certainty about the common law in this field is its implacable hostility to the legality of trade unions and their activities'.[61]

France: Re-establishing the 'Unifying Role of Labour Law'?

The experience of France since the early 1980s makes an interesting contrast. The Socialist labour legislation introduced in 1982 (the Lois Auroux) went decidedly against the grain by attempting to *encourage* collective bargaining and *re-establish* 'the protective and unifying role of labour law'. Yet, as in other areas of Socialist reform in France such as economic and industrial policy, important policy reversals were to occur well before the election of a new right-wing government in March 1986. The most important Socialist reforms—which modified some 400 articles (approximately one-third) of the country's Code du Travail—can be summarized as follows. Collective bargaining was to be encouraged at industry level by an obligation to negotiate pay annually and job grading once every five years while company level bargaining was to be encouraged by a new obligation to negotiate pay and working time in firms with fifty employees or more. Works committees (*comités d'entreprise*) were to be given access to information concerning company strategy and manpower policies. Trade unions would now be able to organize firms with between eleven and forty-nine workers and the atypical work-force—short-term and part-time workers—were to be included in calculating the employee thresholds which trigger entitlement to employment rights, protection, and representation. New 'expression' rights introduced a new form of 'industrial democracy' (by making provision for worker consultation on new technology); and a law on workers' democracy in public sector companies gave workers reinforced rights to board-level representation. Finally, by government decree, the peripheral workforce was to be given the same rights and benefits as full-time workers; and the circumstances in which employers could recruit such labour were restricted—to counteract *de facto* de-regulation through irregular forms of employment.[62]

In principle, these reforms posed a significant challenge to managerial autonomy. In fact, where the new laws have been effectively applied, they have tended to reinforce trends already perceptible in company manpower policies in the late 1970s. As elsewhere, those years had seen the proliferation in France of new company-level social policies. Heavily influenced by American and Japanese techniques of manpower management, these were designed to integrate workers more closely into the firm while minimizing the role of trade unions.[63] In large industrial groups such as those in steel, textiles, chemicals, and electronics, there was an early experimentation with quality and productivity circles which seek to imbue workers with a 'company' ethos. Labour market flexibility was also increased by greater recourse than in the past to non-unionized casual labour, allowing such companies to avoid many of the constraints placed on dismissals by labour legislation in the late 1960s.[64] The highly politicized largest unions—the CFDT and the CGT—had meanwhile abdicated the defence of their members' short-term interests in favour of national political struggle. Initially united behind the Union of the Socialist and Communist Left in its campaign for election victory, after 1977 they fought against each other when unity gave way to internecine conflict. The end of the 1970s saw the French unions in a state of disarray which exceeded that even of their British counterparts. Split profoundly by ideological and strategic disputes, the unions also now faced a crisis of credibility in the eyes of their rank and file—and membership slumped to well below one-fifth of the total work-froce.

The decentralization of bargaining, increasing management autonomy, and the weakness of the unions provided an inauspicious context for industrial relations reform. For employers these reforms were a retrograde step. They were based on an outmoded view of the unions as the legitimate voice of the work-force while membership figures showed they no longer had a mandate; they imposed universal norms at a time when flexibility had become the foremost priority; and they increased labour costs and rigidities when, on the contrary, they should have been reduced. While certain sections of the French *patronat* set about implementing the reforms, their peak organization, the CNPF, launched a campaign for de-regulation, claiming that, once free from regulatory constraint, employers could create 470,000 new jobs (*emplois nouveaux à contraintes allégées*—ENCA) over a two-year period.[65] But this would involve lifting restrictions on employers' freedom to hire and fire; abolishing the system of thresholds whereby firms with more than ten and fifty employees incurred a range of obligations; and freeing from restriction the use of all kinds of short-term and part-time labour. Certain groups within the *patronat*, such as Entreprise et Progrès proposed an alternative: bargained de-regulation. Rather than altering the system of regulation itself, individual companies could opt out of the system through a *contrat collectif d'entreprise*. In essence, this would create a new set of rules specific to the company and tailored closely to its economic and technical needs.[66] Such contracts have been used in Belgium since 1985. The so-called 'Hansenne Experiments' exempt firms from restrictive statutory provisions in the hope of assisting employment creation. But while they have undermined the normal operation of collective bargaining, their job creating potential is dubious.[67]

Yet, the Auroux reforms had hardly revolutionized industrial relations. Indeed in several key respects they conformed to the existing trend towards in-house consultation, and may have weakened the unions further still. Far from counteracting this trend towards decentralized in-house consultation, the Lois Auroux appear to have reinforced it: the number of quality circles in operation had grown from some 500 in 1981 to 10,000 in 1984, involving more than 200,000 people.[68] Moreover, the new regulations on fixed-term and part-time contracts did not prevent recourse to other forms of *de facto* de-regulation, like subcontracting to small, unregulated firms. The company-level consultation encouraged by the law bore little resemblance to West German co-determination. While there were obligations to negotiate and provide access to information, employers were by no means compelled to conclude any form of binding agreement, nor compelled to take works committee opinions into account. As Yves Delamotte observes, 'one of the paradoxes of the new legislation is perhaps that it entangles the employer in a network of obligations without really challenging his prerogatives'.[69]

Finally, the weakness of the labour movement has meant that the potential scope of what is for the most part permissive legislation remains unspoiled. An obligation on an employer to negotiate is much less constraining when his bargaining partners are weak, divided, and lacking an incontrovertible mandate. Thus, while the new legislation was voluminous—'expressing at the most a kind of fetishism regarding legal rules'[70]—its regulatory effect was limited, provoking the political hostility of employers, while doing little in reality to bolster the bargaining power of the unions.

By 1984, the twin pressures of increasing employment and employer lobbying led to a government U-turn on regulation. De-regulation (if possible negotiated) was back at the top of the agenda. Negotiations began in March 1984 to allow a relaxation of the Lois Auroux—especially concerning dismissals and the use of casual labour—but the problems for unions inherent in bargaining away protection for their members provoked a rebellion by the activists of the major union involved—the CFDT—and the negotiations collapsed on the point of agreement.[71] In the absence of agreement, the Socialist Government began in April and May of 1985 to impose de-regulation by decree: the intention now was to promote part-time work rather than discourage it, to allow greater freedom of use for fixed-term contracts, and to lessen constraints on reducing personnel.

With the replacement of the Socialists in government by the Right in March 1986, a new phase of de-regulation began, promising to free employers from most of the restrictions on their rights to hire and fire at will. By the end of 1987, the following changes had occurred. First, procedures governing dismissals became more flexible. According to the terms of an October 1986 agreement between the CNPF and two moderate unions, the CFDT and Force Ouvrière, Labour Inspectorate approval was no longer required for dismissals of less than ten workers. In the case of ten workers or more—where authorization is still required—periods of advance notification of works committees have been reduced. Secondly, the enactment of a new law in 1987 made working hours more flexible, notably by allowing firms to 'annualize' their work schedules (increasing certain working weeks to a total of 44 hours without overtime as long as the annual weekly average of 39 hours is maintained). The 44-hour legal limit can be exceeded if negotiated at branch level. At the same time, restrictions on the use of female labour for night work were removed. Finally, the right to strike in the public sector has been amended. Henceforth, workers are to be penalized by the loss of one-thirtieth of their monthly salary for every day or part thereof spent on strike.

The British and French experiences both reveal the problems confronting trade unions in a period of high unemployment and rapid technological change. In both countries the more traditional forms of unionism are in danger of extinction. The more innovative unions in Britain are attracting support by offering new kinds of services to a wider clientele. But in doing so they risk becoming the modern-day equivalent of Friendly Societies and their loss of bargaining power is unlikely to be restored in a healthier economic climate. The collapse of the French flexibility negotiations in 1984 equally revealed the difficulties created for unions by participating in crisis management—especially when it involves concession bargaining and the exchange of recently won achievements for vague long-term goals. The more limited negotiations on flexibility issues since that date have all involved significant concessions.

West Germany: The Demise of 'Socially Controlled Welfare Capitalism'?

In contrast to Britain and France where the trade unions have been forced into submission by the employers' offensive, in West Germany the flexibility issue has become closely linked to the struggle by the engineering and printers unions (IG Metall and IG Druck) for a 35-hour week. Yet even here, the still strong West German unions have been unable to prevent either *de facto* de-regulation through the development of a dual labour market or the de-regulation of existing arrangements by government legislation.

The traditional system of joint regulation by unions and employers in the past has displayed a great deal of flexibility in the face of technological change. However, the active collaboration of the unions in the process of structural adjustment had been won with the rewards of economic growth—high wages and job security—and had depended as well on the pressure of safety valves such as a large immigrant work-force which could be dispensed with at will. With the recession, however, the countervailing powers of the unions have been weakened by rising unemployment, an increasing lack of discipline within union ranks (notably between national unions and the works councils), and by the multiplication of atypical work contracts which fall neither under union nor works council jurisdiction. The trade unions have been forced in these circumstances to retreat into their citadels of core work-force representation; and in this context, the 35-hour week campaign has been more than a struggle for a shorter working week—it has also been the means by which unions like IG Metall hope to create a new solidaristic base.[72]

Since 1983, the difficulties of the unions have been compounded by the policies of the CDU–FDP Coalition Government, and especially the attitude of its FDP wing which has traditionally been hostile to the unions. But as a number of writers have pointed out, the Christian-Liberal Coalition has not embarked on a Thatcherite strategy of trade-union exclusion: both the Government and employers alike value the regulative function performed by the unions and more especially the works councils in relations between capital and labour.[73] But there lies the rub. As in the other three countries, the pursuit of flexibility requires a decentralization of bargaining and Modell Deutschland Mark II—now oriented more towards 'market-capitalism' than 'socially controlled welfare capitalism'—seems predicated on the weakness rather than the strength, as in the past, of the country's industrial unions.[74] If works councils can be confirmed in their role as co-operative co-managers of internal labour markets, and if their links with national unions are broken down, then the ambivalence of the West German labour movement as both 'counter-power' and 'regulative' force could finally be settled in favour of the latter.

The prospects of this occurring are made more likely by recent trends, such as the abrogation by works councils of national agreements with regard, for example, to wage rates, their autonomy in the larger firms from union financial support, and more recently the greater degree of independence conferred upon them by the 38.5-hour week agreements in the engineering, printing, and furniture industries. These require flexi-time arrangements (the price paid by the unions for employer acceptance of a shorter working week) to be negotiated at the company level by the works councils themselves. IG Metall fiercely resisted this development because it feared the consequences of such decentralization for its campaign to rebuild solidarity. But it has now been forced to acknowledge its loss of control in implementing the programme of working hours reduction, and in the autumn of 1987, the Federal Labour Court upheld the validity of company agreements in this domain.

IG Metall's failure in this respect provides one more example of the problems faced by encompassing industrial unions in retaining organizational strength. Some observers detect in these trends a 'Japanization' of German industrial relations, in which the works councils become the key agents of bargaining, and industrial unions simply passive service organizations.[75] If they are correct, then it would seem that the greater strength of the West German unions, and a high degree of juridification, provide little more defence against a new form of company unionism than the far weaker legal and institutional barriers in Britain and France. Indeed, the dual structure of representation in West Germany provides the institutional basis for a variation of company-based unionism in the form of the *Betriebsräte*. However, the success of the West German unions in the 35-hour week struggle and their continued combativeness suggest that it is much too soon to predict their imminent demise.[76] Indeed, the hazards of making such predictions are also illustrated by their other recent successes. In the banking sector employers failed to win significant union concessions on flexible working time in return for a 1987 wage increase of 3.6 per cent. Employers were equally unsuccessful in their quest for greater flexibility in a new three-year agreement in the engineering sector. In this case, not only was IG Metall able to secure a steady reduction in working hours (to an average of 37 per week by April 1989) but it was also able to ensure that this would occur without loss of pay. The sector's employers, Gesamtmetall, were forced to back down on earlier demands for more flexible working rosters similar to those demanded—and achieved in 1987—by employers in France.

And yet, in exchange for a shorter working week, the unions have had to accept a greater degree of managerial autonomy within the firm over work-time organization, and have had to accept a number of other forms of de-regulation as well. The traditional strength of the 'regulatory system' has not prevented the emergence of an accentuated dualism in the labour market as employers resort increasingly to part-time and fixed-term casual labour—a form of work contract beyond the control of both unions and works councils since such workers are not considered legally part of the firm. Moreover, this *de facto* de-regulation was 're-regulated' in less constraining form by the Government's Employment Promotion Act of April 1985. This Act—unanimously opposed by the unions—relaxed those rules relating to fixed-term contracts, made more flexible provisions for part-time work, and exempted firms of five or fewer workers, from the Protection Against Dismissals Act.[77] In doing so, it followed a similar line to the April and May 1985 decrees in France.

The new measures went some way towards meeting the demands of the German employers' organization, the BDA. But employers have since campaigned for further relaxation of rules governing wages (to allow their adjustment to the conditions of local labour markets), the flexibility of working hours, and the promotion of part-time and diversified work schedules.[78] Greater freedom of action in these areas is the price employers are demanding for any more concessions on their part to union demands for movement towards a 35-hour week. As elsewhere in Western Europe, resistance to such demands for flexibility inevitably attracts the reproach that unions are defending the privileged employed at the expense of those out of work. However, a recent agreement concluded in the chemicals sector between employers and IG Chemie may indicate a solution to this type of dilemma. Under the July 1987 accord, part-time workers (who suffer from reduced protection under the 1985 Employment Promotion Act) will now be covered by collective agreement. This does not secure for them identical rights and protection to those enjoyed by full-time workers, but it does protect them against excessive variations and abuse in working hours. Given other recent successes in the struggle for reduced working hours, this suggests that the scope for bargained flexibility and joint labour market regulation remains strong in the West German system.

Italy: From 'Normative Regulation' to 'Bargained Flexibility'

The Italian unions have been no more successful than their counterparts elsewhere in preventing the emergence of a dual labour market. As in West Germany, dualism has been encouraged by a high degree of protection for the permanent work-force of the larger firms, although these workers too have increasingly been affected by job losses and closures. They may have had more success in negotiating the *form* of flexibility, but in certain sectors like steel this has meant their acceptance of a new role in 'policing the crisis' and in disciplining recalcitrant workers councils. As in West Germany, this creates a threat to internal union cohesion, although the problem in Italy is rather one of 'wildcat conflict' at the base of the labour movement than 'wildcat collusion' between workers councils and firms. The most recent example of this phenomenon has been the 1987 education dispute where rank-and-file committees (*comitati di base*) have rejected an agreement between the Government and the main unions, demanding primarily that all temporary workers immediately be given permanent jobs.[79]

The *garantissimo* established by the Workers' Charter and shop-floor strength in the 1970s already showed signs of giving way after 1975 when a phase of consolidation in union power set in. However, since 1977, the economic costs of free and largely unregulated bargaining have led unions and government to engage in a process of *scambio politico* (political exchange) whereby the former have made concessions with regard, for example, to full wage indexation, in return for government commitments to the creation of youth employment and investment in the South. In particular industrial sectors, trade unions have made concessions on previously rigid shop-floor control, in exchange for influence over company investment strategies. This process of exchange—and the unions' more recent role in policing agreements on restructuring—has allowed them to play a major role in crisis management.[80]

But since the late 1970s, Italian unions have also been on the defensive and as elsewhere have had to cope with a crisis of strategy and organization. The major turning-point seems to have been the defeat of the engineering union, the FLM, in the 1980 Fiat dispute. Before then, most managers of the large public- and private-sector companies accepted union strength as an unpalatable, but inevitable, fact of life. Since 1980, the decline of the FLM both in terms of membership and resources has been emblematic of a more general trend. And, as elsewhere in Europe, the 1980s have seen the state intervene much more directly than in the past both to liberalize legal regulation and to make the rigid norms of Italian industrial relations more flexible. But rather than a universal trend to imposed flexibility by the state, and unilateral change within firms, there is a much more complex shift in Italy from the heavily regulated system of the 1970s to a form of bargained protection and flexibility in the 1980s. In the private sector, certain large companies have attempted to exclude the unions and shop-floor delegates from exerting influence, while in others they have been closely involved in shaping changes to the work process and the adoption of new technology. This has been the case for example in public-sector steel, where extensive rights to information have allowed workers' representatives some say in companies' strategic plans. But, as elsewhere, there has been a growing tendency to divide shop-floor representation from union influence, and new forms of participation, as in Britain and France, have tried to overcome what remains of the heavily politicized unionism of the past.[81]

The principle of political exchange has meant that since the late 1970s flexibility has been a subject for negotiation at the national level alongside the key tripartite negotiations on wage bargaining and indexation. The latter have seen the unions give way progressively to the desire of both the Government and employers to modify the *scala mobile* leading first to the breakdown of union unity in 1983 and then to the imposition by decree of a modified form of wage indexation in 1984. This period also saw union concessions on the use of short-term contracts in particular sectors and the main piece of legislation governing manpower policies in the 1980s—Law 863 of 19 December 1984—made a number of key innovations: relaxing the *collocamento numerico* to allow employers to hand pick up to 50 per cent of their new recruits (although the proportion seems to be much larger in practice); allowing part-time work if covered by collective bargaining at the national and enterprise levels; and creating new forms of 'solidarity' and 'training/work' contracts which modify certain regulatory restraints on employers if they recruit young workers between the ages of fifteen and twenty-nine.[82] Critics claim that such marginal de-regulation reduces the control trade unions can exercise over the employment system, but the degree of union influence in the areas mentioned remains higher than elsewhere.

The most interesting experiments in bargained flexibility—involving a shift from substantive to procedural regulation—have occurred in the public sector. These are regarded by some as a potentially highly successful means of reconciling regulation and union involvement with the need for greater flexibility of adjustment.[83] More critical observers doubt that they are sufficient to prevent the gradual exclusion of Italian unions from decision-making. The most important example of this phenomenon is the Protocollo IRI, an agreement on 'joint mangement' of the state industrial holding IRI's development strategy signed in December 1984 and whose basic principles were extended to the other public sector holdings, ENI and EFIM, in 1986. More recently, there have been attempts to emulate these agreements in *private*-sector engineering and textiles.

In essence, these framework agreements represent a sophisticated form of bargained de-regulation. In addition to creating joint advisory committees at all levels of the groups' hierarchies, they aim to minimize the social consequences of industrial change in return for the suspension of the unions' right to strike (which is enshrined in the Italian Constitution of 1948) while formal dispute procedures are in operation. In this respect, the Protocollo resembles the no-strike agreements made in certain high-technology companies in Britain. Whether the extensive rights to information and participation provided will allow for a significant degree of genuine co-decision-making is, however, a moot point. The fact that IRI's management is required to *consult* the joint advisory committees, but not necessarily follow their advice, suggests not. Moreover, the committees established have met only infrequently and the IRI National Committee—at the summit of the hierarchy—has never been established. Equally, the committees at company, sector, and local levels have had little effect on IRI employment policies, perhaps the main area in which the unions had hoped to wield their influence. Given that the unions are still presented with management strategies as *faits accomplis*, it would seem that the most effective sanction available to the unions will remain that of reclaiming their traditional freedom to strike. Indeed, IRI has accused the unions of breaking the new rules on strikes over 200 times since the Protocollo came into effect.[84]

Conclusions

This chapter began by asking whether the labour market flexibility sought by employers was compatible with collective bargaining and traditional forms of regulation. In all four countries examined, the various forms of flexibility demanded by employers involve significant changes—achieved either by evading regulation entirely or by relaxing its constraints on recruitment, dismissals, and the deployment of labour. The basic principle of statutory protection—the applicability of universal norms—is, therefore, directly undermined, as is the basic tenet of traditional unionism that uniform agreements should be applicable across the board to all workers. Differentiation threatens union control within the regulatory system and weakens solidarity amongst rank-and-file members. In order to adapt and survive, unions need to develop a new type of national unionism compatible with a diversified structure of production and a wide variety of employment contracts, and labour law, which has traditionally been highly rigid, will equally need to be more flexible. As Tiziano Treu observes, 'the common challenge throughout Western Europe is whether or not the various instruments of collective bargaining can become instruments of non-rigid regulation, suited to a context of work not readily submitted to the discipline of generalised norms, capable of influencing decision-making before and during processes of change in technology and production'.[85]

On the face of it, however, it would seem that in those countries where industrial unions have seen their powers eroded by loss of membership and the decentralization of bargaining, the only solution is to find new ways of dealing with management at the lowest levels. This has been the response of the EETPU and the AUEW (now the AEU) in Britain, and in France it would seem that the unions have little choice but to accept the primacy of localized bargaining in conditions set by management. But therein lies the dilemma confronting the unions. Current developments require that they focus their attention more than ever on the lower levels of economic organization—the company and the plant. Yet it is at this level that their independent influence is most fiercely resisted by a growing number of employers whose aim is either to exclude, marginalize, or co-opt their representatives. The danger is that in complying with decentralization and new managerial practices, the unions may well lose their collectivist *raison d'être*. Furthermore, a flexible form of labour law would also need to conform with these trends towards greater decentralization and work-force segmentation, possibly by developing more individualized forms of work contract, although it is hard to see how this could actually operate successfully for more than a small proportion (the élite core) of the labour force. In Britain, for example, this seems to be occurring most frequently at management levels.

But while the future remains unclear, the analysis of current trends in labour market regulation leads one to consider a number of more abstract questions. First, it is likely that the present tendency for *ad hoc* modifications to labour law will entail *more* rather than *less* regulation, leading, as Jean-Claude Javillier points out, to the creation of new norms and the danger of juridical disorder.[86] In this respect, the question remains as to whether the state can intervene to 'de-regulate' and 'de-juridify' in this domain when it is manifestly clear that in their efforts to remove the barriers to market flexibility, the governments of all four countries have *increasingly* intervened in one form or another. In Britain, for example, it is clear that 're-regulating' industrial relations by making unions liable in tort reinforces the labour market freedoms awarded to employers by the removal of certain sections of the work-force from statutory protection. While in the past the law has been used to promote joint regulation, it is now used closely to regulate union conduct and affairs. It also seems clear that, rather than 'less state', de-regulation in the labour market will simply mean a *different form* of state intervention, primarily in assuming the social costs entailed in the expansion of flexible and dual labour markets: the provision of unemployment benefit, state-funded pensions for early retirees, and other forms of welfare support.

Secondly, there may well be a threshold beyond which decentralization, de-regulation, and the weakening of industrial unions becomes counterproductive for employers and governments. In all four countries in this study, unions still play an important regulatory role—albeit to differing degrees—in administering the labour market both within and outside the firm. In their absence, employers could well encounter a new set of rigidities and face increasing costs, not to mention a potential resurgence of undisciplined, localized militancy. This leads us to a final, and more speculative point. De-regulation and decentralization may well *increase* economic costs if they also break down existing structures for the regulation of inflation and employment. As is shown by recent research, those countries scoring worst on the so-called 'misery index' (the sum of the rate of growth of inflation plus the rate of unemployment) have typically been those where, as in Britain, France, and Italy, the degree of neo-corporatism (centralized bargaining, duration of labour contracts, and the regulation of conflict) has been lowest.[87] Current trends in those countries with a low degree of neo-corporatism may simply compound their longer-term macroeconomic problems in the absence of strong social and political control. In countries like West Germany where, on the contrary, neo-corporatism has been strong, the optimum strategy would seem to require a judicious blend of macroeconomic regulation with bargained de-regulation and flexibility at the lower levels of the economy.

Notes

1. A. J. Hingel, 'A Promethean Change of Industrial Relations: A Comparative Study of Western European Unions and Technological Developments', in M. Warner (ed.), *Micro-processors, Manpower and Society: A Comparative, Cross-national Approach* (New York: St Martins Press, 1984), 255–72.
2. For an overview of these developments, see e.g. J. Visser, 'Crisi nella crisi? Le risposte dei sindacati al declino dell' occupazione. 1973–1983', in Quaderni della fondazione G. Brodolini, *Le politiche del lavoro in Europa agli inizi degli anni ottanta* (Milan: Marsilio Editore, 1986), 53–97.
3. See J. J. Oechslin, 'Employment and Flexibility: The Employers Point of View', *Social and Labour Bulletin*, 2 (1985), 176–9. Intellectual support for such demands is provided, for example, by F. A. Hayek, *1980s Unemployment and the Unions: The Distortion of Relative Prices by Monopoly in the Labour Market* (London: The Institute of Economic Affairs, 1980).
4. See M. Rhodes, 'Organised Interests and Industrial Crisis Management: Restructuring the Steel Industry in West Germany, Italy and France', in A. Cawson (ed.), *Organised Interests and the State: Studies in Meso-Corporatism* (London: Sage, 1985), 192–220.
5. J.-D. Reynaud, 'Industrial Relations and Political Systems: Some Reflections on the Crisis in Industrial Relations in Western Europe', *British Journal of Industrial Relations*, 28(1) (Mar. 1980), 8.
6. Ibid. 8.
7. S. Simitis, 'Zur Verrechtlichung der Arbeitsbeziehungen', in Zacher, Simitis, Kübler, Hopt, and Teubner, *Verrechtlichung von Wirtschaft. Arbeit und Sozialer Solidariatät—Vergleichende Analysen* (Baden-Baden: Nomos) 154–5, cited in J. Clark, 'The Juridification of Industrial Relations: A Review Article', *Industrial Law Journal*, 14(2) (June 1985), 71.
8. Clark, 'The Juridification of Industrial Relations', pp. 73–5.
9. Ibid. 85–7.
10. O. Kahn-Freund, *Labour and the Law* (London: Stevens, 1977) 8–9, cited in Lord Wedderburn, R. Lewis, and J. Clark (eds.), *Labour Law and Industrial Relations: Building on Kahn-Freund* (Oxford: Clarendon Press, 1985), 217.
11. The institutional rules and group pressures shaping labour markets are the subject of D. Marsden's *The End of Economic Man? Custom and Competition in Labour Markets* (Brighton: Wheatsheaf, 1986).
12. A. S. Markovits, 'The Legacy of Liberalism and Collectivism in the Labour Movement: A Tense but Fruitful Compromise for Model

Germany', in A. S. Markovits, *The Political Economy of West Germany: Modell Deutschland* (New York: Praeger, 1982), 145.

13. Ibid. 150.
14. Ibid. 151–80, and T. Kirkwood and H. Mewes, 'The Limits of Trade Union Power in the Capitalist Order: The Case of West German Labour's Quest for Co-Determination', *British Journal of Industrial Relations*, 14(3) (Nov. 1976), 295–315. On the importance of law and the labour courts see U. Mueckenberger, 'Labour Law and Industrial Relations', in O. Jacobi, B. Jessop, H. Kastendiek, and M. Regini, *Economic Crisis, Trade Unions and the State* (London: Croom Helm, 1986), 236–57, and E. Blankenburg and R. Rogowski, *West German Labor Courts and the British Tribunal System: A Socio-Legal Comparison*, Working Paper 1984–10 (University of Wisconsin–Madison Law School, 1984).
15. On co-determination, see P. Schwerdtner, 'Trade Unions in the German Economic and Social Order', *Zeitschrift für die Gesamte Staatswissenschaft*, 135 (1979), 454–73, and A. L. Thimm, *The False Promise of Codetermination* (Lexington: D. C. Heath, 1980).
16. On the consequences of economic recession for this system, see W. Streeck, 'Neo-Corporatist Industrial Relations and the Economic Crisis in West Germany', in J. H. Goldthorpe, *Order and Conflict in Contemporary Capitalism* (Oxford: Clarendon Press, 1984), 291–314.
17. See M. Maurice and F. Sellier, 'Societal Analysis of Industrial Relations: A Comparison Between France and West Germany', *British Journal of Industrial Relations*, 17(3) (Nov. 1979), 322–36. For recent overviews of the French labour movement and industrial relations, see J.-D. Reynaud, *Les Syndicats, les patrons et l'état: tendances de la négociation collective en France* (Paris: Les Editions ouvrières, 1978); R. Mouriaux, *Les Syndicats dans la société Française* (Paris: Presses de la FNSP 1983), and G. Adam, *Le Pouvoir syndical* (Paris: Dunod, 1983). On collective bargaining and representation, see G. Adam, 'La Négociation collective en France: éléments de diagnostic', *Droit social* (Dec. 1978), 420–51.
18. Kahn-Freund, *Labour and the Law*, p. 10.
19. See e.g. Adam 'La Négociation collective en France'.
20. See J.-P. Duprilot, 'Le Contrôle administratif des licenciements', *Droit social*, 6 (June 1975), 53–72, and, for a comparative study, M. J. Piore, 'Economic Fluctuation, Job Security and Labour-Market Duality in Italy, France and the United States', *Politics and Society*, 9(4) (1980), 379–407.
21. T. Treu, 'I cinque cerchi della flessibilità', *Politica ed economia*, 3 (Mar. 1987).
22. The CGIL (Confederazione Generale Italiana dei Lavoratori) is close to the Communist Party, the CSIL (Confederazione Italiana Sindicati

Lavoratori) is close to Christian Democratic circles and the UIL (Unione Italiana dei Lavoratori) reflects minority centre and socialist views. For general analyses of Italian industrial relations in English, see P. M. Brandini, 'Italy: Creating a New Industrial Relations System From the Bottom', in S. Barkin (ed.), *Worker Militancy and its Consequences, 1965–1975* (New York: Praeger, 1975), 82–117; P. Lange, G. Ross, and M. Vannicelli, *Unions, Change and Crisis: French and Italian Union Strategy and the Political Economy, 1945–1980* (London: George Allen & Unwin, 1982); and most recently, J. Barkan, *Visions of Emancipation: The Italian Workers Movement since 1945* (New York: Praeger, 1984).

23. See Piore, 'Economic Fluctuation, Job Security and Labour-Market Duality', pp. 384–90, and E. Wolleb, 'D'une institutionalisation tardive au contournement: l'Italie', in R. Boyer (ed.), *La Flexibilité du travail en Europe* (Paris: Editions la découverte, 1986), 153–80.
24. J. Clark and Lord Wedderburn, 'Modern Labour Law: Problems, Functions and Policies', in Wedderburn, Lewis, and Clark (eds.), *Labour Law and Industrial Relations*, pp. 140–1.
25. See D. Soskice, 'Industrial Relations and the British Economy, 1979–1983', *Industrial Relations*, 23(3) (Fall 1984), 309 ff.
26. On the 1971 Industrial Relations Act, see Soskice 'Industrial Relations and the British Economy', and M. Moran, *The Politics of Industrial Relations: The Origins, Life and Death of the 1971 Industrial Relations Act* (London: Macmillan, 1977).
27. Clark and Wedderburn, 'Modern Labour Law: Problems, Functions and Policies' pp. 190–1, and on the power of British shop steward organization, see F. Leijnse, 'Workplace Bargaining and Trade Union Power', *Industrial Relations Journal*, 11(2) (1980), 58–69, and E. Batstone, *Working Order: Workplace Industrial Relations Over Two Decades* (Oxford: Basil Blackwell, 1984).
28. See Rhodes, 'Organised Interests and Industrial Crisis Management', for an analysis of the West German, French, and Italian metal unions.
29. On the general decline of centralized bargaining in Western Europe, see T. Treu, 'Centralizazzione e decentramento nella contrattazione collettiva: riflessioni comparate', in *Giornale di diritto del lavoro e di relazioni industriali*, 27 (1985), 495–527. On West Germany, see Streeck, 'Neo-Corporatist Industrial Relations', and W. Sengenberger 'West German Employment Policy: Restoring Worker Competition', *Industrial Relations*, 23(3) (Fall 1984), 323–43.
30. Rhodes, 'Organised Interests and Industrial Crisis Management', 218–19, and C. Crouch, 'The Future Prospects for Trade Unions in Western Europe', *The Political Quarterly*, 37(1) (Jan.–Mar. 1986), 5–17.
31. Streeck, 'Neo-Corporatist Industrial Relations', pp. 307–8.

32. Rhodes, 'Organised Interests and Industrial Crisis Management', pp. 217–20.
33. Simitis, 'Zur Verrechtlichung der Arbeitsbeziehungen', p. 131, cited in Clark, 'The Juridification of Industrial Relations', p. 77.
34. E. Córdova, 'Atypical Employment Patterns: Significance and Repercussions', *Social and Labour Bulletin*, 1 (1986), 19.
35. See C. Offe, 'The Future of the Labour Market', in his *Disorganised Capitalism* (Cambridge: Polity Press, 1985), 71 (my emphasis).
36. Ibid.
37. Simitis, 'Zur Verrechtlichung der Arbeitsbeziehungen', pp. 113–20, summarized by Clark, 'The Juridification of Industrial Relations', pp. 77–8. On the concept of social closure, see F. Parkin, *Marxism and Class Theory: A Bourgeois Critique* (London: Tavistock Publications, 1979).
38. C. Offe, 'The Political Economy of the Labour Market' in his *Disorganised Capitalism*, 33–4.
39. On the emergence of 'flexible specialization' see the theses of C. F. Sabel, *Work and Politics: The Division of Labour in Industry* (Cambridge: Cambridge University Press, 1982), and M. J. Piore and C. F. Sabel, *The Second Industrial Divide: Possibilities for Prosperity* (New York: Basic Books, 1984).
40. A. J. M. Roobeck, 'The Crisis in Fordism and the Rise of a New Technological Paradigm', *Futures*, 19(2) (Apr. 1987), 129–54. The literature on 'Fordism' has been developed largely by French and West German economists such as M. Aglietta, *Regulation et crise du capitalisme* (Paris: Calmann-Levy, 1976), R. Boyer and J. Mistral, *Accumulation, inflation, crises* (Paris: PUF, 1983), A. Lipietz, 'Towards Global Fordism: Marx or Rostow?', *New Left Review*, 132 (Mar.–Apr. 1982), and J. Hirsch, 'Fordismus und Postfordismus: Die gegenwärtige gesellschaftliche Krise und ihre Folgen', *Politische Vierteljahresschrift*, 26(2) (1985), 160–82. Also see Sabel, *Work and Politics*, esp. ch. 5, and the collection edited by R. Boyer, *La Flexibilité du travail en Europe* (Paris: Éditions la decouverte, 1986).
41. See B. Gustavsen, 'Evolving Patterns of Enterprise Organisation: The Move Towards Greater Flexibility', *International Labour Review*, 125(4) (July–Aug. 1986), 367–82, and K. H. Ebel, 'The Social and Labour Implications of Flexible Manufacturing Systems', *International Labour Review*, 124(2) (Mar.-Apr. 1985), 133–45. On the applicability of traditional forms of labour law, R. Blanpain, 'Structural Adjustment and Industrial Relations: Labour Law Aspects', *Labour and Society*, 10(2) (May 1985), 175–93.
42. See NEDO, *Changing Working Patterns: How Companies Achieve Flexibility to Meet New Needs* (London: National Economic Development Office, 1986), 2–13.

43. The original model was developed by J. S. Atkinson, *Flexibility, Uncertainty and Manpower Management*, IMS Report No. 89 (Brighton: Institute of Manpower Studies, 1984). This summary is derived from NEDO, *Changing Working Patterns*, pp. 2–13.
44. NEDO, *Changing Working Patterns*, pp. 4–5.
45. Wolleb, 'D'une institutionalisation tardive au contournement', and M. Salvati, *Il sistema economico italiano* (Bologna: Mulino, 1975).
46. Piore, 'Economic Fluctuation, Job Security and Labour-Market Duality', pp. 391–8.
47. H. Müller-Vogg, 'Federal Republic', in B. C. Roberts (ed.), *Industrial Relations in Europe* (London: Croom Helm, 1985), 78–82.
48. See J. Evans, 'Flexibility and Jobs: ETUC Looks at Myths and Realities', *Social and Labour Bulletin*, 3–4 (1985), 70–4, for a summary of this argument.
49. For an overview of the various flexibility strategies adopted in the 1980s, see P. Perulli, 'Le relazioni industriali e i due fronte della flessibilità', *Giornale di diritto e di relazioni industriali*, 29 (1986), 85–105.
50. On the distinction between negotiated and imposed flexibility, see J.-C. Javillier, 'Ordre juridique, relations professionnelles et flexibilité. Approches comparatives et internationales', *Droit social*, 1 (Jan. 1986), 56–65.
51. On the general impact of the recession on British industrial relations, see D. Bright, D. Sawbridge, and B. Rees, 'Industrial Relations of Recession', *Industrial Relations Journal*, 14(3) (1983), 24–33, and W. Brown and K. Sisson, 'Industrial Relations in the Next Decade: Current Trends and Future Possibilities', *Industrial Relations Journal*, 14(1) (1983), 9–21.
52. According to the Department of Employment, the UK part-time labour force expanded by 16% between 1981 and 1985, accounting for a total of 8.1m. or 34% of those in work by 1985. *Financial Times*, 5 Feb. 1987.
53. For general analyses of trends in collective bargaining, see J. Purcell, 'The Management of Industrial Relations in the Modern Corporation: Agenda for Research', *British Journal of Industrial Relations*, 21(1) (1983), 1–16, and N. J. Kinnie, 'Changing Management Strategies in Industrial Relations', *Industrial Relations Journal*, 16(4) (1985), 17–24. On 'Japanization', see P. J. Turnbull, 'The "Japanisation" of Production and Industrial Relations at Lucas Electrical', *Industrial Relations Journal*, 17(3) (Autumn 1986), 193–206, and K. Bradley and S. Hill, ' "After Japan": The Quality Circle Transplant and Productive Efficiency', *British Journal of Industrial Relations*, 21(3) (1983), 291–311.
54. See R. Williams and F. Steward, 'Technology Agreements in Great

Britain: A Survey 1977–1983', *Industrial Relations Journal*, 16(3) (1985), 58–73.

55. 'Flexibility Agreements—the End of Who Does What?', *Industrial Relations—Review and Report*, 316 (20 Mar. 1984), 2.
56. On the so-called 'new realism' in British industrial relations see P. Bassett, *Strike Free: New Industrial Relations in Britain* (London: Macmillan, 1986). On the spread of 'new realism' from high-tech to mainstream manufacturing, see 'Single Status, "No-Strike" Deals Spread into Steel?', *Industrial Relations—Review and Report*, 368 (20 May 1986), 8–11.
57. Bassett, *Strike Free*, and on inter-union conflict see the articles by P. Bassett, C. Leadbetter *et al.* in the Labour Section of the *Financial Times*.
58. See G. Standing, 'Meshing Labour Flexibility with Security: An Answer to British Unemployment', *International Labour Review*, 125(1) (Jan.–Feb. 1986), 87–106.
59. For an overview of these developments, see Lord Wedderburn, 'The New Industrial Relations Laws in Great Britain', *Labour and Society*, 10(1) (Jan. 1985), 45–61, and B. C. Roberts, 'Recent Trends in Collective Bargaining in the United Kingdom', *International Labour Review*, 123(3) (May–June 1984), 287–306.
60. See Low Pay Unit, *Part-timers Under Pressure*, London, 1987, *IDS Focus*, 42 (Dec. 1986), 5–11, and S. Keevash, 'Wages Councils: An Examination of Trade Union and Conservative Government Misconceptions about the Effect of Statutory Wage Fixing', *Industrial Law Journal*, 14(4) (Dec. 1985), 217–32.
61. Clark and Wedderburn, 'Modern Labour Law', p. 141.
62. For an overview of these reforms and their implementation, see M. Rhodes, 'Labour and Industry: The Demise of Traditional Unionism?', in M. Newman and S. Mazey, *Mitterand's France* (London: Croom Helm, 1987), 56–80. It should be noted that originally the Socialists proposed to make strikers and unions immune from legal liability, as has traditionally been the case in the UK. However, this was withdrawn when opposed by the French Constitutional Court (the Conseil constitutionnel) on the grounds that it conflicted with one of the fundamental norms of administrative and constitutional law in France—the principle of *égalité*. See M. Forde, 'Bill of Rights and Trade Union Immunities: Some French Lessons', *Industrial Law Journal*, 13(1) (Mar. 1984), 40–9.
63. See J. Freyssinet, 'La Déstabilisation des formes d'emploi: stratégies patronales et stratégies syndicales', *Critique de l'économie politique*, 23/24 (Apr.–Sept. 1983), 111–24, and P. Morville, *Les Nouvelles Politiques sociales du patronat* (Paris: Editions la découverte, 1985).

64. On the strategies of these large companies, see J. Freyssinet *Politique d'emploi des grands groupes français* (Grenoble: PUG, 1982).
65. For the best account of this campaign, see H. Weber, *Le Partie des patrons: le CNPF (1945–1986)*, (Paris: Editions du seuil, 1986), 344–82.
66. Ibid. 387–90, and J.-C. Guibal, 'Point de vue: plaidoyer pour un "contrat collectif d'enterprise" ', *Droit social*, 7–8 (July–Aug. 1986), 602–4.
67. On the Belgian 'Hansenne Experiments', see F. Vandamme and J.-F. Tempels, 'Greater Flexibility in Worktime Arrangements—the Hansenne Experiments', *Social and Labour Bulletin*, 2 (1986), 189–93, and 'Belgium: Further Results of Working Time Experiments', *European Industrial Relations Review*, 149 (June 1986), 15–18.
68. See *European Industrial Relations Review*, 126 (July 1984), and 128 (Sept. 1984).
69. Y. Delamotte, 'Recent Trends in the Statutory Regulation of Industrial Relations in France', *Labour and Society*, 10(1) (Jan. 1985), 23.
70. Ibid. 25, and P. Petit, 'Heurs et malheurs de l'état face au rapport salarial: la France', in R. Boyer (ed.), *La Flexibilité du travail en Europe*, pp. 55 ff.
71. For an analysis of the flexibility negotiations, see R. Soubie, 'Après le négociations sur la flexibilité', *Droit social*, 2 (Feb. 1985), 3 (Mar. 1985), and 4 (Apr. 1985).
72. Streeck, 'Neo-Corporatist Industrial Relations', and F. Furstenberg, 'The Regulation of Working Time in the Federal Republic of Germany', *Labour and Society*, 10(2) (May 1985), 133–50.
73. See J. Esser, 'State, Business and Trade Unions in West Germany after the "Political Wende" ', *West European Politics*, 9(2) (Apr. 1986), 198–214, and D. Webber, 'Eine Wende in der Deutschen Arbeitsmarktpolitik? Sozialliberale und christlich-liberale Antworten auf die beschäftigungskrise', mimeo (University of Sussex, 1986).
74. Sengenberger, 'West German Employment Policy', and G. Leithauser, 'Des flexibilités . . . et pourtant une crise: la République Fédérale d'Allemagne', in R. Boyer (ed.), *La Flexibilité du travail en Europe*, pp. 181–205.
75. Streeck, 'Neo-Corporatist Industrial Relations', and Esser, 'State, Business and Trade Unions in West Germany', pp. 211–14.
76. On the 35-hour week struggle, see M. Weiss 'Tendances récentes des négociations collectives en République Fédérale d'Allemagne', *Droit social*, 11 (Nov. 1985), 757–62, and G. Bosch, 'The Dispute over the Reduction of the Working Week in West Germany', *Cambridge Journal of Economics*, 10(3) (Sept. 1986), 271–87. On recent successes of unions in banking and engineering, see *European*

Industrial Relations Review, 161 (June 1987), 10–11, and 162 (July 1987), 4.

77. On the growing recourse in West Germany to casual contract labour, see R. Dombois and M. Osterland, 'Neue Formen des Flexiblen Arbeits Krafteeinsatzes: Teilzeitarbeit und Leiharbeit', *Soziale Welt*, 3–4 (1982), 466–81. On the 1985 Employment Promotion Act and other flexibility measures see Webber, 'Eine Wende in der Deutschen Arbeitsmarktpolitik?', 12–14, 19–20, and W. Daubler and M. Le Friant, 'Un récent exemple de flexibilisation legislative: la loi allemande pour la promotion de l'emploi du 26 avril 1985', *Droit social*, 9–10 (Sept.–Oct. 1986), 715–20. In a survey of the impact of the 1985 Act, the commerce, banking, and insurance union, HBV, claims that it has contributed to the growth in atypical casual contracts and left the decline in the creation of full-time jobs unchanged. See *European Industrial Relations Review*, 150 (July 1986), 4.
78. See Bundesvereinigung der Deutschen Arbeitgeberverbande (BDA), *Zwanzig-Punkte-Programme: Für mehr Beschäftigung*, Cologne, 1985.
79. Rhodes, 'Organised Interests and Industrial Crisis Management', pp. 209–16, and on the Italian education dispute, *European Industrial Relations Review*, 162 (July 1987), 6.
80. See Wolleb, 'D'une institutionalisation tardive au contournement', and U. Runggaldier, 'Tendances actuelles du droit du travail italien', *Droit social*, 12 (Dec. 1985), 856–62.
81. For a useful account of these changes in English, see F. Butera, 'Italy', in B. C. Roberts (ed.), *Industrial Relations in Europe* (London: Croom Helm, 1985), 137–58. On the implications for labour law and collective bargaining, see G. Ghezzi, 'L'assetto giuridico delle relazioni industriali. Dallo statuto dei lavoratori all'accordo scotti del 22 Gennaio 1983', in *Problemi del socialismo*, 27–8 (May–Dec. 1983), 113–32, and G. Trioni, 'Il sistema del diritto sindacale dalla rappresentanza alla rappresentività', *Giornale di diritto del lavoro e di relazioni industriali*, 27 (1985) 529–600.
82. T. Treu, 'Recent Developments of Italian Labour Law', *Labour and Society*, 10(1) (Jan. 1985), 27–43, and *European Industrial Relations Review*, 151 (Aug. 1986), 13–14. On the measures to de-regulate the labour market, see M. Tortorella, 'Aprite le gabbie del collocamento', *Mondo economico* (28 Apr. 1986), 20–3, and on the evolution of national bargaining, M. Regini, 'Relazioni industriali e sistema politico: l'evoluzione recente e le prospettive degli anni ottanta', in G. Ferrante (ed.), *Il futuro del sindacato* (Rome: Ediesse, 1986), 139–63.
83. See Treu, 'I cinque cerchi della flessibilità', and E. Reyneri, 'Le politiche del lavoro in Italia: verso la deregolazione strisciante o una nuova regolazione flessibile e contrattata?', in Quaderni della fonda-

zione G. Brodolini, *Le politiche del lavoro in Europa agli inizi degli anni ottanta*, 163–85.

84. For details of public sector agreements and the Protocollo IRI, see *Social and Labour Bulletin*, 3–4 (1984), and 2 (1985). On the agreements in ENI and EFIM and the Protocollo IRI in practice, see *European Industrial Relations Review*, 154 (Nov. 1986), 5–6, and 164 (Sept. 1987) 15–17.
85. Treu, 'Centralizzazione e decentramento nella contrattazione collettiva', p. 527.
86. Javillier, 'Ordre juridique, relations professionnelles et flexibilité', p. 65.
87. On this wider issue and debate, see E. Tarantelli, 'The Regulation of Inflation and Unemployment', *Industrial Relations*, 25(1) (Winter 1986), 1–15.

PART 4
Conclusions

10

Organizing Regulatory Space

Leigh Hancher and Michael Moran

Introduction

Regulation is virtually a defining feature of any system of social organization, for we recognize the existence of a social order by the presence of rules, and by the attempt to enforce those rules. Whether the matter concerns the control of sexual morality, the flow of traffic, the licensing of drugs, or the imposition of taxation, the core of the activity remains constant: it involves the design of general rules, the creation of institutions responsible for their implementation, the clarification of the exact meaning of a general rule in particular circumstances, and the enforcement of the rule in those circumstances. As a large and rich literature testifies,[1] there is much to be gained from exploring these common features of regulation, and from comparing the experience of rule-making and implementation in different settings.

Within the broad field of regulation, however, a special place is occupied by the processes which are the subject of the preceding chapters: the regulation of economic activity in Western capitalist societies, where organization on market principles is combined with a high level of industrial development. Economic regulation under advanced capitalism has several distinctive features, and these features in turn shape the character of regulatory activity. The purpose of this concluding chapter is to bring together those features identified elsewhere in this book, and to sketch out their more important implications for the connections between capitalism, culture, and regulation.

We begin by identifying the most distinctive features of economic regulation; go on to suggest that regulation is best understood through the analytical device of 'regulatory space'; and then sketch how national political and legal settings, historical timing, organizational structure, the character of markets, and the nature of issue arenas all influence the shape of regulatory space and the allocation of power within that space.

Regulation and Economic Regulation

The most striking single feature of economic regulation to emerge from the preceding chapters is that it is dominated by relations between large, sophisticated, and administratively complex organizations performing wide-ranging economic and social tasks. Such bodies obviously include the various agencies of the state—government departments, quangos, and specialized regulatory bodies—but they also encompass organized interest groups, trade unions, and firms. The importance of the large firm in the regulatory process is particularly notable. Indeed an important theme of the contributions to this volume is the central place of the large, often multinationally organized, enterprise as a locus of power, a reservoir of expertise, a bearer of economic change, and an agent of enforcement in the implementation process. Understanding economic regulation, then, means understanding a process of intermediation and bargaining between large and powerful organizations spanning what are conventionally termed the public and private domains of decision-making. But this understanding points to an important, related, feature. The economies of advanced capitalist societies have been universally marked by a high level of state intervention. Regulation is embedded in the practices of the interventionist state. The aims of regulation—as the contributions of Wilks and of Cawson and his colleagues make clear—are commonly only explicable by reference to the wider structures and more general aims of the interventionist system. As we see from Cawson's study, the French Government's attempts, for instance, to intervene in the affairs of Thomson can only be understood in the context of its wider sectoral policy ambitions.

Economic regulation under advanced capitalism—its formation as much as its implementation—invariably involves interdependence and bargaining between powerful and sophisticated actors against a background of extensive state involvement. But the particular character of the individual nation-state adds two other distinctive features, the first to do with the role of law, the second with the allocation of sovereign authority. Nations with advanced capitalist economies are almost universally governed, or claim to be governed, according to some principles of constitutional democracy. The exercise of public power, in other words, rests on legal authority, and this legal authority is made legitimate in turn by appeal to popular will. Of course by no means all economic regulation is cast in the form of legal rules, but the central importance of the principle of constitutionalism means that the range and form of regulation is deeply influenced by the particular conception of the scope and purpose of law which prevails in any particular community at any particular time. To put the point more technically, the purpose and character of economic regulation is in part a function of the nature of the surrounding legal culture, as the chapters by Rhodes and by Hancher both illustrate.

Conceptions of the proper role of law are in turn intimately connected with notions about the appropriate allocation of sovereign authority. Economic regulation is practised in a highly developed form in societies combining organization on market principles, domination of many sectors by giant firms, and political rule according to formally democratic principles. The combination of these three features sets up great tensions in the regulatory process, a tension reflected in much of the literature on the subject. Democracy, especially in the Anglo-Saxon tradition, is closely associated with parliamentarianism: that is, with the assumption that a monopoly of legitimate authority flows from the command of popular and legislative majorities. Regulation, on this conception, is a process by which popular and public control is exercised over the workings of private power in the market-place. The idea was well expressed by one of the most eloquent defenders of American regulation under the New Deal, when he spoke of the regulatory agencies created in that period as 'the outposts of capitalism' designed to control the market-place 'lest capitalism by its own greed, fear, avarice and myopia destroy itself.'[2]

The notion that economic regulation is a process by which sovereign public authority disciplines and controls private interests has exercised a particularly strong influence over American thinking about the subject. Since the literature on regulation, in the English language at least, is largely American inspired, the notion has in turn deeply influenced debates about the historical development of economic regulation and about its proper place in modern democratic systems. The most important consequence has been an instinctive belief that 'private' influence over the regulatory process is illegitimate. If regulation is assumed to be an activity in which some ideal of the public interest is pursued at the expense of the private, then evidence that private interests benefit from regulation, or that they exercise a strong influence over the regulatory process, is naturally treated as a sign that the purpose of the activity has been distorted.

These notions are particularly marked in the long-running debate about 'capture' in regulation. The very idea of 'capture' betrays an assumption that there is a sphere of public regulatory authority which ought to be inviolate from private influence. Both Kolko's historical interpretation of regulation as a response to the needs of powerful corporate interests, and the vast literature 'exposing' particular instances of regulatory capture, are united by the belief that the practise of regulation has involved the subordination of public authority to sectional interest.[3] Likewise the most influential critique of the interventionist regulatory state produced by a political scientist—Lowi's *End of Liberalism*—rests on the argument that there once existed, and should exist again, a liberal constitution possessing an inviolable public core, bounded by law, and clearly distinct from the private sphere.[4] Even observers sceptical of 'capture' theories have shared the assumptions of their opponents: debate has typically turned on attempts to rebut the empirical accuracy of capture theory, rather than on attempts to question the assumption that there should indeed exist an inviolable public sphere.

It is undoubtedly the case that arguments about the capture or otherwise of the regulatory process raise important issues of both constitutional principle and substantive outcome. Questions about who benefits from regulation, and who is allowed to shape the decisions made by regulatory agencies, are plainly central to understanding and evaluation. Yet to couch the discussion in terms suggesting the necessity of identifying and defending a clearly delimited sphere of public authority is unhelpful. It rests on the culturally restricted constitutional assumption that the roles of 'public' and 'private' in the regulatory process can be authoritatively distinguished. But as we explore below, there actually exist significant national variations in how the public–private divide is conventionally drawn. More seriously, the 'capture' debate obscures perhaps the single most important feature of economic regulation under advanced capitalism: that the most important actors in the process are organizations, and organizations which, regardless of their formal status, have acquired important attributes of public status. Of the formally 'private' organizations with public status, none is more important than the large firm.

The role of the large firm is unique. Whereas the regulation of the behaviour of individual 'private' actors is concerned with the imposition of a public or general will on private citizens, large firms cannot be described as private 'takers' of regulation in this sense. They have acquired the status of 'governing institutions'.[5] As Lindblom has argued, in a market economy firms carry out functions of an essentially public character. Their decisions on investment, employment, and output have important allocational and distributional implications which resonate in the 'public' sphere.[6] As we have seen time and time again in this volume, the corporate strategy of individual firms is a major determinant of the direction of the regulatory process. Public governmental agencies do not merely act upon firms as, so to speak, external agents. Corporations are major centres of expertise, and they constitute significant independent social and administrative hierarchies. Their integration into the implementation of regulation is very often a precondition of its success. This is so even where the ownership structure of a firm is independent of a (state) public agency; but as Prosser, Cawson *et al.*, and Wilks all demonstrate, the fusion of private and public ownership is actually now a common feature of advanced capitalist economies.

Economic regulation of markets under advanced capitalism can thus be portrayed as an activity shaped by the *interdependence* of powerful organizations who share major public characteristics. In the economic sphere no clear dividing line can be drawn between organizations of a private nature and those entitled to the exclusive exercise of public authority. The fusion is made more complete by one of the features remarked on earlier: economic regulation is an integral part of the activities of the modern interventionist state. While much economic regulation does indeed involve the making of rules and the enforcement of standards, this occurs within a framework of much more diffuse intervention, concerned with a wide range of often unstated and even contradictory objectives. Economic rule-based regulation is not a distinct activity; it is woven into a larger fabric of intervention. The overall pattern is marked by a high level of social and administrative complexity. In regulation much of the most important activity consists in the routinized application of general principles, which may be devised by the regulatory authority or alternatively may be little more than the company's standard operating procedures, officially endorsed as general principles. Hence we say that certain ways of doing things become 'institutionalized'. At the same time, however, organizational alliances are constantly forming and reforming without any reference to a conventional public–private divide. Parties bargain, co-operate, threaten, or act according to semi-articulated customary assumptions. The allocation of roles between rule makers, enforcers, and bearers of sectional interests constantly shifts, again obeying no obvious public–private dichotomy. In such a world firms are not bearers of some distinct private interest which is subject to public control; they are actors in a common sphere with other institutions conventionally given the 'public' label.

Economic regulation under advanced capitalism is therefore best conceived as an activity occurring in economies where the public and private are characteristically mixed, where the dominant actors are powerful and sophisticated organizations, and where the biggest firms have taken on many of the features of governing institutions. In this world the language of regulatory capture is largely devoid of meaning. Questions about who participates in and benefits from regulation are certainly important: explaining the complex and shifting relationships between and within organizations at the heart of economic regulation is the key to understanding the nature of the activity. But little can be gained by depicting the relationship in the dichotomous language of public authority versus private interests. On the basis of the evidence collected in this volume we can see that different institutions have come to inhabit a common regulatory space. The critical question for the analyst of the European regulatory scene is not to assume 'capture', but rather to understand the nature of this shared space: the rules of admission, the relations between occupants, and the variations introduced by differences in markets and issue arenas. The character of regulatory space is our next theme.

Public Space and Regulatory Space

Framing the problem in this way mirrors the approach recently adopted by Crouch in his attempt to make sense of different national configurations in the place given to organized interests in the policy process. Crouch begins with the notion that it is possible in any particular community at any particular time to identify a 'public space', which he describes as the 'range of issues over which general universal decisions are made within a given political unit.'[7] He then explores the historical experiences which have, in different European countries, allowed different groups of participants into this public space. We can likewise speak of a 'regulatory space' whose dimensions and occupants can be understood by examining regulation in any particular national setting, and by analysing that setting in terms of its specific political, legal, and cultural attributes.

The concept of 'regulatory space' is an analytical construct. It is defined, to adapt Crouch's language, by the range of regulatory issues subject to public decision. A number of obvious consequences follow from this. First, precisely because it is a space it is available for occupation. Secondly, because it is a space it can be unevenly divided between actors: there will, in other words, be major and minor participants in the regulatory process. Thirdly, just as we can identify a general concept of regulatory space in operation in a particular community we can also speak of specific concepts of regulatory space at work in individual sectors: in pharmaceuticals, for instance, issues of safety and price control are subjects, or potential subjects, of regulatory activity, whereas in the automobile sector only the former set of issues are included. Fourthly, because 'regulatory space' is an image being used to convey a concept, it can be augmented by similar images: thus because an arena is delineated space we sometimes speak of a 'regulatory arena'. The boundaries which demarcate regulatory space are defined in turn by a range of issues, so it is sensible to speak of regulatory space as encompassing a range of regulatory issues in a community. In these terms regulatory space may be furiously contested. Its occupants are involved in an often ferocious struggle for advantage. Any investigation of the concept involves examining the outcomes of competitive struggles, the resources used in those struggles, and the distribution of those resources between the different involved institutions. In other words, the play of power is at the centre of this process.

Discovering who has power in regulation involves paying close attention to the relations between the organizations which at any one time occupy regulatory space. But the idea of a space also directs us to a far more important aspect of power. It encourages us not only to examine relations between those who enjoy inclusion, but also to examine the characteristics of the excluded. That the structure of power is shaped by modes of exclusion from any political process is an elementary truth. In the case of economic regulation, however, the observation has a particularly sharp point. When we speak of the politics of economic regulation under advanced capitalism we are speaking of a set of power relationships dominated by large organizations. These complex organizations—the biggest firms, representative associations, regulatory agencies, central departments of state—are organized in administrative hierarchies whose method of doing business is shaped by standard operating procedures. Institutional procedure, that is, the routine application of established practices, rather than individual choice, is the dominant influence in deciding who is taken into, or kept out of, regulatory space. Since the rules of organizational life have a routinized character, exclusions tend to be systematic. Understanding who is in, and who is out, is therefore particularly vital, and depends crucially on analysing the customary patterns of organizational relationships in any particular regulatory space.

If groups can be organized into, or organized out of, regulatory space, the same can be said of issues. There are no obvious natural limits of boundaries to regulation. Notions of what is 'regulatable' are plainly shaped by the experience of history, the filter of culture, and the availability of existing resources. The fact that economic regulation is predominantly regulation by and of large organizations means, however, that notions about appropriate scope are routinized, and are embedded in organizational procedures. Understanding why some issues are prioritized, included, or excluded, at different times and in different places, thus demands an exploration of how organizations become committed to, and maintain a commitment to, particular definitions of the scope of regulatory space. Likewise, understanding changes in the notion of what issues should be included demands attention to the shifting balance of power within and between institutional actors inside the common regulatory space.

The factors determining the shape of this space, and the relative position of its occupants, are many and complex. Here only a sketch of the main influences can be offered. But the gist of understanding lies in one simple observation: the most important relationships in economic regulation are relationships between organizations. Thus the key matters requiring explanation—inclusion and exclusion, the relative power of the included, the scope of regulatory issues—will be illuminated in terms of the characteristics of the operating organizations: the cultural environment within which they work, their standard operating procedures, the customary assumptions which govern their interaction, and the resources at their disposal. Understanding economic regulation therefore involves understanding the terms under which organizations enter regulatory space, and defend their position within it. This is in turn heavily influenced by the prevailing general political attitudes and legal traditions existing in any community to the place of organized interests in the policy process. In other words, *place* matters in determining the nature of regulation, an insight also central to Crouch's exploration of national peculiarities and public space. We therefore next sketch the importance of place.

National Peculiarity and Regulatory Space

The central problem examined in Crouch's analysis is the character of the transition from competitive to organized capitalism—from economies marked by comparatively unregulated competition between a large number of actors to economies where a small number of organizations dominate a closely regulated economic environment. The political response to this transformation has been highly varied: in some communities the legitimacy of certain actors, including peak associations, unions, and large corporations, in policy-making is largely denied; in others their incorporation, though thorough, is accomplished informally; in others there still exist developed, statutorily based forms of incorporation. (Rhodes's chapter on the regulation of labour markets illustrates precisely such divergences at work.) These variations are largely a reflection of national differences in the strength of what Maier calls the 'parliamentary parenthesis': that episode in the history of political development when state institutions claimed a monopoly of authority legitimized by command of parliamentary majorities.[8] Crouch explores the varying strength of the parliamentary parenthesis, tracing the differing capacities of individual states to command a continuing monopoly over 'public space' to a range of deeply rooted historical experiences: the character of pre-capitalist group organization, the timing and incidence of the transition to capitalism, the route taken to organized capitalism, and the varying legacies of fascism.

Our sketch only gives the outline of Crouch's subtle argument, but it serves to highlight one key feature: although the economies of advanced capitalist nations exhibit similar patterns of extensive regulation dominated by a small number of large organizations, there exist significant national variations in the political and constitutional responses to these similarities. Different national traditions conceive of the public–private authority in different ways; and different national traditions likewise allow access to regulatory space to different constellations of actors. The differences are summed up in the importance given to concepts of legal and political culture. Though some argument exists about the independent explanatory power of cultural variables, there can be no doubt that they are at the very least important in mediating the influence of historical experiences. Recognizing the significance of cultural variations means recognizing, in Hayward's words, 'the operation of culturally based dominant values that inhibit or preclude some kinds of arrangements but favour others'.[9]

In regulation, culturally formed assumptions about the purpose and role of law are particularly significant. These assumptions can determine whether regulation happens at all, its scope, how far it is embodied in statute or formal rules, and how far the struggles for competitive advantage which are a part of the regulatory process spill over into the Courts. The variables grouped under the umbrella of legal culture have been well summarized by Friedman, who speaks of

> the values and attitudes which bind the system together and determine the place of the legal system in the culture of society as a whole . . . Do groups or individuals willingly go to court? For what purpose do they make use of lawyers? . . . What is the relationship between class structure and the use or non-use of legal institutions? What informal special controls exist in addition to or in place of formal ones? Who prefers which kind of controls and why?[10]

One of the most striking illustrations of the significance of these kinds of variables is provided by a comparison of Anglo-American and European conceptions of public law. In the Anglo-American tradition, where a legal concept of the state is either absent or only weakly present, public law has been essentially concerned with the pragmatic control of public power, especially of the kind of discretionary power which is embedded in the process of economic regulation. As Graham notes in his chapter, in the UK especially, law has not been viewed as 'the great interpreter of politics'. The continental European tradition, more firmly rooted in Roman law, by contrast assigns a central place to the state both as idea and as institution. This establishes the 'unique character of public authority in terms of sovereignty and/or function.'[11] The jurisprudence of public law, enforced through a distinct and specialized court structure in France and West Germany, is developed independently of private law norms, whereas in the United Kingdom and the United States the control of public authority has been characteristically secured through the ordinary courts.[12]

Within these broad traditions, distinct national configurations abound. Vogel has recently explored the striking differences produced by British and American attitudes to the relevance of litigation in the regulatory process, contrasting the detailed rules and adversarial enforcement common in the United States with the discretionary guidelines and co-operative implementation characteristic of so much British regulation.[13] Within the European tradition very different national patterns also exist. In France the ideal of a unitary state and the 'paternalistic conception of a state prerogative police power, conceived as the general regulation of French society for the public good' still permeates public law theory and practice.[14] The constitution is viewed, not so much as a source of legitimate authority, but rather as an expression of the idea of the unity of the state. In such circumstances, especially in the sphere of economic regulation, administrative courts are considered to be of relatively limited value in challenging the rulings of administrations 'addicted to discretionary adaptation of the rules to suit the political convenience of governments'.[15] This truncated approach to constitutional values is reflected in public law procedures and norms. The administrative courts may review the legality of a decision but will not, except in very unusual circumstances, substitute their own evaluation of the facts for that of an administration. The Council of State—the highest administrative 'court'—has indeed consistently refused to interfere in economic decisions involving the exercise of discretion.[16]

The place of the constitution and constitutional values in shaping the practise of regulation in West Germany stands out in sharp contrast. The Basic Law of 1949 is viewed as embodying a juristic idea of the state. When combined with Roman law traditions of deductive legal reasoning from a unified set of principles, this has meant that the 'constitution has acquired an imperative character and policy has become highly judicialised'. The West German Constitution is seen 'not just as a general framework establishing a minimum consensus about certain principles'—in the manner of, for instance, the American Constitution—but as a 'political programme containing particular substantive goals'.[17] As Hancher's chapter on price control of prescription drugs shows, this commitment to legalism and formalism has limited the exercise of executive power and given the Courts a prominent role in controlling the scope of regulatory activity and the range of regulatory discretion. Equipped with highly generalized constitutional principles such as the right to equal treatment, the freedom to own property, and the freedom to pursue a profession, the German Courts have not hesitated to invalidate both administrative regulation and legalisation.

This sketch illustrates some of the important ways in which the character of a legal culture mediates the regulatory process, fixing the scope of regulatory space and influencing who gains entry and on what terms. Variables attributable to distinctive legal cultures may also determine the ability of 'excluded' interests to challenge the existing distribution of power within the common regulatory space. Legal culture may further operate as an important variable in determining the way in which the different rules interact to create a regulatory framework. For instance, as Rhodes shows in his chapter, the interplay of rules established by collective bargaining and the rules established by statute or common law in the regulation of labour markets, varies considerably between the large European democracies. Similar variations exist in financial regulation: some disclosure practices which are simply the standard operating procedures of large firms in the UK have become 'juridified', or expressed as legally binding rules, in the USA.

A similar observation can be made about the more general influence of political culture, conceived as the prevailing set of beliefs and assumptions about the nature of political authority in a community. As an explanatory tool, however, political culture is most useful when disaggregated into its constituent parts: in other words, when we examine the attitudes to such matters as the role of law and the Courts, the place of organized interests, and the appropriate terms for the exercise of legitimate authority.

It might be thought that an emphasis on the mediating power of cultural assumptions overstates the consensual and stable character of regulatory practise, at the expense of the bitter struggles and often rapid changes which can occur in regulatory arenas. But this danger only occurs, first, if culture is indeed assumed to have a changeless, timeless character, and secondly, if we fail to appreciate the sectoral specificity of regulatory arenas. In reality, a consideration of the changing impact of culture on the shape and occupation of the common regulatory space can be particularly illuminating. In the United Kingdom many of the most important regulatory arrangements—for instance, in the financial community and in the professions—were evolved in a political culture marked by a deferential attitude on the part of mass publics towards authority, and by a preference for informal and private regulation on the part of élite groups. These factors ensured that regulation was conducted inside enclosed regulatory communities shielded from the attention of democratic politics. This is what the characteristic British preference for 'self-regulation' amounted to. In the last couple of decades the deferential and secretive character of the political culture has been subjected to some strain, as a result of a combination of government policy failures, changes in social structure, and wider alterations in the character of popular values. One of the most important consequences—illustrated to perfection by the experience of the financial services industry—has been the invasion of regulatory space by organizations (such as central departments of state and highly organized pressure groups) previously excluded under the assumptions of a deferential and secretive culture. (Though, as Prosser's analysis of the newly privatized British Telecom shows, those traditional assumptions remain powerful.)

Regulation occurs, it is a truism to observe, in particular places, and therefore place matters. The most important delineation of place is provided by the boundaries of the nation-state. Nations arrange their regulatory spaces in distinctive ways. Yet it is also plain that national peculiarities are by no means the whole story. Within particular countries the characters of different regulatory communities show great variety. Many influences shape these variations, but one of the most important is time—for regulation is practised in time as well in space. The historical timing of regulatory initiatives and development can thus be critical. To this we now turn.

Historical Timing and Regulatory Space

Why is the British insurance industry subject to much tighter statutory regulation than is banking in the United Kingdom? Why are banks in the United States much more tightly controlled by law than are securities firms? Why was a model of central banking regulation initially evolved in the UK during the middle and later decades of the nineteenth century later widely copied in different national settings? The observations prompting these questions illustrate the importance of historical timing in the shaping of regulatory space.

The significance of timing arises from an elementary characteristic of regulation as an activity: it has to be organized. Without appropriate institutional arrangements implementation simply does not take place. The act of organization in turn demands resources: the knowledge to create or to copy regulatory institutions; the money and people to run those institutions; the expertise to devise rules, and to monitor and police their enforcement. The organization that controls these resources will dominate regulatory space; and the organization that commands the necessary resources at the historical moment when regulation is initiated has a good chance of exercising a continuing dominant influence. (For example, as Hancher shows in her chapter, the British ABPI has been able to retain continuing control over the regulation of profits on the sale of its member companies drugs to the NHS, stemming from its initial historical domination.) The significance of timing is emphasized by the nature of regulation itself. Regulation is largely a matter of organizational routine, of institutionalized procedures, punctuated by occasional crises, economic or political. Such crises serve the function of inducing change, or at least initiating a search for alternative institutional arrangements, as in the case of the regulation of international taxation discussed by Picciotto. In between periods of crisis, the more dominant organizations can retain and consolidate their position of superiority, so that alternative mechanisms of regulation are ignored or suppressed. The moment of historical origin of regulation can thus be of the utmost significance.

Regulation almost always happens because some sense of crisis is precipitated, but the crisis can occur at very different historical moments: extensive national regulation of banking in the United

States began in the critical atmosphere of the American Civil War; extensive national regulation of the British banking industry had to wait the atmosphere created by the international banking collapse of the 1970s. The balance of institutional forces at the moment of crisis is plainly of enduring importance. In some sectors at the crucial initial moment the state commands the necessary regulatory resources, and its own agencies or actors dominate the process. In the creation of new institutional frameworks to regulate telecommunications, for instance, the state has been the major actor in the United Kingdom. In others—the examples of pharmaceuticals and securities examined in this volume illustrate the point—the control of expertise and personnel gives the regulatory initiative decisively to firms. The key analytical point is that understanding regulatory arrangements in the present depends on understanding the historical configuration out of which they developed.

It will be plain that, in respect both of nations and of particular sectors, there are 'early' and 'late' regulators. This simple fact of historical timing has profound implications for regulatory arrangements, because it intimately affects the international diffusion of regulatory forms. The most casual acquaintance with any important substantive area of regulation soon reveals that institutions and rules are widely imitated. Copying is obviously an economical way of solving the problem of regulatory design. Since regulation typically is begun under pressure of time, or in conditions of crisis, the incentive to imitate is great. The result is that 'early' regulators often provide a model for countries following later along the regulatory road. De-regulators follow a similar path as the 'export' to Europe of many American de-regulatory models illustrates.

The process by which regulatory design is diffused internationally is little understood, but it is apparent that models emanating from countries exercising great economic and political power are most likely to be the objects of emulation. This is part of the explanation for the widespread diffusion in the past of the English model of central banking. Wilks's study of the motor industry in this volume likewise identifies the United States as a world leader in control of emissions standards. In her study of telecommunications regulation and deregulation Hills has identified a similar pattern, involving the export of American standards and market practices to the industries of competitors. This pattern of imitation is confirmed by Prosser's study of the industry in this volume.[18] (Although, in addition, he clearly demonstrates the impact of British legal culture which has militated against a straightforward transplantation of the American institutional model.)

Regulation takes place in particular places and in particular times, and these two factors have an immense influence on the shape of regulatory space. But there exists a further important consideration. Regulatory space is dominated by organizations. The implications of this are examined in our next section.

Organizational Structure and Regulatory Space

Economic regulation is predominantly regulation by and through organizations. In any particular arena the character of these organizations will vary; the variations in turn influence the nature of the activity. The most fundamental effect governs who or what exercises any power in the regulatory process. The everyday practise of regulation of course involves dealings between individuals. But these individuals characteristically only enjoy access to regulatory space because they have some organizational role: as employees of firms, as the voice of an organized interest, as servants of the state. Private citizens rarely have a significant legitimate role in the formulation and implementation of regulatory policy. Intellectuals may occasionally contribute to the shaping of regulatory ideologies, though even in such cases their influence depends heavily on their identification with the organizational bearers of scholarly knowledge, such as universities and professional associations. Individual political entrepreneurs like Nader in the United States can likewise periodically intervene, though as the history of Nader's campaigns indicates continuing influence depends heavily on the ability to embody activity in organizational form.

Organizational status is thus the most important condition governing access to regulatory space. Private individuals who do not perform organizational roles, or who are not bearers of organizational interests, enjoy limited and usually temporary success in any attempt to intervene. Citizens are 'takers' of regulation; organizations are makers and shapers. Very occasionally private citizens may succeed in mounting a successful legal challenge to a regulatory programme, but sustained or permanent participation is precluded.

The organizations typically dominant in regulatory space,

whether they are conventionally labelled 'private' or 'public', share important characteristics. They are usually big—in the case of the state and the largest firms very big indeed—and are marked by the elaborate internal division of administrative labour and extended administrative hierarchies. These features impose both co-operative and conflictual elements on the practise of regulation. When regulatory space is dominated by large, hierarchical bodies regulation inevitably becomes a co-operative matter, because only by such a means can it be accomplished. Almost nothing of significance is done in regulation as the result of the actions of any single individual or simple organizational entity. The regulatory task is subjected to an elaborate and elongated division of labour. Even the design and implementation of comparatively simple standards (like the introduction of transparency guidelines to advise doctors on prescribing) depends on co-operation between large numbers of individuals occupying very different roles in the hierarchies of different organizations. This observation merely serves to reinforce one of our earlier points: that the big firms who are major occupiers of regulatory space can in no sense be pictured as mere 'takers' of regulation. Even if they are not explicitly involved in the formal process of rule-making, nothing would happen to promulgated rules without their extensive co-operation.

In economic regulation, therefore, the most important parties are bound together in relations of exchange and interdependence. But the co-operation enforced by the division of administrative labour should not conceal the way the organizations who inhabit regulatory space are riven by competition and conflict. Indeed the essence of regulatory politics is the pursuit of institutional advantage: the pursuit of advantage in the market-place, measured by indices like market share and profit; and the pursuit of command over the regulatory process itself, as measured by the right to make rules and to command their means of implementation. Regulation—and the rules and distribution of power through which it operates—is always a 'stake' of industrial or political struggle.

Organizational status as a condition of access to regulatory space; large-scale, extended hierarchies; a refined division of administrative labour; enforced co-operation in the implementation of regulation; the relentless pursuit of institutional advantage: these are the most important consequences of the organizational character of economic regulation under advanced capitalism. But of course these shared institutional characteristics still allow for considerable diversity, and this diversity influences not only the allocation of power within the regulatory space but also perceptions about what should be regulated, and how the necessary tasks should be accomplished. Four influences are particularly important: the way organizational procedures impose different views about the substance of regulation; the variations introduced by governmental structure and structure of ownership; variations in the internal cohesion of firms; and variations in the social and cultural cohesion and economic strength of industries and sectors.

Powerful organizational structures not only dictate, through their standard operating procedures, how things are to be done; they also impose beliefs about what *can* be done. As Hall expresses it, organizational structures 'tend to impose certain perceptions, responsibilities and interests on the actors'.[19] The most distinctive feature of organizations is, of course, precisely that they are indeed formally organized. But organization involves not only a set of procedures for taking decisions; it also involves customary assumptions, often barely articulated, about the substantive purposes of the activities which are being pursued. Understanding economic regulation thus demands not only an examination of national cultural traits; it also necessitates an exploration of the distinctive subcultures within leading organizations in the regulatory process. For instance, the phenomenon of *pantouflage* (the career movement of civil servants out into industry) has produced precisely such a distinctive subculture in France.

These variations in organizational subculture are obviously linked to national variations in institutional structures, that is, to routinized forms of rule-making and rule application. The nature of these structures in any particular regulatory space will be in part a product of external factors. In political systems like that of the United States, for instance, where government structures are highly fragmented, the same pattern of fragmentation tends to be repeated inside individual regulatory arenas. The results include perpetual contests for authority between different Federal agencies, and constant demarcation disputes between Federal and state agencies. The structure of governmental agencies often in turn imposes a particular organizational pattern on an industry or an industry's peak association because, especially in respect of the formal organization of interest groups, there is a pronounced tendency for such arrangements to mirror those of the state. The fragmented, competitive pattern of state organization in the United States is thus likewise reflected in the balkanized character of pressure group organization.

Intervention in regulation by international or supranational agencies such as the European Commission has, contrary to what may be commonly assumed, exacerbated the patterns of fragmentation and competition within the state. In some sectors, such as consumer electronics, the process of internationalization has weakened the regulatory capacity of national governments and enhanced the importance of self-regulation by the firms as they make their own response to market pressures. As Cawson *et al.* note in the extreme case of the capture of a state agency by a firm such as Thomson, a firm in nominal state ownership, this can amount to the regulation of government by the firm.

In an equally obvious way the structure of ownership in a regulated industry also shapes the nature of its organizational world. Since firms are among the key actors in regulatory space, the degree of concentration of ownership is critical. The domination of industries by a small number of giant firms is one of the commonest features of market organization in advanced capitalist economies, but the extent of this domination varies significantly between industries. The individual studies of earlier chapters show a pattern varying from comparative dispersion (in the securities industry) to oligopoly (automobiles and pharmaceuticals) to monopoly (telecommunications).

Nor is the degree of concentration of market power the only way in which firms shape the organizational character of regulatory space. The internal political character of individual firms, though little investigated, is also a crucial variable. In some firms hierarchical control is strong and the regulatory response of the institution is co-ordinated in a unified fashion. In others formal organizational unity only conceals deep differences between functional divisions, or even between warring factions. It is perfectly possible for separate divisions to operate independently of, and indeed in competition with, each other in the struggle for regulatory advantage.

It will be plain that the internal social and political cohesion of the biggest firms in an industry is an important influence on the kind of organizational life which develops in a particular regulatory arena. The same observation may be made about the social character of an industry as a whole, for different parts of the economy plainly vary greatly in their social cohesion. Some—like the banking industries of many advanced industrial nations—exhibit high social and cultural unity. Such industries are typically dominated by a social élite, enjoying shared life experience and social origins, and often bound by similar ties to élites in state institutions. The possibility that this sort of social cohesion can add cement to organizational structures is plainly contingent on the economic and social history of particular parts of economies.

Economic regulation under advanced capitalism is largely transacted through big organizations. The structure of these organizations, their internal cohesion and their capacity to co-operate with each other, is a function of a wide range of factors in their environment. But one final important consideration should be noticed. Although the organization of a particular regulatory space can plainly only be understood by reference to the social structure of industrial and state élites, it is not simply a product of these features. Patterns of organization can themselves be self-sustaining, and thereby institutionalized. In economic regulation control of the means of organization is itself a major resource. This is in part due to the instrumental resources—of money, information, and personnel—which organizations command. But it is also due to the special legitimacy which attaches to institutional status in regulatory worlds where the key transactions are those involving organizations. Institutions develop their own independent interests and, in the world of economic regulation, have powerful means of ensuring their continuing defence. As Rhodes points out in his chapter, the history of the regulation of British industrial relations, for instance, is inexplicable without reference to the fragmented and dispersed character of British trade-union organization, and to the capacity of the numerous unions to defend their institutional autonomy. This process of fragmentation is exacerbated in labour markets, so that for trade unions, as Rhodes observes, 'external exclusion is an organisational prerequisite for building internal solidarity'. Likewise in the American financial services industry, the historical fragmentation of markets, and the equally dispersed nature of the organizations involved in regulation, are explicable only in terms of the capacity of competing institutions to maintain the existing fragmented structures.

Understanding the nature of the regulatory process in advanced capitalist economies involves, above all, understanding the character of the organizational forms dominant in regulatory arenas. Our sketch shows that the allocation of power and influence within regulatory space is influenced both by legal tradition and by a wide range of social, economic, and cultural factors. But the character of the transactions between organizations is also affected by a more immediate set of influences: by the particular kinds of issues which arise in regulation and by the particular areas where those issues are dealt with. Common issues and common arenas bind actors together in relations of interdependence. Analysis of the process of regulation from the perspective of interdependence is by no means new, but the concept of regulatory space offers additional insights into the character of interdependence.

Interdependence and Regulatory Space

Over two decades ago Lowi developed the notion that patterns of politics were in part determined by the kinds of policies which were at issue—in other words, that 'policies make politics'.[20] He also identified a particular pattern associated with the politics of regulation. Within such a broad schematic framework, however, in any particular regulatory arena there exists a diversity of organizations which interact through a range of networks or linkages of varying density of formality. As we have observed, these linkages may be articulated in terms of formal, binding legal rules, standard operating procedures, or indeed in the form of mere conventions. The range of those involved in the regulatory process will not only vary from issue to issue but will also be deeply influenced by convention or constitutional practice, or by prior patterns of regulatory practice. Inter-organizational linkages are the subject of a large, existing literature on network theory which demonstrates the significance of policy communities and networks within which 'élite coalitions' allocate issues to particular arenas, manage the policy agenda, and control the range of participants allowed into decision-making.[21]

The plurality of the regulatory process, its openness to a variety of actors, is itself a function of bureaucratic and legal traditions and of past regulatory practice. Network analysis offers useful insights into the impact of such traditions on the organizational aspect of regulation. Its aim is to identify or map patterns of dependent relations between key personalities, but it takes as a central premiss the notion that these relations are predicated upon the acceptance of certain internal 'rules of the game' which evolve within stable communities.

One advantage of approaching the subject of interdependence through the concept of 'regulatory space' is that it alerts us to the problem of defining the character of the social relations between the occupants of that space. The notion of a 'regulatory space' focuses attention not only on who the actors involved in regulation are, but on structural factors which facilitate the emergence and development of networks and which contribute to the institutionalization of linkages. In taking the nature of the links between actors as the starting-point of analysis, it offers the chance of developing a systematic comparison of their character in different industrial sectors and within different national settings.

Network analysis offers the undoubted advantage of highlighting the functional importance of informal links between actors. It plainly can be misleading to assume that formal regulatory arrangements are the only kind of institutionalized relationships. Indeed, as Rhodes's description of the legal framework of industrial relations in France illustrates, formal arrangements may not be institutionalized at all: notwithstanding the plethora of formal rules on representation and the various substantive rights enshrined in the legal code, French industrial relations have remained fragmented and the unions have been unable to exert sufficient economic power to mobilize their legal rights.

Our sketch shows that the allocation of power and influence within regulatory space is influenced both by legal tradition and by a wide range of social, economic, and cultural factors which go beyond narrow 'rules of the game'. But the character of the transactions between organizations is also affected by a more immediate set of influences: by the particular kind of issues which arise in regulation and by the particular areas where those issues are dealt with. This is what we next examine.

Issues, Arenas, and Regulatory Space

While it is a truism to say that the nature of a regulatory issue intimately affects the range of those who participate in its resolution, it is plain that the nature of any single issue is not 'given'. The definition of the character of a regulatory issue is itself an important part of the process by which it is allocated to the domain of certain organizations and removed from the domain of others. Most problems in economic regulation are both complex in their intrinsic character and wide ranging in their social and economic consequences. It is thus rare for an issue to be 'obviously' in a particular domain. For instance, does the regulation of work practices belong to 'industrial relations' or, since it affects the health of the economy, should it be assigned to the sphere of economic management? The very process of issue definition will itself be heavily influenced by different national conceptions as to the legitimate exercise of regulatory power. As this process of defining or 'labelling' an issue develops, the policy network to which it is appropriate may become evident.

A second and equally important act of definition involves the distinction between what are in everyday language loosely described as 'technical' and 'political' issues. The distinction is particularly crucial in the field of regulation, where much of the most important activity consists in the routinized application of general principles to particular circumstances. The distinction between technical and political issues is also typically a distinction between a 'high' and 'low' politics of regulation. Where an issue is identified as technical, it is commonly consigned for resolution to a very different organizational network from that concerned with resolving 'political' issues held to involve questions of principle. The separation can be crucial in determining who controls the regulatory process. The point is vividly illustrated by the regulation of financial services, where matters critical to the wider economic health of the community—entry into markets, the degree and kind of competition in those markets, the standards of honesty demanded of market participants—have traditionally been defined as technical problems of market control, and thus safely assigned to the 'low politics' of regulatory routine. The identification of the issue, and its allocation to a particular organizational arena are not the subject of constant debate in the regulatory process. On the contrary: issue identification and definition are done largely unthinkingly as a result of customary assumptions and organizational routine. It could not be otherwise because, were it necessary to argue at length about the appropriate identification of every new issue, the activity of regulation would simply grind to a halt. Institutional inertia, the shaping power of professional ideologies, and the underlying force of customary assumptions about what is, and is not, 'political' are all vital to ensuring some continuing routine in the regulatory process.

Expressed thus, our account conveys the importance of custom and convention in deciding how regulatory issues are to be processed—and thus in deciding which organizations are to have the largest say in their resolution. But there is another face to regulation under advanced capitalism. The most highly developed market economies are also extraordinarily dynamic. Since the end of the Second World War they have been marked by historically high rates of growth, profound structural change, and rapid innovation in both technology and market practices. This has far-reaching consequences for the character of regulatory issues, and for the arenas in which they are settled.

This is made particularly evident in the two chapters which deal with financial regulation. In the first place, as Moran's chapter shows, one of the most striking recent changes is the redefinition of these issues as involving 'high' politics and their reassignment to new arenas, disrupting the old policy networks. In the second place, as Picciotto emphasizes in his chapter, rapid change may erode the narrow basis of legitimation on which 'technical' or bureaucratic regulation rests, thus forcing regulatory issues (once again) into the political arena.

The dynamic nature of the market economy disturbs the routine processing of issues and their routine assignment to particular spheres. Growth, innovation, and structural change all magnify the complexity of the issues which arise in economic regulation. This growth in complexity has three dimensions: intellectual, social and administrative. The growth of intellectual complexity happens because economic innovation typically involves the application of the most advanced technical and scientific processes to the creation and marketing of products. One of the most striking features of regulatory debates is the growing extent to which they are expressed in languages of technical complexity and legal discourse often far removed from everyday lay political argument.

The growing intellectual complexity of the issues at the heart of economic regulation is in many respects matched by the growth in social complexity. The economies of advanced capitalist nations are characterized by relations of interdependence, at the root of which is the ever more refined and elaborate division of labour. The result in the sphere of regulation is that decisions cannot be made, let alone implemented, by involving only a small group in the regulatory process. Social complexity ensures that effective regulation typically demands the co-operation of countless interdependent social actors, often including those well beyond the boundaries of any conventionally defined regulatory community. (The recent intervention of the European Community in the regulation of subsidies to car manufacturers, documented in Wilks's chapter, in a case in point.)

Administrative complexity is in many respects a mirror of this growing social complexity. It refers not only to the substance of rules—though these can be dauntingly elaborate—but also to the administrative apparatus which increasingly surrounds the activity of regulation. Regulatory space is dominated by organizations, many of which possess elaborate internal hierarchies and numerous points of decision, linked in a network to the numerous points of decision in the other organizations populating regulatory space.

The innovative nature of markets under advanced capitalism therefore constantly disturbs the routine identification of regulatory issues, and their ready assignment to organizational domains. But there is also a more profound sense in which the delineation of regulatory arenas is disrupted. Economic innovation means, quite simply, the invention of new products, and new means of manufacture and marketing. The new products can be anything from a new drug to a novel financial instrument. Innovations in market practice can range from the adoption of a single new sales technique to the creation of whole new social arenas and new social institutions. In financial services, for instance, the innovations span the gamut from 'cold calling'—a marketing device made popular and effective by the spread of telephone ownership—to the invention of whole new markets, like those in financial futures. Every innovation in turn raises two immediate problems: is it to be regulated, and by whom? In regulatory politics most of the contests for authority to settle issues surround newly invented products or marketing forms, for which some regulatory arena has to be found.

The connection between the effects of structural change and innovation, and the determination of regulatory domain, is particularly well illustrated by attempts to regulate the most advanced parts of market economies, those organized on a multinational scale. The problem is a recurrent theme of several of the contributions to this volume, including Wilks's discussion of the automobile sector and Cawson and his colleagues' analysis of the consumer electronics industry. It is also the dominant theme of Picciotto's chapter. Some early accounts of the significance of the development of multinational institutions, especially of multinational business corporations, suggested that institutions had been created which reduced the nation-state to insignificance. As our contributions—notably Picciotto's—show time and again, this is far from the case: national governments are major players in the multinational arena. Nevertheless, this particular regulatory space has two distinctive characteristics, concerning the character of authority and the nature of the parties to regulation. The rules of decision and the lines of authority in the regulatory process are even less clear than is the case within national regulatory communities. Inside nations the sovereign authority of the state is, as we showed earlier, often closely circumscribed by the realities of organized power. Nevertheless, there does characteristically exist some sovereign authority able to act as a 'tie breaker' in disputes, and able to provide a fountain of legitimacy for the exercise of regulatory authority. No such sovereign centre exists in multinational regulatory space; what cannot be bargained is for the most part deadlocked.

The parties to bargaining also have special characteristics. If domestic economic regulation is dominated by organizations, the same is even more emphatically the case in the multinational arena. The only realistic mode of entry into regulatory debates is as a bearer of organizational interests—indeed, usually of the interests of corporations or government departments. These actors have structural and cultural features which, though present in many domestic regulatory arenas, exist in the multinational sphere in particularly highly developed forms. All organizations involved in regulation are bearers of complex arrays of interests, but this feature is especially notable when the organizations are themselves governments trying to distil some national interest out of the wide range of conflicting domestic forces to which they are subject. All domestic regulatory arenas are likewise marked by a degree of cultural diversity, but in the supranational sphere the range of diversity and the consequent potential for clashes is greatly magnified, while the pressure for compromise is weaker.

The connection between issues, arenas, and the character of economic regulation is shaped by both ideological and structural factors. Regulatory 'issues' are in an important sense ideological constructions: their recognition depends on social actors construing the world in a particular way; their allocation to a particular regulatory arena is likewise the result of a process of ideological construction. But these acts of issue recognition and definition are underpinned by the structural forces at work in the economy. The most important of these forces is provided by the dynamic character of the economy of advanced capitalism, which constantly creates new regulatory problems, new regulatory arenas, and new organizations ready and available to compete in those arenas.

Conclusion

Economic regulation is, we have stressed, predominantly regulation by and through organizations. The analyst of contemporary regulation is confronted with the task of understanding the networks of interdependence in the arenas of negotiation and compromise—in a phrase the patterns of power brokerage. The study of regulation thus involves the concepts traditionally central to the disciplines of law and of politics. In this chapter we have argued that the study of regulatory power cannot be furthered by an artificial division between 'public' and 'private' spheres. An organizational perspective on regulation allows us to go beyond 'capture' theory, to examine the process by which powerful organizations, both state and non-state, gain, maintain, and sometimes lose their dominant positions within regulatory space. It also highlights in a new way some very traditional concerns of both law and political science—the definition of the legitimate scope of power, and the quest for meaningful accountability on the part of regulatory institutions. Indeed the problems of accountability and legitimacy can only be fully addressed if the process of power brokerage between powerful institutions in advanced capitalism is made central to the analysis. In this concluding chapter we have drawn attention to some of the themes emerging from current work on regulation, in the hope that they will serve as pointers for future study and analysis.

Notes

1. For a bibliographic survey see e.g. B. Mitnick, *The Political Economy of Regulation* (New York: Columbia University Press, 1980).
2. J. Allen (ed.), *Democracy and Finance: The Addresses and Public Statements of William O. Douglas* (New Haven: Yale University Press, 1940), 244.
3. G. Kolko, *Railroads and Regulation 1877–1916* (Princeton: Princeton University Press, 1965); and G. Kolko, *The Triumph of Conservatism* (New York: Free Press, 1963). The capture literature is critically examined in G. Wilson, 'Social Regulation and Explanations of Regulatory Failure', *Political Studies*, 32 (1984), 203–25.
4. T. Lowi, *The End of Liberalism: The Second Republic of the United States* (New York: Norton, 1979).
5. The phrase is from R. K. Middlemas, *Politics in Industrial Society* (London: Deutsch, 1979).
6. C. Lindblom, *Politics and Markets* (New York: Basic Books, 1977).
7. C. Crouch, 'Sharing Public Space: States and Organised Interests in Western Europe', in J. Hall (ed.), *States in History* (Oxford: Basil Blackwell, 1986), 177–210. The quotation is on p. 180.
8. C. Maier, ' "Fictitious Bonds . . . of Wealth and Law": On the Theory and Practice of Interest Representation', in S. Berger (ed.), *Organising Interests in Western Europe* (Cambridge: Cambridge University Press, 1981).
9. J. Hayward, 'Institutional Inertia and Political Impetus in France and Britain', *European Journal of Political Research*, 4 (1976), 341–59.
10. L. Friedman, 'Legal Culture and Social Development', *Law and Society Review*, 6 (1969), 19–46 at p. 19.
11. K. Dyson, *The State Tradition in Western Europe* (Oxford: Martin Robertson, 1980), 207.
12. See generally C. Harlow and R. Rawlings, *Law and Administration* (London: Weidenfeld and Nicholson, 1983).
13. D. Vogel, *National Styles of Regulation* (Cornell: Cornell University Press, 1986).
14. J. Hayward, *Governing France: The One and Indivisible Republic*, 2nd edn. (London: Weidenfeld and Nicholson, 1983), 133.
15. Ibid. 134.
16. A. Bockel, 'Actualité et perspective du contrôle de l'interventionisme économique', *Actualité juridique du droit administratif*, 8 (1985), 8–21.
17. Dyson, *The State Tradition in Western Europe*, p. 213.
18. J. Hills, *Deregulating Telecoms: Competition and Control in the United States, Japan and Britain* (London: Frances Pinter, 1986).

19. P. Hall, *Governing the Economy* (Cambridge: Polity Press, 1986), 265.
20. T. Lowi, 'Four Systems of Policy, Politics and Choice', *Public Administration Review*, 32 (1972), 298–310.
21. For a survey see e.g. S. Wilks and M. Wright, *Comparative Government—Industry Relations: Western Europe, the United States, and Japan* (Oxford: Clarendon Press, 1987).

Index

Note: The following abbreviations are used:
UK = United Kingdom
FRG = Federal Republic of Germany